"This is a very practical and entertaining window into the baby's first year and a half. Van de Rijt and Plooij have observed and found the vulnerable times in an infant's development that I independently came to in my book, Touchpoints (Perseus). The authors' observations and practical suggestions are wonderful."

—T. Berry Brazelton, M.D., Professor Emeritus, Harvard Medical School

"Anyone who deals with infants and young children will want to read The Wonder Weeks. This book will open parents' eyes to aspects of their children's growth, development, changing behavior, and emotional responsiveness that they might otherwise not notice or find puzzling and distressing."

—Catherine Snow, Ph.D., Shattuck Professor of Education,
Harvard Graduate School of Education

"Van de Rijt and Plooij's work on infant development has enormous value for clinical use and scientific application. Not only have they explained the periods of puzzling, difficult behavior in infancy which so worry parents, they have also shown how these behaviors mark developmental leaps and have described the stages in the infant's understanding. Together, this gives parents and professionals soundly based insight into babies' developing minds. What's more, Van de Rijt and Plooij have described the play and communication that work best with babies at different ages and thus helped parents understand and connect sensitively with their babies. This parent-child connection is the major prerequisite for the development of secure, well-adjusted children. The Wonder Weeks is essential reading for everyone who works with infants—pediatricians, social workers, psychologists, and, of course, parents."

—John Richer, Ph.D., Dip. Clin. Psychol., Consultant Clinical Psychologist and Head of Pediatric Psychology, Department of Pediatrics, John Radcliffe Hospital, Oxford, England

"Van de Rijt and Plooij will help you see the world the way an infant sees it. As the child grows, displays of emotion (such as crying) tell us the child is summoning reserves of energy and is calling out for help in finding new ways to perceive the changing world. Because Van de Rijt and Plooij have discovered predictable stages in the widening of the infant's perceptions and skills, they can enable you, with their superb examples, to recognize the onset of these stressful episodes and to join your child in coping with them. So rich, indeed, are the implications of finding new perceptions and new skills in the midst of stress that whether or not you are a parent, it can never be too early or too late to profit from this book."

—Philip J. Runkel, Ph.D., Professor Emeritus of Psychology and Education, University of Oregon

To our children, Xaviera and Marco,
and to our grandchildren, Thomas, Victoria and Sarah,
from whom we have learned so much

"Portrait of the first author, Hetty van de Rijt, created by her grandson Thomas on September 12, 1998, when he was 23 months old. Grandson and Grandma had a very close relationship and during her last seven years he was the sunshine in Hetty's life, which was restricted by disease.

On September 29, 2003, Hetty passed away. Untill the very last moment she worked on the extended edition of this book in Dutch. When she died, the first draft of the last chapter was ready. Through her life's work Hetty hoped to empower parents and give them peace of mind and self-confidence in their role as upbringer and socializer in such a way that they could enjoy their little sunshine."

The Wonder Weeks

How to stimulate the most important developmental weeks
in your baby's first 20 months and turn these 10 predictable,
great, fussy phases into magical leaps forward.

EXTRA: Insights, Tips & Tricks for Sleep and Leaps.

Hetty van de Rijt, Ph.D., and Frans Plooij, Ph.D.
with Xaviera Plas-Plooij

The WonderWeeks

Copyright © 2017 Kiddy World publishing
10 9 8 7 6 5
Illustrations by Hetty van de Rijt, Vladimir Schmeisser
Cover and internal design by Sumedia
Layout by Andrei Andras
Translation by Stephen Sonderegger and Gayle Kidder
Printed in Turkey

First published in 1992 as Oei, ik groei! by Zomer & Keuning Boeken BV,
Ede and Antwerp.

This book is intended as a reference volume only, not as a medical manual. The information given here is designed to help you make informed decisions about your baby's health. It is not inteded as a substitute for any treatment that may have been prescribed by your doctor. If you suspect a medical problem, we urge you to seek competent medical help. Any mention of specific companies, organizations, or authorities in this book does not imply endorsement by the publisher, nor does the mention of specific companies, organizations, or authorities imply that they endorse this book.

Kiddy World Publishing
Van Pallandtstraat 63
6814 GN Arnhem
The Netherlands

WWW.THEWONDERWEEKS.COM

Worldwide best-selling baby app #1

Contents

About this Book

Having completed our studies in Educational Psychology, Physical Anthropology and Behavioral Biology, and just married, my wife Hetty van de Rijt and I left for the Gombe National Park, Tanzania, East Africa to study chimpanzees with Jane Goodall. The particular research project we had prepared for proved impossible under the prevailing circumstances, so we had to change topic. There and then we realized that there was no better place on earth where one could observe freeliving newborn chimpanzee babies at such close range. We did not have any theory or hypothesis at hand for testing, but we were trained in systematic, direct observation of animal behavior in the field, in the tradition of Nobel Laureate Niko Tinbergen. So that is what we did for nearly two years. When we returned to Europe to work in Robert Hinde's Medical Research Council-Unit on the Development and Integration of Behavior, University Sub-department of Animal Behavior in Madingley, Cambridge, England, we had to analyze reams of data. Out of this analysis emerged the notion of regression periods – difficult periods where the baby clings more closely to the mother. Previously, such regression periods had been found by others in no less than 12 other primate species. The results of the data analysis also supported the idea that in the course of early octogeny, a hierarchical organization emerges in the central nervous system that underlies the behavioral development of the free-living chimpanzee babies and infants. It was only after we had analyzed our data and discerned a hierarchical organization that our friend and colleague Lex Cools, a neurobiologist, suggested that we compare our findings about the capabilities of infants at the different stages of development to the levels of perception spelled out by Hierarchical Perceptual Control Theory (PCT) developed by William T. Powers. PCT turned out to explain our findings very well. In the following years, the core postulates of PCT have been further tested by other researchers and results published in the scientific literature. Readers who are interested can go to the website www.livingcontrolsystems.com for an overview of PCT. Once we had earned our Ph.D. degrees in Cambridge, England (Hetty) and Groningen, the Netherlands (Frans), we moved on to observe and film human mothers and infants in their home environment. These studies demonstrated clearly that human babies, too, go through difficult, age-linked regression periods in a similar way. With each difficult period, babies make a leap in their mental development. Each time another layer of perceptual control systems is superimposed onto the already existing, hierarchically organized layers of perceptual control systems.

Based on our research, Hetty and I wrote the original Dutch version of The Wonder Weeks, published in 1992 and followed in subsequent years by German, French, Swedish, Italian, Danish, Spanish, English, Japanese, Korean, and Russian editions. Our original research in the Netherlands has been replicated and confirmed by other researchers in Spain, Britain and Sweden. For information about the research upon which The Wonder Weeks is based, and about editions in various languages, see www.thewonderweeks.com. Unfortunately, Hetty contracted a rare tropical disease during our stay in Tanzania and following a long, brave battle with the disease, she passed away in 2003. Hetty's legacy is alive as well as her life's work continues to bear fruit and The Wonder Weeks continues to make life easier for parents and contribute to the healthy development of children.

Frans Plooij
Arnhem, the Netherlands

Introduction

Jolted from a deep sleep, the new mother leaps from her bed and runs down the hall to the nursery. Her tiny infant, red-faced, fists clenched, screams in their crib. On instinct, the mother picks up the baby, cradling them in her arms. The baby continues to shriek. The mother nurses the baby, changes their diaper, then rocks them, trying every trick to ease their discomfort, but nothing seems to work. "Is there something wrong with the baby?" the mother wonders. "Am I doing something wrong?"

Parents commonly experience worry, fatigue, aggravation, guilt, and sometimes even aggression toward their inconsolable infants. The baby's cries may cause friction between the parents, especially when they disagree on how to deal with it. Well-meant but unwelcome advice from family, friends, and even strangers only makes things worse. "Let them cry, it's good for their lungs" is not the solution mothers and fathers wish to hear. Disregarding the problem does not make it go away.

The Good News: There is a Reason

For the past 35 years, we have studied the development of babies and the way their caregivers respond to their changes. Our research was done in homes, where we observed the daily activities of mothers and children. We gleaned further information from more formal interviews.

Our research has shown that from time to time all parents are plagued by a baby who won't stop crying. In fact, we found that, surprisingly, all normal healthy babies are more tearful, troublesome, demanding, and fussy at the same ages, and when this occurs they may drive the entire household to despair. From our research, we are now able to predict, almost to the week, when parents can expect their babies to go through one of these "fussy phases."

During these periods, a baby cries for a good reason. They are suddenly undergoing drastic changes in their development, which is upsetting to them. These changes enable the baby to learn many new skills and should therefore be a reason for celebration. After all, it's a sign they are making wonderful progress. But as far as the baby is concerned, these changes are bewildering. They are taken aback – everything has changed overnight. It's as if they have entered a whole new world.

It is well known that a child's physical development progresses in what we commonly call "growth spurts." A baby may not grow at all for some time, but then they'll grow a quarter of an inch in just one night. Research has shown that essentially the same thing happens in a child's mental development. Neurological studies have shown that there are times when major, dramatic changes take place in the brains of children younger than 20 months. Shortly after each of them, there is a parallel leap forward in mental development. This book focuses on the 10 major leaps that every baby takes in their first 20 months of life. It tells you what each of these developments mean for your baby's understanding of the world about them and how they use this understanding to develop the new skills that they need at each stage in their development.

What This Means for You and Your Baby

Parents can use this understanding of their baby's developmental leaps to help them through these often confusing times in their new lives. You will better understand the way your baby is thinking and why they act as they do at certain times. You will be able to choose the right kind of help to give them when they need it and the right kind of environment to help them make the most of every leap in their development.

This is not a book about how to make your child into a genius, however. We firmly believe that every child is unique and intelligent in their own way. It is a book on how to understand and cope with your baby when they are difficult and how to enjoy them most as they grow. It is about the joys and sorrows of growing with your baby.

All that's required to use this book is:
- One (or two) loving parent(s).
- One active, vocal, growing baby.
- A willingness to grow along with your baby.
- Patience.

How to Use This Book

This book grows with your baby. You can compare your experiences with those of other parents during all stages of your baby's development. Over the years, we've asked many mothers and fathers of new babies to keep records of their babies' progress and also to record their thoughts and feelings as well as observations of their babies' behavior from day to day. The diaries we've included in this book are a sample of these, based on the weekly reports of mothers of 15 babies – eight girls and seven boys. We hope you will feel that your baby is growing alongside those in our study group and that you can relate your observations of your baby to those of other mothers.

This book is not just for reading, however. Each section offers you the opportunity to record the details of your baby's progress. By the time a baby has grown into middle childhood, many parents yearn to recall all of the events and emotions of those first all-important years. Some parents keep diaries, but most mothers and fathers who are not particularly fond of writing or who simply lack the time – are convinced they will remember the milestones and even the minor details in their babies' lives. Unfortunately, later on they end up deeply regretting the fact that their memories faded faster than they could ever have imagined.

The next chapter, "Growing Up: How Your Baby Does It" explains some of the research on which this book is based and how it applies to your baby. You will learn how your baby grows by making "leaps" in their mental development and how these are preceded by stormy periods when you can expect them to be fussy, cranky, or temperamental.

The chapter "Newborn: Welcome to the World" describes what a newborn's world is like and how they perceive the new sensations that surround them. You will learn how nature has equipped them to deal with the challenges of life and how important physical contact is to their future development. These facts will help you get to know your new baby, to learn about their wants and needs, and to understand what they are experiencing when they take the first leap forward.

Subsequent chapters discuss the Wonder Weeks – the 10 big changes your baby undergoes in the first 20 months of life, at around 5, 8, 12, 19, 26, 37, 46, 55, 64 and 75 weeks. Each chapter tells you the signs that will let you know that a major leap is occurring. Then they explain the new perceptual changes your baby experiences at this time and how your baby will make use of them in their development.

Each leap is discussed in a separate chapter, consisting of four sections:

"This Week's Fussy Signs" describes the clues that your baby is about to make a developmental leap. Reflections from other mothers about their babies' troublesome times offer sympathetic support as you endure your baby's stormy periods.

In this section, you'll also find a diary section titled "Signs My Baby Is Growing Again." Check off the signs you've noticed that indicate your baby is about to experience a big change.

"The Magical Leap Forward" discusses the new abilities your baby will acquire during the current leap. In each case, it's like a new world opening up, full of observations they can make, and skills they can acquire. In this section, you will find a diary section, "How My Baby Explores the New World," which lists the skills that babies can develop once they have made this developmental leap. As you check off your baby's skills on the lists, remember that no baby will do everything listed. Your baby may exhibit only a few of the listed skills at this time, and you may not see other skills until weeks or months later. How much your baby does is not important – your baby will choose the skills best suited to them at this time. Tastes differ, even among babies! As you mark or highlight your own baby's preferences, you will discover what makes your baby unique.

"What You Can Do to Help" gives you suggestions for games, activities, and toys appropriate to each stage of development which will increase your baby's awareness and satisfaction – and enhance your playtime together.

"After the Leap" lets you know when you can expect your baby to become more independent and cheerful again. This is likely to be a delightful time for parents and babies, when both can appreciate the newly acquired skills that equip the baby to learn about and enjoy their world. This book is designed to be picked up at any point in your baby's first 20 months when you feel you need help understanding their current stage of development. You don't have to read it from cover to cover. If your baby is a little older, you can skip the earlier chapters.

Bonus: Sleep and Leaps

Sleep, and the lack of sleep… that's something we all have to deal with when we have a baby. As a bonus, we've added an additional chapter at the end of the book about this (on page 443). It includes everything about the relationship between sleep and leaps, as well as unique insight into your baby's sleeping behavior.

What This Book Offers You

We hope that you will use this knowledge of your child's developmental leaps to understand what they are going through, help them through the difficult times, and encourage them as they take on the momentous task of growing into a toddler. Also, we hope that this book helps provide the following.

Support in times of trouble. During the times you have to cope with crying problems, it helps to know that you are not alone, that there is a reason for the crying, and that a fussy period never lasts more than a few weeks, and sometimes no longer than several days. This book tells you what other parents experienced when their babies were the same age as yours. You will learn that all parents struggle with feelings of anxiety, aggravation, and a whole range of other emotions. You will come to understand that these feelings are all part of the process, and that they will help your baby progress.

Confidence. You will learn that you are capable of sensing your baby's needs better than anyone else. You are the expert, the leading authority on your baby.

Help in understanding your baby. This book will tell you what your baby endures during each fussy phase. It explains that they will be difficult when they are on the verge of learning new skills, as the changes to their nervous system start to upset them. Once you understand this, you will be less concerned about and less resentful of their behavior. This knowledge will also give you more peace of mind and help you to help them through each of these fussy periods.

Hints on how to help your baby play and learn. After each fussy period, your baby will be able to learn new skills. They will learn faster, more easily, and with more pleasure if you help them. This book will give you insight into what is preoccupying them at each age. On top of that, we supply a range of ideas for different games, activities, and toys so that you can choose those best suited to your baby.

A unique account of your baby's development. You can track your baby's fussy phases and progress throughout the book and supplement it with your own notes, so that it charts your baby's progress during the first 20 months of their life.

We hope that you will use this knowledge of your child's developmental leaps to understand what they are going through, help them through the difficult times, and encourage them as they take on the momentous task of growing into a toddler. Also, we hope you will be able to share with them the joys and challenges of growing up.

Most of all, we hope you will gain peace of mind and confidence in your ability to bring up your baby. We hope this book will be a reliable friend and an indispensable guide in the crucial first 20 months of your baby's life.

This Book is Gender-Neutral

We are very proud that this book has been written in gender-neutral language. There are no references to 'him' or 'her' but we use 'they' to refer to both boys and girls. You may need to get used to this when reading the book, but this enables us to emphasize what we stand for, and that applies to girls and boys: *a smart start for a happy beginning*.

Leap Alarm!

A mother sent us this letter:

Dear Frans and Hetty,

I always noticed that my baby was difficult for a few days before I realized that he was making a leap. I was irritated for a few days, but kept the feeling to myself until the proverbial straw broke the camel's back. At that point, I became very angry with him, and my own reaction scared me. When this had happened three times, I wrote down all the leaps in my calendar. That way, I can read the next chapter in time for the next leap. It may seem crazy, but I think I can handle his difficult periods much better now. I know what will happen before it does. I won't be surprised any more.

Sincerely, Maribel

To us, this was a very special letter. Maribel described what many parents feel – their baby's leaps can be overwhelming!

This is why we developed the Leap Alarm. It's easy to use. Just enter your data (due date, not birth date!) at www.thewonderweeks.com. Each email will feature a short description of your baby's imminent leap in mental development. And of course, this service is *completely free!*

Growing Up

How Your Baby Does It

For many parents, watching their baby grow is one of the most interesting and rewarding experiences of their lives. Parents love to record and celebrate the first time their baby sits up, crawls, says their first words, feeds themselves, and a myriad of other precious "firsts." But few parents stop to think about what's happening in their baby's mind that allows them to learn these skills when they do. We know that a baby's perception of the world is growing and changing when they are suddenly able to play peek-a-boo or recognize Grandma's voice on the telephone. These moments are as remarkable as the first time they crawl, but even more mysterious because they involve things happening inside their brain that we cannot see. They're proof that their brain is growing as rapidly as their chubby little body. But sooner or later every parent discovers that the first 20 months of life can be a bumpy road. While parents revel in their child's development and share their joy as they discover the world around them, they also find that at times, that the joyfulness can suddenly turn to abject misery. A baby can seem as changeable as a spring day. At times, life with baby can be a very trying experience. Inexplicable crying bouts and fussy periods are likely to drive both mother and father to desperation, as they wonder what's wrong with their little tyke and try every trick to soothe them or coax them to happiness, to no avail.

Crying and Clinging Can Simply Mean They're Growing

For 35 years, we have been studying interactions between parents and babies. In objective observations, from personal records, and on videotape, we have documented the times at which mothers report their babies to be "difficult." These difficult periods are usually accompanied by the three C's: Clinginess, Crankiness, and Crying. We now know that they are the telltale signs of a period in which the child makes a major leap forward in their development. It's well known that a child's physical growth progresses in what are commonly called "growth spurts." A child's mental development progresses in much the same way. Recent neurological studies on the growth and development of the brain support our observations of mother and baby interactions. Studies of the physical events that accompany

mental changes in the brain are still in their infancy. Yet, other scientists have identified major changes in the brain at six of the ten difficult ages we see take place in the first 20 months. Each major change announces a leap forward in mental development of the kind we are describing in this book. We expect that studies of other critical ages will eventually show similar results. It is hardly surprising, when you think of the number of changes that your baby has to go through in just the first 20 months of life, that they should occasionally feel out of sorts. Growing up is hard work!

The Fussy Signs that Signal a Magical Leap Forward

In this book, we outline the ten major developmental leaps that all babies go through in the first 20 months of their lives. Each leap allows your baby to assimilate information in a new way and use it to advance the skills they need to grow, not just physically but also mentally, into a fully functioning, thinking adult.

Each leap is invariably preceded by what we call a fussy phase or clingy period, in which the baby demands extra attention from their caregiver. The amazing and wonderful thing is that all babies go through these difficult periods at exactly the same time, give or take a week or two, during the first 20 months of their lives.

These ten developmental leaps that infants undergo are not necessarily in sync with physical growth spurts, although they may occasionally coincide. Many of the common milestones for a baby's first 20 months of development, such as cutting teeth, are also unrelated to these leaps in mental development. Milestones in mental development can, on the other hand, be reflected in physical progress, although they are by no means limited to that.

Signs of a Leap

Shortly before each leap, a sudden and extremely rapid change occurs within the baby. It's a change in the nervous system, chiefly the brain, and it may be accompanied by some physical changes as well. In this book we call this a "big change." Each big change brings the baby a new form of perception and alters the way they perceive the world. And each time a new form of perception swamps your baby, it also brings with it the means of learning a new set of skills appropriate for that world. For instance, at approximately 8 weeks, the big change in the brain enables the baby to perceive simple patterns for the first time. During the initial period of disturbance that always accompanies a big change, you may already notice new behaviors emerging. And you most certainly will shortly afterwards. In week eight, for example, your baby will suddenly show an interest in visible shapes, patterns, and structures, such as cans on a supermarket shelf or the slats on their crib. You might see physical developments as well. For example, they may start to gain some control over their body, since they now recognize the way in which their arms and legs work in precise patterns and they are able to control them. So, the big change alters the perception of sensations inside the baby's body as well as outside it. The major sign of a big change is that the baby's behavior takes an inexplicable turn for the worse. Sometimes it will seem as if your baby has become a changeling. You will notice a fussiness that wasn't there in the previous weeks and often there will be bouts of crying that you are at a loss to explain. This is very worrisome, especially when you encounter it for the first time, but it is perfectly normal. When their babies become more difficult and demanding than usual, many parents wonder if their babies are becoming ill. Or they may feel annoyed, not understanding why their babies are suddenly so fussy and trying.

The Timing of the Fussy Phases

Babies all undergo these fussy phases at around the same ages. During the first 20 months of a baby's life, there are ten developmental leaps with their corresponding fussy periods at the onset. The fussy periods come at 5, 8, 12, 15, 23, 34, 42, 51, 60, and 71 weeks. The onsets may vary by a week or two, but you can be sure of their arrival. In this book, we confine ourselves to the developmental period from birth to just' after the first year and a half of your baby's life. This pattern does not end when your baby has become a toddler, however. Several more leaps have been documented throughout childhood, and even into the teenage years.

The initial fussy phases your baby goes through as an infant do not last long. They can be as short as a few days – although they often seem longer to parents distressed over an infant's inexplicable crying. The intervals between these early periods are also short – three or four weeks, on average. Later, as the changes your infant undergoes become more complex, they take longer for them to assimilate and the fussy periods may last from one to six weeks. Every baby will be different, however. Some babies find change more distressing than others, and some changes will be more distressing than others. But every baby will be upset to some degree while these big changes in their life are taking place.

Every big change is closely linked to changes in the developing infant's nervous system, so nature's timing for developmental leaps is actually calculated from the date of conception. In this book, we use the more conventional age calculation from a baby's birth date. Therefore, the ages at which developmental leaps occur are calculated for full-term babies. If your baby was premature or very late, you should adjust the ages accordingly. For example, if your baby was born two weeks late, their first fussy phase will probably occur two weeks earlier than we show here. If they were four weeks early, it will occur four weeks later. Remember to make allowances for this with each of the 10 developmental leaps.

Your Baby's
10 Great Fussy Phases

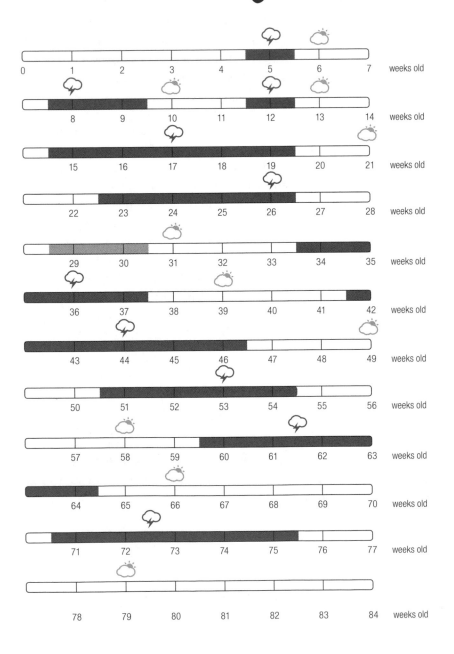

- [ ] Your baby is probably going through a comparatively uncomplicated phase

- ◧ Fussy and irritable behavior at around 29 or 30 weeks is not a telltale sign of another leap. Your baby has simply discovered that their mommy can walk away and leave them behind. Funny as it may sound, this is progress. It is a new skill: they are learning about distances.

- ■ Your baby may be fussier now than before.

- ⚡ Around this week, a "stormy" period is most likely to occur.

- ☁ Around this week, it is most likely that your baby's sunny side will shine through

Not a Single Baby Escapes

All babies experience fussy periods when big changes occur in their development. Usually calm, easygoing babies will react to these changes just as much as more difficult, temperamental babies do. But not surprisingly, temperamental babies will have more difficulty in dealing with them than their calmer counterparts. Mothers and fathers of "difficult" babies will also have a harder time as their babies already require more attention and will demand even more than usual when they have to cope with these big changes. These babies will have the greatest need for their mother and father, the most conflict with their parents, and the largest appetite for learning.

The Magical Leap Forward

To the baby, these big changes always come as a shock, as they turn the familiar world they have come to know inside out. If you stop to think about this, it makes perfect sense. Just imagine what it would be like to wake up and find yourself on a strange planet where everything was different from the one you were used to. What would you do? You wouldn't want to calmly eat or take a long nap. Neither does your baby.

All they want is to cling tightly to someone they feel safe with. To make matters more challenging for you and your baby, each developmental leap is different. Each gives the baby a new form of perception that allows them to learn a new set of skills that belong to the new developmental world – skills they could not possibly have learned at an earlier age, no matter how much encouragement you gave them.

We will describe the perceptual changes your baby undergoes in each developmental leap, as well as the new skills that then become available to them. You will notice that each world builds upon the foundations of the previous one. In each new world, your baby can make lots of new discoveries. Some skills they discover will be completely new, while others will be an improvement on skills they acquired earlier.

No two babies are exactly the same. Each baby has their own preferences, temperament, and physical characteristics, and these will lead them to select things in this new world that they, personally, find interesting. Where one baby will quickly sample everything, another will be captivated by one special skill. These differences are what make babies unique. If you watch, you will see your baby's unique personality emerging as they grow.

What You Can Do to Help

You are the person your baby knows best. They trust you more and have known you longer than anyone else. When their world has been turned inside out, they will be completely bewildered. They will cry, sometimes incessantly, and they will like nothing better than to simply be carried in your arms all day long. As they get older, they will do anything to stay near you. Sometimes they will cling to you and hold on for dear life. They

Quality Time: An Unnatural Whim

When a baby is allowed to decide for themselves when and what sort of attention they prefer, you'll notice this differs from one week to the next. When a big change occurs within a baby they will go through the following phases.

- A need to cling to mommy or daddy.
- A need to play and learn new skills with mommy or daddy.
- A need to play on their own.

Because of this, planned playtimes are unnatural. If you want your baby's undivided attention, you have to play when it suits them. It is impossible to plan having fun with a baby. In fact, they may not even appreciate your attention at the time you had set aside for "quality time." Gratifying, tender and funny moments simply happen with babies.

may want to be treated like a tiny baby again. These are all signs that they are in need of comfort and security. This is their way of feeling safe. You could say that they are returning to home base, clinging to their mommy. When your baby suddenly becomes fussy, you may feel worried or even irritated by their troublesome behavior. You will want to know what's wrong with them, and you'll wish that they would go back to being their old self again. Your natural reaction will be to watch them even more closely than before. It's then that you are likely to discover that they know much more than you thought they did. You may notice that they're attempting to do things you have never seen them do before. It may dawn on you that your baby is changing, although your baby has known it for some time already. As parents, you are in the best position to give your baby things they can handle and to meet their needs. If you respond to what your baby is trying to tell you, you will help their progress. Obviously, your baby may enjoy certain games, activities, and toys that you, personally, find less appealing, while you may enjoy others they don't like at all. Don't forget that caregivers are unique, too. You can also encourage them if they lose interest or want to give up too easily. With your help, they will find the whole play-and-learn process more challenging and fun, too. When your baby learns something new, it often means that they have to break an old habit. Once they can crawl, they are perfectly capable of fetching their own playthings, and once they can walk quite confidently on their own, they can't expect to be carried as often as before. Each leap forward in their development will make them more capable and more independent. This is the time when a mother or father and baby may have problems adjusting to one another. There is often a big difference in what baby wants and what their mother or father wants or thinks is good for the baby, and this can lead to anger and resentment on both sides. When you realize what new skills your baby is trying to exercise, you will be better equipped to set the right rules for each developmental stage and alter them as needed as they grow.

After the Leap

The troublesome phase stops just as suddenly as it started. Most parents see this as a time to relax and enjoy their babies. The pressure to provide constant attention is off. The baby has become more independent, and they are often busy putting their new skills into practice. They are more cheerful at this stage, too. Unfortunately, this period of relative peace and quiet doesn't last long – it's just a lull before the next storm. Nature does not allow babies to rest for long.

Newborn:

Welcome to the World

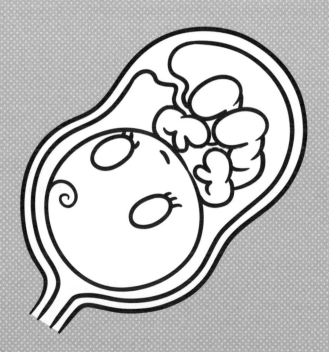

Watch any new parent when they hold their baby for the first time. Chances are they will follow this particular pattern: First they will run their fingers through the baby's hair. Then they will run a finger around the baby's head and over their face. After this, they will feel the baby's fingers and toes. Then they will slowly move toward the baby's middle, along their arms, legs, and neck. Finally, they will touch the baby's tummy and chest. The way in which parents generally touch their newborn babies is often very similar, too. First a new mother or father will touch their infant with fingertips only, stroking and handling them very gently. Slowly but surely, as they become more comfortable, they will use all of their fingers and may sometimes squeeze their baby. Finally, they will touch them with the palm of their hand. When they eventually dare to hold their baby by the chest or tummy, the new parent will be so delighted that they may exclaim what a miracle it is that they have produced something as precious as this.

Ideally, this discovery process should occur as close to birth as possible. After a mother and father's first encounter with their baby, they will no longer be afraid to pick them up, turn them around, or put them down. They will know how their little one feels to the touch.

Every baby looks and feels different. Try picking up another baby if their parents will allow it, and you'll find that it's a strange experience. It will take a minute or two to get used to the other infant. This is because you have become so accustomed to *your* baby.

Take Charge Early

The sooner parents become confident handling their baby, the quicker they can begin responding sensitively to their needs. A baby shouldn't be dumped in their mother or father's arms; they should be allowed all the time they need to take the baby into their arms by themselves.

Those Important First Hours

A mother is usually extremely perceptive to her newborn baby in the first hours after birth. Try to have your baby with you at this critical time to get to know each other. Your newborn baby is often wide awake during this period. They are aware of their surroundings, they turn towards quiet sounds, and they fix their gaze on the face that happens to hover above them. Most mothers love it if the father is there, too, so they can share this experience as a brand-new family.

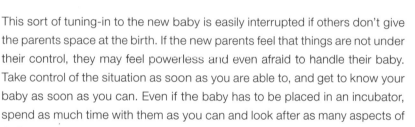

This sort of tuning-in to the new baby is easily interrupted if others don't give the parents space at the birth. If the new parents feel that things are not under their control, they may feel powerless and even afraid to handle their baby. Take control of the situation as soon as you are able to, and get to know your baby as soon as you can. Even if the baby has to be placed in an incubator, spend as much time with them as you can and look after as many aspects of their care as you are able to do. Talk to your baby to let them know you are there when you are not able to touch them. Be sure to speak up. If you want to have your baby near you, or if you want to be alone with them for a while, say so. *You* decide how often you want to pick them up and cuddle them.

The majority of mothers whose early contact with their newborns was thwarted by hospital procedures or others around them say that they regret not having spent more time alone with their babies during this period. Many mothers feel resentful about this for quite some time. The maternity period wasn't like they imagined. Instead of enjoying a well-earned rest, they felt harassed. They had wanted to have their babies near them all the time, especially when their little one was crying. If they were not allowed to hold their babies, the new mothers felt disappointed and annoyed. They felt as if they were being treated like immature, helpless children who were incapable of deciding for themselves what was best for them and their babies. These feelings have also been expressed by fathers, too, who felt overwhelmed by hospital rules and frustrated by meddling from others.

"I had to do as I was told. I wasn't just told how to sit during nursing, but also when I could nurse, and for how long. I also had to allow my baby to cry whenever it wasn't "his time" yet. I was annoyed most of the time, but I didn't want to be rude, so I nursed him in secret. I just couldn't stand hearing him cry, and I wanted to comfort him. My breasts kept swelling and shrinking all day long. I'd really had more than I could take. I was the one who had given birth, and I wanted my baby. I was so angry that I just started crying. But of course they had a name for that, too – 'maternity tears.' That was the last straw. All I wanted was my baby and a bit of peace and quiet."

Paul's mom

"I had a long delivery. Our baby was taken away from us immediately. For hours, we assumed we'd had a baby boy. When I got my baby back later on, it turned out to be a girl. We were shocked. It wasn't that we didn't want a girl, but we had started getting used to the idea that we had a son."

Jenny's mom

"When I nursed my baby, I liked to snuggle up to her and get nice and close. But the maternity nurse wouldn't let me. She made me lean back into the cushions on the sofa. It felt so unnatural – detached and unemotional."

Nina's mom

When parents have problems with their baby shortly after the birth, they often say this is because they don't feel completely confident. They are afraid of dropping them or holding them too tightly. They haven't learned to assess their baby's needs and responses to certain situations. They feel they are failing as mothers and fathers.

Some parents think this has to do with the fact that they saw so little of their baby just after the birth. They would have loved to have spent more time with their baby back then, but now they feel relieved when the baby is back in their crib. They've become afraid of parenthood.

"Because I had a difficult birth, we had to stay in the hospital for 10 days. I was only allowed to see my baby during the day, at nursing times. Nothing was the way I had imagined it would be. I'd planned to breastfeed, but sometimes the staff gave my baby a bottle on the sly, to make things easier for themselves. At night, they always gave her bottles. I wanted to have her near me more often, but they wouldn't allow it. I felt helpless and angry. When I was allowed to go home, I felt that they might as well keep her. By that time, she felt like a stranger, like she wasn't mine."

Juliette's mom

Do Remember

Cuddle, rock, caress, and massage your baby when they are in a good mood, because this is the best time to find out what suits them and what relaxes them most. When you know their preferences, you will be able to use these methods to comfort them later on when they are upset. If you only cuddle, rock, caress, and massage them only when they are in a bad mood, your "comforting" will cause them to cry even longer and louder.

"The maternity nurse was a nuisance. She stayed when I had company, did most of the talking, and went on and on telling everyone about every case she'd been on that had ever gone just the slightest bit wrong. For some reason, she was overly concerned that my healthy baby would turn yellow. She would check on her every hour, sometimes every 15 minutes, and tell me she thought she'd seen the first signs of jaundice. It made me so nervous. When I tried to breastfeed, the nurse kept interrupting by whisking my hungry baby off to be weighed. This upset me every time, and my baby didn't seem too pleased about it, either. She wriggled around on the scales, so it would take even longer for the nurse to see whether she had taken 1.4 or 1.5 ounces of milk. Meanwhile, my baby's desperate screams made me even more nervous, so I finally decided to stop breastfeeding. When I look back on it, I feel terrible. I would have liked so much to nurse my little girl."

Emily's mom

"With my second child, we were determined to do everything exactly the way we wanted. When the baby started crying, I would simply feed her a little. For nearly two weeks, we had been told to let our eldest cry and go hungry for no reason, as it later turned out. With the first baby, you tend to take advice from everyone. The second time, I listened only to myself."

Eve's mom

Getting to Know and Understand Your Baby

In some ways, you already know your baby. After all, they were with you day and night for nine months. Before they were born, you wondered what kind of baby you would have and whether you would recognize any traits you thought they had while in your womb. But once they are born it's different – totally different, in fact. You see your baby for the first time, and your baby also finds themselves in completely new surroundings. Most mothers look for familiar traits in their tiny newborns. Are they the peaceful little person she expected them to be? Do they kick at certain times of the day like they did before they were born? Do they have a special bond with their dad? Do they recognize his voice?

Often parents want to "test" their baby's reactions. They want to find out what makes their children happy and contented. They will appreciate advice, but not rules and regulations. They want to get to know their baby and see how their baby respond to them. They want to find out for themselves what is best for their children. If they're right about their likes and dislikes, they feel pleased with themselves, as it shows how well they know their baby. This increases their self-confidence and will make them feel they are perfectly able to cope after they take their infants home. Seeing, hearing, smelling, and feeling your baby during those first few days has a tremendous impact on your relationship with your baby. Most mothers instinctively know how important these intimate "parties" are. They want to experience everything their baby does. Just looking at them gives them enormous pleasure. They want to watch them sleep and listen to them breathe. They want to be there when they wake up. They want to caress them, cuddle them, and smell them whenever they feel like it.

"My son's breathing changes whenever he hears a sudden noise or sees a light. When I first noticed this irregular breathing, I was really concerned, but then I realized he was just reacting to sound and light. Now I think it's wonderful when his breathing changes, and I don't worry about it anymore."

Bob's mom

Your Baby Gets to Know and Understand You

When a new parent gazes down into their baby's face, it often seems as if the baby, gazing steadily back with wide, astonished eyes, is thinking: "What a strange and wonderful world this is!"

Indeed, a newborn baby's world is an astonishing place of new and strange sensations. Light, sound, motion, smells, the sensations on their soft skin – it is all so new that they can't separate all the different things. Sometimes, snuggled tightly up against their mother's breast, it all feels so wonderfully good. They feel full, warm, sleepy, and soothed by the softness around them.

At other times, their whole world seems utterly shattered, and they can't figure out what's making them feel so miserable. Something is wet, cold, hungry, noisy, blindingly bright, or just desperately unhappy, and all they can do is wail.

During the first five weeks of your baby's life, they will slowly become familiar with the world around them. You will get to know each other more intimately than anyone else in your shared world at this time. Soon they will make the first major leap in their development.

But before you are able to understand what your baby will experience when they are five weeks old and take their first leap forward, you need to know what your newborn baby's world is like now and how they are equipped to deal with it. Also, to help them meet their new challenges, you need to know how important physical contact is and how to use it.

Your New Baby's World

Babies are interested in the world around them from the moment they are born. They look and listen, taking in their surroundings. They try very hard to focus their eyes sharply, which is why babies frequently look cross-eyed as they strain to get a better look. Sometimes they tremble and gasp in sheer exhaustion from the effort. A newborn often looks at you as if they are staring, transfixed with interest.

Your new baby has an excellent memory, and they are quick to recognize voices, people, and even some toys, such as an especially colorful stuffed animal. They also clearly anticipate regular parts of their daily routine, such as bath-time, cuddle-time, and nursing-time.

Even at this age, a baby mimics facial expressions. Try sticking your tongue out at them while you sit and talk to them, or open your mouth wide as if you are going to call out. Make sure that they are really looking at you when you try this, and give them plenty of time to respond. Most of your baby's movements are very slow by adult standards, and it will take them several seconds to react.

A young baby is able to tell their parents just how they feel – whether they are happy, angry, or surprised. They do this by slightly changing the tone of their murmuring, gurgling, or crying and by using body language. You will quickly get to know what they mean. Besides, the baby will make it perfectly clear that they expect to be understood. If they aren't, they will cry angrily or sob as if heartbroken.

Your newborn baby has preferences even at this tender age. Most babies prefer to look at people, rather than toys. You will also find that if presented with two playthings, they are able to express a preference by fixing their gaze on one of them.

Your new baby is quick to react to encouragement. They will adore being praised for their soft baby fragrance, their looks, and their achievements. You will hold their interest for longer if you shower them with compliments! Even though your baby's senses are in full working order, they are unable to process the signals their senses send to their brain in the same way adults do. This means they aren't able to distinguish among their senses. Babies experience their world in their own way, and it's quite different from ours. We *smell* a scent, *see* the flower spreading it, *touch* its soft, velvety petals, *hear* a bee buzzing towards it, and know we are *tasting* honey when we put it into our mouths. We understand the difference among all of our senses, and so we are able to distinguish the differences.

(continued on page 31)

New Baby's Senses

Young babies can already see, hear, smell, taste, and feel a variety of things, and they are able to remember these sensations. However, a newborn baby's perception of these sensations is very different from the way they will experience them as they get older.

WHAT BABIES SEE

Until recently, scientists and doctors believed that new babies were unable to see. This is not true. Parents have known all along that newborns love to look at faces, although it is true that vision is the last sense to reach full capacity. Your newborn can see most clearly up to a distance of about a foot. Beyond that, their vision is probably blurred. Sometimes they will also have difficulty focusing both eyes on whatever they are looking at, but once they have, they can stare at the object intently. They will even stop moving briefly. All their attention will be focused on the object. If they are very alert, they will sometimes be able to follow a moving toy by moving their eyes, turning their head, or sometimes by doing both together. They can manage to do this whether the object is moved horizontally or vertically. The important thing is that the object is moved very slowly and deliberately. If they lose track after a few moments, they pick up their gaze again and try it even more slowly.

The object that your baby will be able to follow best is a simple pattern with the basic characteristics of a human face – two large dots at the top for the eyes and one below for the mouth. Babies are able to do this within an hour of birth. Many of them have their eyes wide open and are very alert. Fathers and mothers are often completely fascinated by their newborn baby's big, beautiful eyes. It is possible that babies are

attracted to anything that even vaguely resembles a human face when they are this young. Your baby will be particularly interested in sharp contrasts – red and white stripes will probably hold their attention for longer than green and blue ones. The brighter the color contrasts, the more interested they will be. Black and white stripes actually hold a baby's attention longest because the contrast is strongest.

WHAT BABIES HEAR

At birth, your new baby can already clearly distinguish between different sounds. They will recognize your voice shortly after birth. They may like music, the hum of an engine, and soft drumming. This makes sense, because these sounds are already familiar to them. In the womb, they were surrounded by the constant thump, rustle, grumble, wheeze, and squeak of heart, veins, stomach, lungs, and intestines. They also have a built-in interest in people's voices and find them soothing. By and large babies will feel comfortable in environments similar to those that they were used to in the womb. For example, a baby whose mother spent a lot of time in noisy surroundings while she was pregnant may be quite upset by a room that is too quiet.

Your baby also recognizes the difference between deep and high-pitched voices. High-pitched sounds will draw their attention more quickly. Adults sense this and speak to babies in high-pitched voices, so there is no need to be ashamed of your "oochykoochycooing." Your baby is also able to differentiate between soft and loud sounds and does not like sudden, loud noises. Some babies are easily frightened, and if this is the case for your baby, it is important that you do nothing that will frighten them.

WHAT BABIES SMELL

Your new baby is very sensitive to smells. They do not like pungent or sharp odors. These smells will make them overactive. They will try to turn away from the source of the smell, and they may start to cry, too.

Your baby can smell the difference between your body scent and breast milk and those of other mothers. If they are presented with several items of worn clothing, they will turn toward the article that you have worn.

WHAT BABIES TASTE

Your baby can already distinguish between several different flavors. They have a distinct preference for sweet things and will dislike anything that tastes sour or acidic. If something tastes bitter, they will spit it out as fast as they can.

WHAT BABIES FEEL

Your baby can sense changes in temperature. They can feel heat, which they put to good use when searching for a nipple if it is not put in their mouth, since the nipple is much warmer than the breast. They simply move their head in the direction of the warmest spot. Your baby can also sense cold. But if they are allowed to become cold, they will be unable to warm themselves, because at this age they can't shiver to get warm as a means of controlling their own body temperature. Their parents need to consider their bodily warmth. For instance, it's not very sensible to take a baby for a long walk through snow and ice, no matter how well wrapped up they are, because they may become too cold and show signs of hypothermia. If your baby shows distress of any kind, hurry inside where it is warm. Your baby is extremely sensitive to being touched. Generally, they love skin contact, whether it's soft or firm. Find out what your baby prefers. They will usually enjoy a body massage in a nice warm room, too. Physical contact is simply the best possible comfort and amusement for them. Try to find out what type of contact makes your baby sleepy or alert, since you can put this knowledge to good use in troublesome times.

Your new baby is not yet able to make this distinction, however. They experience the world as all one universe – a mish-mash of sensations that changes drastically as soon as a single element changes. They receive all these impressions but cannot distinguish among them. They do not yet realize that their world is made up of signals from individual senses and that each sense conveys messages about a single aspect of it.

To make matters even more confusing for your infant, they cannot yet make a distinction between themselves and their surroundings, and they are not yet aware of being an independent person. Because of this, they are also unable to make a distinction between sensations that originate within their own body and those that come from outside it. As far as they are concerned, the outside world and their body are one and the same. To them, the world is one big color-cuddle-smell-and-sound sensation. What their body feels, they assume everyone and everything else feels.

Because a newborn baby perceives the world and themselves as one and the same, it is often difficult to discover the reason why they are crying. It could be anything inside or outside of them. No wonder their crying fits can drive their parents to distraction.

Your New Baby's Tool Kit

If you were to experience the world in the same way your baby does, you too would be incapable of acting independently. You would not know that you have hands to grasp things with and a mouth to suck with. Only when you understand these things will you be able to do things deliberately.

This does not mean, however, that newborn babies are completely incapable of reacting to the world. Fortunately, your baby comes equipped with several special features to compensate for these shortcomings and help them survive this initial period.

Their Reflexes Tell Them What to Do

Babies have several reflex reactions to keep them safe. For example, a newborn baby will automatically turn their head to one side to breathe freely when lying face down. In some ways, this reflex is similar to the way a puppet reacts to its strings being pulled. They do not stop to think, "I'm going to turn my head." It simply happens. As soon as a baby learns to think and respond, this reflex disappears. It is a perfect system. (Of course, when it's time for your baby to go to sleep, be sure to place them on their back.) Newborn babies also turn their heads toward sound. This automatic reaction ensures that a baby will shift their attention to the place of interest closest by. For many years, doctors overlooked this reaction because a newborn's response to sound is delayed. It takes five to seven seconds before the baby starts to move their head, and it takes another three to four seconds to complete the movement. This reflex disappears somewhere between the 5th and 8th week after birth. Here are some of your baby's other reflexes:

As soon as the mouth of a hungry newborn comes in contact with an object, their mouth will close around it, and they will start to suck. This reflex provides the baby with an incredibly strong sucking ability. It disappears as soon as a baby no longer needs to suckle. Babies also have a strong gripping reflex. If you want your baby to grasp your finger, just stroke the palm of their hand. They will automatically grab your finger. If you do the same with their feet, they will use their toes to grab your finger. This gripping reflex is thought to date back to prehistoric times, when hominid mothers were covered with thick body hair. Because of this reflex, babies were able to cling to their mothers hair shortly after birth. A baby will use this gripping reflex during the first two months of life, especially if they sense you want to put them down when they would much rather stay with you!

A baby shows a reaction called the Moro reflex when they are frightened. They look as if they are trying to grab at something during a fall. They arch their back, throw their head back, and wave their arms and legs about, outward

Babies Get Bored, Too

Your tiny infant is not yet able to amuse themselves. Lively, temperamental babies in particular make no secret about wanting some action as soon as they are awake. Here are some ways to keep your baby entertained.

- Explore the house with them. Give them the opportunity to see, hear, and touch whatever they find interesting. Explain the items you come across while exploring. No matter what it is, they will enjoy listening to your voice. Pretty soon, they will start recognizing objects themselves.

- Have a quiet "chat." Your baby enjoys listening to your voice. But if you also have a radio playing in the background, they will have difficulty concentrating on your voice. Although young babies are able to make a distinction between different voices when they hear them one at a time, they cannot distinguish one from the other when hearing them simultaneously.

- Place interesting objects in convenient places for your baby to look at when they are awake. At this age, they won't be able to search for them by themselves, so for them it's "out of sight, out of mind."

- Experiment with music. Try to discover their favorite music and play it to them. They may find it to be very soothing. In all activities, let your baby's responses guide you.

at first, then inward, before crossing them across their chest and stomach. All of these baby reflexes disappear when they are replaced by voluntary responses. But there are other automatic reflexes that remain for life, such as breathing, sneezing, coughing, blinking, and jerking back a hand from a hot surface.

Their Cries Get Your Attention

The reflexes mentioned above are your new baby's way of restoring an uncomfortable situation to normal. Sometimes these reflexes are not enough – for instance, if they are too hot or cold, if they are not feeling well, or if they are bored. In these cases, the baby employs another strategy: They wail until *someone else* rectifies the situation. If no one helps them, the baby will cry incessantly until they are completely exhausted.

"My son's crying fits started in his second week. He yelled day and night, even though he was nursing well and growing steadily. When I took him to the clinic for his regular checkup, I mentioned that perhaps he was bored. But the pediatrician said that was impossible because babies keep their eyes closed for the first 10 days, and even if my baby had his eyes open, he still wouldn't be able to see anything. Last week, I put a rattle in his crib anyway. It seems to be helping. He's certainly crying less. So he was bored after all!"

Paul's mom, 4th week

Their Appearance Melts Your Heart

In order to survive, your baby has to rely on someone else to attend to their every need, morning, noon, and night. Therefore, nature has supplied them with a powerful weapon that they continually put to use – their appearance. Nothing is cuter than a baby. Their extraordinarily large head makes up almost one third of their total length. Their eyes and forehead are also "too big," and their cheeks are "too chubby." Furthermore, their arms and legs are "too short and too plump." Their cute looks are endearing. Designers of dolls, cuddly toys, and cartoons are quick to copy them. This look sells! This is exactly how your baby sells themselves, too. They are sweet, tiny, and helpless – a little cutie, just begging for attention. They will charm you into picking them up, cuddling them, and taking care of them.

Throughout the world, babies have been seen smiling before they are six weeks old. Smiling babies have even been filmed in the womb. Even so, this

is a very rare occurrence in babies this young. Nevertheless, you may be one of the lucky parents who has witnessed an early smile. Newborn babies smile when touched, when a breath of fresh air brushes their cheeks, when they hear human voices or other sounds, when they see faces hovering over their cribs, or simply when they are full of milk and feeling content. Sometimes they even smile in their sleep.

Your New Baby's Biggest Need

Even before they were born, your baby perceived their world as one whole. At birth, they left their familiar surroundings and for the first time were exposed to all kinds of unknown, completely new things. This new world was made up of many new sensations. Suddenly, they are able to move freely, sense heat and cold, hear a whole range of different and loud noises, see bright lights, and feel clothes wrapped around their body. Besides these impressions, they also have to breathe by themselves and get used to drinking milk, and their digestive organs have to process this new food, too. All these things are new to them. Because they suddenly have to cope with these enormous changes in lifestyle, it's easy to understand why they need to feel safe and secure.

Close human contact is the best way of imitating your baby's secure world inside the womb. It makes them feel safe. After all, your womb hugged their body, and your movements kneaded it, as far back as they can remember. It was their home. They were part of whatever took place in there – the rhythmical beating of your heart, the flow of your blood, and the rumbling of your stomach. Therefore, it makes perfect sense that they will enjoy feeling the old, familiar physical contact and hearing those well-known sounds once more. It is their way of "touching base."

Touch: Simply the Best Comfort

Besides food and warmth, nothing is more important to your infant than snuggling close to you during the first four months of their life. As long as they experience lots of physical contact, their development will not be delayed, even if you don't have much opportunity to play with them. A young baby generally loves lying close to you and being carried around. At the same time, this is also a good opportunity for them to learn to control their body.

Another idea is to give them a relaxing massage. Make sure the room is warm. Pour some baby oil into your hands and softly massage every part of their naked body. This is a nice way of helping them to grow accustomed to their body, and it will make them wonderfully drowsy.

At this age, a baby loves to be picked up, cuddled, caressed, and rocked. They may even enjoy soft pats on their back. They can't get enough physical contact now. Don't worry about whether you're doing the right thing – they will soon let you know what they like best and what comforts them most. In the meantime, they are learning that they have a wonderful home base to which they can safely return when they are upset.

Wonder Week 5

The World of Changing Sensations

"
AS IF YOUR BABY
HAS BEEN REBORN

For much of the past four or five weeks, you have watched your infant grow rapidly. You have become acquainted with each other, and you have learned all of their little ways. At this point in time, it is hard for adults to imagine what the baby's world is like. It's in soft focus and its qualities are undefined – in some ways, there are similarities to their life in your womb.

Now, before the mists that envelop their infant world part and allow them to start making sense of all the impressions they have been busy absorbing in the past few weeks, they will need to go through their first major developmental leap. At about five weeks, and sometimes as early as four, your baby will begin to take the first leap forward in their development. New sensations bombard your baby inside and out, and they are usually bewildered by them. Some of these new things have to do with the development of their internal organs and their metabolism. Others are a result of their increased alertness – their senses are more sensitive than they were immediately after birth. So it's not so much the sensations themselves that are changing, but rather the baby's perceptions of them.

This rapidly changing world is very disturbing at first. Your baby's first reaction will be to want to return to the safe, warm, familiar world they so recently left, a world with its parents at its center. Suddenly, your infant may seem to need more cuddles and attention than they did before. While eating and sleeping and being well-looked after physically were enough to lull them with a sense of well-being before, they now seem to need more from you. Although your baby has been very close to you since their birth, this might be the first time you think of them as fussy or demanding. This period may last only a day, but with some babies it lasts a whole week.

As this clinginess begins to ease, you will notice that your baby is just a little more grown-up in a way that you find hard to put your finger on. They seem more alert and aware of the world around them than they were.

Do Remember

If your baby is fussy, watch them closely to see if they are attempting to master new skills.

This Week's Fussy Signs

Even very young babies of five weeks can sense the changes occurring inside their tiny bodies. Having just gotten used to a world outside the warm embrace of your body, your baby is now finding their world changing for a second time. It's important to understand that although everything seems the same to you, to them everything they see, feel, hear, smell, or taste is different somehow. They may like some of these changes, but they might dislike others because they don't yet know how to cope with them. They are still too young to turn to you for help, and they certainly can't ask you what is going on.

How You Know it's Time to Grow

Even though your baby can't form the words to tell you what's going on, they are able to communicate quite a bit in other ways. Here are some signs that they are preparing to make their first leap.

They May Be Highly Upset

At this point in time, it's very likely your baby will yell, cry, scream, and refuse to go to sleep in their crib until they have driven the entire household crazy. These are the clues that your baby is about to make their first leap! With a bit of luck, their distress will have you running to them, picking them up, holding them tight, and letting them snuggle up.

They May Crave Closeness with You

If they are even luckier, after you pick them up, you might also nurse them. Sometimes they will only drift off to sleep if they are snuggled up to mommy in the closest way possible – latched onto the breast. Providing this sort of physical comfort with a breast or bottle may be the only way to create the safe world they are so desperate for at this time.

"Normally, my baby is very easy, but she suddenly started crying non-stop for almost two days. At first I thought it was just stomach cramps. But then I noticed she stopped whenever I had her on my lap, or when I let her lie in between us. She fell asleep right away then. I kept asking myself if I was spoiling her too much by allowing it. But the crying period stopped just as suddenly as it started, and now she's as easygoing as she was before."

Eve's mom, 5th week

How This Leap May Affect You

As these major changes in your baby affect them, they're bound to have an effect on you as well. Here are some emotions you might feel.

You May Feel Insecure

All parents want to find out why their babies are being troublesome and restless so that they can make it better for them. Usually, they will first try to see if the baby is hungry. Then they check if the diaper has come loose. They change the diaper. They try to comfort their baby with all the love and soothing they can muster in those trying moments. But it isn't easy. Pretty soon they discover that all the best care and comfort in the world doesn't really stop the little bundle from resuming their relentless crying. Most parents experience a sudden change in their babies' behavior as a miserable experience. It undermines their confidence and is very distressing.

"My son wanted to be with me all of the time, and I either held him against my chest or on my lap, even when we had company. I was terribly concerned. One night I hardly slept at all. I just spent the whole night holding and cuddling him. Then my sister came and took over for a night. I went in the other bedroom and slept like a log the whole night. I felt reborn when I woke up the next day."

Bob's mom, 5th week

You May Feel Very Concerned

Often, mothers and fathers are afraid that something is wrong with their tiny screamers. They think they are in pain, or that they might be suffering from some abnormality or disorder that has gone undetected until now. Others worry that the milk supply from breastfeeding alone is not sufficient. This is because the baby seems to crave the breast constantly and is always hungry. Some parents take their babies to a doctor for a checkup. Of course, most babies are pronounced perfectly healthy and they are sent home to worry alone. (But, when in doubt, always consult your family doctor or go to the childcare clinic.)

"My daughter was crying so much that I was afraid something was terribly wrong. She wanted to breastfeed constantly. I took her to see the pediatrician, but he couldn't find anything wrong with her. He said she just needed time to get used to my milk and that many infants went through a similar crying phase at five weeks. I thought that it was a strange thing to say, because she hadn't had any problems with my milk until then. Her cousin, who was the same age, kept crying, too, but he was being bottle-fed. When I told the doctor that, he pretended he hadn't heard. I didn't push the subject, though. I was happy enough just knowing it wasn't anything serious."

Juliette's mom, 5th week

Because your baby senses something is changing, they feel insecure and have a greater need for close skin-to-skin contact. This close embrace seems to be the most powerful kind of calming physical contact when they are upset. Give them all the cuddling they need and all the contact you feel you can handle at times like these. They need time to adjust to these new changes and grow into their new world. They are accustomed to your body scent, warmth, voice, and touch, so with you, they will relax a little and feel contented again. You can provide the tender loving care they really need during this trying period.

"Sometimes my daughter will nurse for half an hour and refuse to come off the breast. Just take her off after 20 minutes, and let her scream. She'll soon learn." is the advice people give me. But secretly I think, 'They can say what they like; I decide what's best."

Nina's mom, 5th week

You may notice that close physical contact helps during these crying fits, and that a noisy little creature will respond better and quicker when they are with you than if you try anything else. Try carrying your baby around in a sling if you can while you go about your chores, or keep them on your lap while you read or do other sedentary activities. A gentle massage or stroking can be helpful too.

"When my baby was crying all the time, she seemed so lost. I had to massage her for a long time before she calmed down a bit. I felt exhausted but extremely satisfied. Something changed after that. It doesn't seem to take as long to soothe her now. When she cries now, I don't find it such an effort to put her world to rights again."

Nina's mom, 4th week

Mothers and fathers who carry their babies around whenever they are in a fussy mood may label them "extremely dependent." These babies like nothing better than lying quietly against their mother or father and being stroked, rocked, or cuddled. They might fall asleep on their mother or father's lap, but start crying again as soon as furtive attempts are made to sneak them back into their cribs.

Parents who stick to feeding and sleeping schedules often notice their babies fall asleep during feeding. Some wonder if this is because the baby is so exhausted from crying and the lack of sleep that they have no energy left to nurse. This may seem logical, but it may not be the whole story. It's more likely that the baby falls asleep because they are where they want to be. They are finally with mommy, and they're content, so they're able to fall asleep.

Soothing Tips

When you want to comfort a tiny baby, a gentle rhythm can play a very important role. Hold your baby close to you, with their bottom resting on one arm while your other arm supports their head resting against your shoulder. When they are in this position, they can feel the soothing beat of your heart.

Here are a few other methods recommended by parents to soothe a tiny screamer.

- Cuddle and caress them.
- Rock them gently in your arms, or sit in a rocking chair with them.
- Walk around slowly with them.
- Talk or sing to them.
- Pat them gently on the bottom.

Not all of these ideas will suit your baby personally, so if you don't succeed at first, keep trying until you find out what works for them. The most successful way of comforting a crying baby is to do the things they enjoy most when they are in a cheerful mood.

How to Make a Sling

Slings are extremely easy to make and cozy for you and your new baby. A sling will help to give your arms a break by supporting your baby's weight and it will make your baby feel safe and secure. Plus, they cost only a few dollars to make. You can use a sling with your baby almost immediately after birth since it allows them to lie flat. Here's how to make one:

Use a sturdy piece of material, 1 yard by 3 1/2 yards. Drape the cloth over your left shoulder if you are right-handed, or over your right shoulder if you are left-handed, and knot the ends together at the opposite hip. Turn the knot towards your back. Check to see if the length of the sling feels right. If it does, the sling is ready for use. Pop your baby inside and support them with your hands. It's that easy!

"The first two days my son cried so much. I was doing my best to stick to the proper bedtimes, but it turned out to be a total disaster. It drove us both up the wall. Now I keep him on my lap for as long as he wants without feeling guilty. I feel good about it. It's nice and warm and cozy. It's obvious he loves it. The feeding schedule's gone out the window, too. I didn't stick to it. Now he just lets me know when he's hungry. Sometimes he nurses for a long time, but sometimes he doesn't. He's much more contented now, and I am, too."

Steven's mom, 5th week

The Magical Leap Forward

There are a number of indications in babies aged approximately four to five weeks that show they are undergoing enormous changes that affect their senses, metabolism, and internal organs. This is when the first leap occurs – the baby's alertness in the world of sensations increases dramatically. At this point your baby is losing some of their newborn skills. They will no longer follow a face with their eyes or turn towards a sound. These early skills were controlled by primitive centers in the lower brain, and they disappear to make way for developments in the higher levels of the brain. Soon you will see similar behaviors emerge, but this time they will seem to be much more under your baby's control than ever before. At this age, your baby is also likely to outgrow problems with their digestive system that they may have had initially.

Sleeping Tips

A baby with sleeping problems will often fall asleep quickly when they are with you. The warmth of your body, your gentle movements, and your soft sounds will help soothe them. Here are some tips on the best ways to get them to sleep.

- Give them a warm bath, put them on a warm towel, and then massage them gently with baby oil.
- Breast or bottle-feed them, since sucking will help to relax and soothe them.
- Walk around with them, either in a sling or baby carrier.
- Push them around in their stroller.
- Take them for a ride in the car.
- Pop them into bed beside you.

Between four and five weeks old, your baby goes through a whole set of changes that affect their senses – the way they experience the world, the way they feel, even the way they digest their food. Their whole world feels, looks, smells, and sounds different all of a sudden. Some of these changes have direct consequences that you can see. For example, this may be the first time that you notice them crying real tears. They may stay awake for longer periods and seem more interested than before in the world around them. Just after birth, they were only able to focus on objects that were up to a foot away, but now they can focus at a longer distance. It's not surprising, therefore, that a baby feels it's time for some action.

Five- to six-week-old babies are even prepared to work in order to experience interesting sensations. In a laboratory experiment, babies showed that they could adjust the focus of a color movie by sucking harder on a pacifier. As soon as the baby stopped sucking, the picture blurred. Babies at this age have difficulty sucking and watching at the same time, so they could keep this up only for a few seconds. To check this was really what they were trying to do, the babies were then required to stop sucking in order to bring the picture into focus. They could do that, too!

Babies can also start using their smile in social contact to influence their experiences. Your baby's smiles change from something superficial, almost robot-like, into social smiles around this age. Mothers and fathers become very excited when they see a smile at an earlier age, but once they have seen the "social smile," they will admit it's a different type of smile.

Brain Changes

At approximately three to four weeks, there is a dramatic increase in a baby's head circumference. Their glucose metabolism, in the brain, also changes.

My Diary

How My Baby Explores the New World of Changing Sensations

Check off the boxes below as your baby changes compared to how they were before. Stop filling this out once the next stormy period begins, heralding the next leap.

Their interest in their surroundings

- ☐ Looks at things longer and more often
- ☐ Listens to things more often and pays closer attention
- ☐ Is more aware of being touched
- ☐ Is more aware of different smells
- ☐ Smiles for the first time, or more often than before
- ☐ Gurgles with pleasure more often
- ☐ Expresses likes or dislikes more often
- ☐ Expresses anticipation more often
- ☐ Stays awake longer, and is more alert

Their physical changes

- ☐ Breathes more regularly
- ☐ Startles and trembles less often
- ☐ Cries real tears for the first time, or more often than before
- ☐ Chokes less
- ☐ Vomits less
- ☐ Burps less

OTHER CHANGES YOU NOTICE

Your Baby's Choices: A Key to Their Personality

All babies' senses develop rapidly at this time, and it will become apparent they are now more interested in their surroundings. It may or may not seem obvious at first, but every baby will have their own preferences. Some bright-eyed infants really enjoy looking at and watching everything and everyone around them. Others will listen keenly to music and sounds around them and will find sound-producing objects such as rattles more appealing than anything else. Another group of babies will love to be touched, and they would like nothing better than to play games that involve being touched and caressed by someone. Some babies don't have any clear preference. Even at this very young age, you will find that every baby is different.

As you go through the "My Diary" list on page 47, you may want to mark or highlight the items that apply to your baby at this time. They may display only a few of the behaviors, and others may not appear for several weeks. An infant who is more interested in certain sensory experiences in their world than others is showing you that they are already an individual.

"I take my daughter along to my singing classes every day. During the first few weeks, she hardly reacted to sounds at all, and I felt quite concerned, to be honest. Now suddenly, she's totally preoccupied by noises of any kind when she is awake. If she wakes up in a bad mood and I sing to her, she stops crying immediately. She doesn't stop when my friends sing, though!"

Hannah's mom, 6th week

Rocky Times for Everyone

Going through a big change can be a stressful event for your baby and for you, and you may both find the strain unbearable at times. You may become exhausted from the lack of sleep or because anxieties are preventing you from sleeping well. Here's an example of how this vicious cycle can work.

- The baby is confused and cries.
- Constant crying makes their mother and father feel insecure and anxious.
- Tension builds, and the parents finds themselves unable to cope, and so baby cries even louder than before.
- The cycle repeats, again and again.

If the strain gets to be too much, remember that it's normal to feel this way. Try to take time out to relax. Your baby will benefit from it as much as you will. Use physical contact and attention to comfort your baby. This will make it easier for them to adapt to all the changes at their own pace, and it will also give them self-confidence.

They will know that someone is there for them whenever they need comfort. As their parents, you need support, too, not criticism, from family and friends. Criticism will only undermine your already battered self-confidence, support will enable you to cope better with the difficult periods.

What You Can Do to Help

The very best way to help your baby is to give them tender loving care and support. It's impossible to spoil them at this age, so never feel guilty about comforting them, especially when they cry. Help your baby on their voyage of discovery. You'll find that they are generally more interested in the world around them now. They are more perceptive, and they are often awake for a longer period to enjoy their surroundings at this time. Try to find out what activities they like best by watching their reactions carefully. As small as they are, they are still able to let you know what pleases or displeases them. Once you know what your baby likes, you'll be able to gradually introduce new activities, games, and toys.

How Can You Tell What They Like Best?

Your baby will smile when given the things that they enjoy. It could be something they see, hear, smell, taste, or feel. Because their senses have developed and they are now able to perceive a little more of their world, they will also smile more often now. It will be very rewarding to experiment and discover which activities produce these wonderful smiles.

"I dance around with my baby, and when I stop, he smiles."

John's mom, 6th week

"When I put my face close to my daughter's and smile and talk to her, she makes eye contact and grins. It's wonderful."

Laura's mom, 5th week

"My daughter smiles at her dolls and teddy bears."

Jenny's mom, 6th week

That's Just How Babies Are

Babies love anything new, and it's important you acknowledge your baby's new skills and interests. They will enjoy it if you share these new discoveries, and your encouragement will accelerate their learning progress.

Help Your Baby Explore the New World Through Sight

Your baby looks longer at objects that interest them than before. The brighter the colors, the more fascinating they will find them. They also like striped and angular objects. And your face, of course.

If you walk around with your baby, you'll automatically discover what they like looking at best. Give them enough time to have a good look at things – and don't forget that their range of focus is not much more than a foot. Some babies like looking at the same objects time and time again, while others get bored if they are not shown something different each time. If you notice that your baby is getting bored, show them objects that are similar to the ones they like, but just slightly different.

"My baby is much more aware of everything she sees now. Her favorites are the bars of her crib, which contrast with the white walls; books on the bookshelf; our ceiling, which has long wooden slats with a dark stripe in between; and a black-and-white ink drawing on the wall. At night, lights seem to interest her the most."

Emily's mom, 5th week

"My son stares right into my face and gazes at me for quite some time. He thinks it's funny when I eat. He looks at my mouth and watches me chew. He seems to think it's fascinating."

Kevin's mom, 6th week

"When I move a green and yellow ball slowly from left to right, my daughter turns her head to follow it. She seems to think it's great fun, although this proud mom probably enjoys it more than she does."

Ashley's mom, 5th week

Help Your Baby Explore the New World Through Sound

Sounds usually fascinate babies. Buzzing, squeaking, ringing, rustling, or whizzing sounds are all interesting. Babies find human voices very intriguing, too. High-pitched voices are extremely captivating, although nothing can beat the sound of their mother's voice, even if she's not a natural soprano. Even at five weeks old, you can have cozy little chats with your baby.

Pick a comfortable place to sit and put your face close to theirs. Chat to them about how beautiful they are, about everyday events, or whatever comes to mind. Stop talking once in a while to give them a chance to "reply."

"I really think my son is listening to me now. It's remarkable."
Matt's mom, 5th week

"Sometimes my baby chats back to me when I'm talking to her. She talks for longer now, and sometimes it seems as if she's really trying to tell me something. It's adorable. Yesterday, she chatted to her rabbit in her crib."
Hannah's mom, 5th week

Help Your Baby Explore the New World Through Touch

All babies become more aware of being touched at this age. Too many cuddling visitors may suddenly become 'too much' for one baby, whereas another may enjoy the attention tremendously. Every baby is different! You might hear your baby laughing out loud for the very first time now, perhaps when they are being tickled. Although generally, babies of this age do not particularly appreciate being tickled.

"My daughter laughed out loud, really roared, when her brother started tickling her. Everyone was startled, and it went dead quiet."
Emily's mom, 5th week

Baby Care

Don't Overdo it

Let your baby's responses guide you. Your baby has become more sensitive now, so you need to be careful not to overstimulate them. Bear this in mind when you play with them, cuddle them, show them things, or let them listen to things. You have to adapt to them. Stop as soon as you notice something is getting too much for them.

Your baby is still unable to concentrate for a long period of time, so they will need short rest breaks. You may think they have lost interest, but they haven't. Be patient. Usually, they'll soon be raring to go again if you let them rest for a short while.

Let Them Know You Understand Them

Your baby may use a greater range of crying and gurgling sounds than before, and they may produce these sounds more frequently at this age. They may have different sounds for different situations. Babies will often make a whimpering sound before falling asleep. If a baby is really upset, you'll be able to tell by the way they cry, because it's a totally different sound. They are telling you that something is wrong. Your baby may also make other noises, such as gurgling sounds to show they are happy, especially when they are looking at or listening to something. These sounds will help you to understand them better. If you understand what your baby is trying to tell you, let them know. Babies adore interaction.

"I know exactly when my baby is gurgling with pleasure or grumbling because she's angry. Sometimes she gurgles with pleasure when she sees her mobile, and she loves it when I imitate the sounds she makes."

Hannah's mom, 6th week

After the Leap

At around six weeks, the leap has ended, and a period of comparative peace dawns. Babies are more cheerful, more alert, and more preoccupied with looking and listening than before. Many parents claim that their baby's eyes seem brighter. Babies are also capable of expressing their likes and dislikes at this age. In short, life seems a little less complicated than before.

"We communicate more now. Suddenly, the hours that my son is awake seem more interesting."

Frankie's mom, 6th week

"I feel closer to my baby. Our bond is stronger."

Bob's mom, 6th week

LEAP 2

Wonder Week 8

The World of Patterns

"

YOUR BABY FEELS, HEARS AND SEES
THEM... FOR THE FIRST TIME

Sometime around eight weeks, your baby will begin to experience the world in a new way. They will have the capacity to recognize simple patterns in the world around them and in their own body. Although it may be hard for us to imagine at first, this happens with all the senses, not just vision. For example, they may discover their hands and feet and spend hours practicing the skill of controlling their arms or legs in certain positions. They'll be endlessly fascinated with the way light displays shadows on the wall of their bedroom. You might notice them studying the cans on the grocery store shelf in detail or listening to themselves making short bursts of sounds, such as ah, uh, ehh.

Any of these things – and lots of others – signal a big change in your baby's mental development. This change will enable them to learn a new set of skills that they would have been incapable of learning at an earlier age, no matter how much help and encouragement you gave them. But just as in their previous developmental leap, adjusting to this new world will not come easily at first.

The change in the way your baby perceives the world around them will initially make them feel puzzled, confused, and bewildered as their familiar world is turned upside down. They suddenly see, hear, smell, taste, and feel in a completely new way, and they will need time to adjust. To come to terms with what is happening to them, they need to be somewhere safe and familiar. Until they begin to feel more comfortable in this new world, they will want to cling to their mommy for comfort. This time, the fussy phase could last anywhere from a few days to two weeks.

Note: *This leap into the perceptual world of "patterns" is age-linked and predictable. It sets in motion the development of a whole range of skills and activities. However, the age at which these skills and activities appear for the first time varies greatly and depends on your baby's preferences, experimentation and physical development. For example, the ability to perceive patterns emerges at about eight weeks, and is a necessary precondition for "sitting with minimal support," but this skill normally appears anywhere from two to six months. The skills and activities in this chapter are stated at the earliest possible age they could appear so you can watch for and recognize them. (They may be rudimentary at first.) This way you can respond to and facilitate your baby's development.*

If you notice your baby is more cranky than usual, watch them closely. It's likely they're attempting to master new skills. Once you're over the hump, however, you will probably experience this second leap as a real milestone in your child's development. As they begin to learn to control their body and use their senses to explore what interests them, they will start to express their own preferences. You'll learn what they like and don't like, whether they listen more keenly to particular kinds of sounds, which colors they prefer, what kinds of toys or activities they enjoy, and whose face makes them light up most – beside yours, of course. These are the first signs of your baby's newly emerging personality.

This Week's Fussy Signs

Sometime between seven and nine weeks of age your baby may become more demanding than they were. They might cry more often now, as this is their way of expressing how stressful these changes are to them. At this age, crying is the most effective way to show they feel lost and need attention. More sensitive babies will sob and scream even more than they did before and drive their mothers and fathers to distraction. Even when everything possible is done to console these tiny screamers, they may still continue to wail. Most babies will calm down, however, when they experience close physical contact, although for some babies it can never be close enough. If such a tiny cuddler had their way, they would crawl right back into their mommy. They would like to be totally enveloped in their mother's arms, legs, and body. They may demand their mother's undivided attention and will protest as soon as it wavers.

How You Know it's Time to Grow

It's time to change again! Here are some clues that this leap is approaching.

They May Demand More Attention Than Before

Your baby may want you to spend more time amusing them than they did before. They might even want you to be totally absorbed in them, and only them. At this time, many babies no longer want to lie in their cribs or on blankets on the floor, even if they had always been happy to do so until now. They might not object to lying in baby chairs, just as long as their parents are close by. But their ultimate goal is to be with their mothers and fathers. They want their parents to look at them, talk to them, and play with them.

"Suddenly, my baby doesn't like going to bed at night. She becomes restless and starts screaming and crying and refuses to settle down. But we need some peace and quiet too. So we keep her with us on the couch, or hold and cuddle her, and then she's no trouble at all."

Eve's mom, 8th week

They May Become Shy with Strangers

You may notice that your friendly bundle may not smile so easily at people they do not see often, or they may need more time to warm to them than before. Occasionally, some babies will even start crying if other people try to get near them when they are lying contentedly snuggled up to their moms. Some think this is a pity: "They always used to be so cheerful." Others are secretly pleased: "After all, I'm the one who's there for them all the time."

"My daughter seems to smile more for me than anyone else. It takes her a little longer to loosen up with other people now."

Ashley's mom, 9th week

They May Lose Their Appetite

At this time, it may seem that if your baby had their way, they'd be on the breast or bottle all day long. But although they are latched onto the nipple, you might notice that they hardly take any milk at all. Many babies will do this now. As long as they feel a nipple in or against their mouths, they are content. But as soon as they are taken off the breast or the bottle, they start protesting and continue to cry until they feel the nipple again. This generally only occurs in babies who are nursed on demand. Some mothers who breastfeed might start to think that there is something wrong with their milk supply, while other mothers question whether the decision to breastfeed was the right one after all. It's not necessary to stop breastfeeding at this point; on the contrary, this would not be a very good time to choose to wean your baby. During this stormy period, the baby is demanding the breast less for nutritional purposes and more as a comfort. This explains why some babies will suck their thumbs or fingers more often during this period.

"Sometimes I feel like a walking milk bottle, on standby 24 hours a day. It really irritates me. I wonder if other mothers who breastfeed go through the same thing."

Matt's mom, 9th week

They May Cling to You More Tightly Now

Your baby might hold on to you even tighter than they did before when they sense they are about to be set down. Not only will they cling to you with their fingers, they may even cling to you with their toes! This show of devotion often makes it difficult for a mother or father to put their baby down, both literally and figuratively. You may find it touching and heart-wrenching at the same time.

"When I bend over to put my infant down, she clutches at my hair and clothes as if she's terrified to lose contact. It's really sweet, but I wish she wouldn't do it, because it makes me feel so guilty about setting her down."

Laura's mom, 9th week

They May Sleep Poorly

At a difficult time like this, your baby may not sleep as well as they did before. They might start crying the moment you carry them into their bedroom, which explains why parents sometimes think their babies are afraid of their cribs. Various sleeping problems may affect your little one. Some babies have difficulty falling asleep, while others are easily disturbed and sleep for short periods. Whatever sleeping problems your baby might have, they all have the same result: a lack of sleep for everybody in the house. Unfortunately, this also means that your baby is awake for longer periods now, giving them more opportunities to cry.

They May Just Cry and Cry

At approximately eight weeks, it's normal for your baby to have an urgent desire to go "back to mommy." Some infants, of course, will demonstrate this need more than others. Crying and clinging might become part of your everyday life around this age. It's a sign that your baby is making healthy progress, that they are reacting to the changes within them, and that they are taking a leap forward in their development.

Your little one is upset simply because they haven't yet had time to adjust to these changes and are still confused. This is why they need to have you around. They want to return "home," to their safe haven, where they can feel secure in familiar surroundings. With you, they will gain enough confidence to explore their new world.

Imagine what it must be like to feel upset with no one around to comfort you. You'd feel the tension mounting and not know what to do. You'd need all your energy just to cope with the stress, and you'd have little strength left to solve your problems. Your baby is no different. To them, every time a big change in their mental development occurs, they feel as if they have woken up in a brand-new world. They will be confronted with more new impressions than they can handle. They cry, and they will continue to cry until they become accustomed enough to their new world to feel at ease. If they are not comforted, they will use all their energy crying, and they will be wasting valuable time that they could put to much better use discovering their new and puzzling world.

My Diary

Signs My Baby is Growing Again

Between seven and nine weeks, you may notice your baby starting to show some of the following behaviors. They are probably signs that they are ready to make the next leap, when the world of patterns will open up to them.

Check off the boxes next to the behaviors your baby shows:

☐ Cries more often than before

☐ Wants you to keep them busy

☐ Loses appetite

☐ Is shyer with strangers all of a sudden

☐ Clings more than usual

☐ Sleeps poorly

☐ Sucks their thumb, or more often than before

OTHER CHANGES YOU NOTICE

How This Leap May Affect You

These major changes in your baby will have a tremendous impact on you as well. Here are some of the ways they might affect you.

You May Feel Worried

When a baby goes through an inexplicable crying fit, life can unravel for everyone around them. Babies who cry a lot more than they used to can wear down even the most confident parents. If you are in this situation, you may begin to wonder whether you're really fit for the job. But don't despair: Your experience is very normal. The average baby will cry noticeably more and will also be a lot more difficult to comfort than usual at this time. Only a small number of mothers and fathers are lucky enough to have no particular worries about their babies at this age. These parents have infants who are unusually easygoing or quiet, who don't cry much more than usual, and who are generally easy to comfort.

Temperamental, irritable babies are the most difficult ones to deal with. They will seem to cry 10 times louder and more frequently than other babies, and they will thrash around as if they were in a boxing ring. Their mothers often worry that the whole family will fall apart.

"It's a nightmare, the way my baby goes on and on. She cries all of the time and hardly sleeps at all at the moment. Our marriage is going to pieces. My husband comes home in the evening, dragging his feet, because he can't face another night of torment. We're having constant arguments about how to stop her awful crying."

Jenny's mom, 7th week

"When my son won't stop crying, I always go to him, although I've reached the stage where I could agree with statements such as 'Children just need to cry sometimes.' I feel so drained. But then I start thinking about how thin these apartments walls are, and so I end up going to him again, hoping I'll be able to get him to settle down this time."

Steven's mom, 9th week

At this time, when your baby cries more than usual, you might be desperate to figure out why. You may wonder, "Is my milk supply drying up? Are they ill? Am I doing something wrong? Do they have a wet diaper? When they're on my lap, they're fine – does this mean I'm spoiling them?" When every other avenue has been explored, some parents finally decide that their baby must be upset due to colic. Their tiny screamers do seem to be writhing around a lot, after all. Some mothers and fathers even have a good cry themselves. It is a particularly hard time for first-time mothers, who tend to blame themselves. Occasionally, parents will go to see the doctor, or they will bring the problem up with the pediatrician.

"Sometimes, when my daughter cries and won't stop no matter what I do, I get so upset that I take it out on my poor husband. I often have a good cry myself, which does help to relieve the tension a bit."

Emily's mom, 10th week

"Some days when I'm at a low ebb, I wonder if I'm doing the right thing, if I'm giving my son enough attention or too much. It's so typical that it was on one of those difficult days that I read that babies smile at their mothers when they're six weeks old. Mine never did. He only smiled to himself, and that really undermined my confidence. Then suddenly, this evening, he grinned at me. Tears welled up in my eyes, it was so touching. I know this sounds ridiculous, but for a moment I felt like he was trying to tell me it was okay, that he was with me all the way."

Bob's mom, 9th week

"Normally my baby never cries. He's so easygoing, as easy as they come. But this week he had terrible problems: stomach cramps, I presume."

John's mom, 9th week

Whatever you do, don't despair – tell yourself it is not your fault! Try to remember this is your young baby's way of telling you that they are now capable of learning new skills, which means that their mind is developing well. At this age, their crying is normal and only temporary.

You May Be Irritated and Defensive

As soon as you are convinced that your noisy little infant has no valid reason to keep crying and clinging to you, you might feel irritated. You may think that they're ungrateful and spoiled. You still have so much work to do, and their crying is driving you mad. Plus, you're exhausted. Well, you're not alone. Most parents have these feelings. Many mothers worry that their baby's fathers, family, friends, or neighbors may regard "mommy's little sweetheart" as a "complete nuisance." They may become defensive when other people tell them to be stern with their babies.

"Is this what I gave my job up for–eight weeks of crying? I'm at my wit's end. I really don't know what more I can do."

Jenny's mom, 8th week

"It really drives me up the wall when I finally get my baby to sleep after comforting her for an hour, and she starts whimpering again the moment that I set her down. She's only happy when I'm holding her. This irritates me to no end. I don't get a chance to do anything else."

Laura's mom, 8th week

"I had to keep my son occupied all day long. Nothing really helped. I tried walking around, stroking him, and singing. At first I felt completely helpless and depressed, and then suddenly, I felt really frustrated. I sat down and just started sobbing. So I asked the day care center if they would have him for two afternoons a week, just to give me a few hours to recharge my batteries. His crying sometimes drains me completely. I'm so tired. I'd just like to know how much both of us can take."

Bob's mom, 9th week

Baby Care

Shaking Can Be Harmful

Having aggressive feelings towards a demanding little screamer is not dangerous, but acting on those feelings is. Whatever you do, don't ever let yourself get into such a state that you might harm them. Never shake a baby. Shaking a young child is one of the worst things that you can do. It could easily cause internal bleeding just below the skull, which can result in brain damage that may lead to learning difficulties later on or even death.

You May Really Lose it

Only rarely will a mother or father admit to having been a bit rougher than necessary when pulling their baby down because they were so irritated by the baby's screaming and crying. If this does happen, it is always a disturbing experience, especially because it seemed to be a gut reaction at the time.

"My daughter cried even more this week than she did last week. It drove me crazy. I had more than enough to do as it was. I had her in my arms, and on the spur of the moment, I threw her onto her changing mat on the dresser. Afterward, I was shocked by what I'd done, and at the same time I realized it hadn't helped the situation at all. She screamed even louder. After it happened, I understood what drives some parents to abuse their children during these 'colic fits,' but I never thought I'd do something like that myself."

Juliette's mom, 9th week

How Your Baby's New Skills Emerge

You will automatically keep an extra close eye on your baby when you are concerned about their clinginess. At the back of your mind, you may have these nagging doubts: "What is the matter with them?"

Why are they being so troublesome? What can I do? Am I spoiling them? Should they be doing more at this age? Are they bored? Why are they unable to amuse themselves? Soon you'll realize what's really going on – your infant is attempting to master new skills.

At approximately eight weeks, you will notice that your baby is opening up to their new world: a world of observing and experimenting with simple patterns. They will be ready to acquire several pattern skills at this time, but your baby, with their unique inclinations, preferences, and temperament, will choose which discoveries they want to make. You can help them with what they are ready to do.

Don't try to push them. While you may think they should be practicing holding a ball (for their future softball career), they might prefer to make their first attempts at talking by babbling to their toys. Let them go at their own pace and respect their preferences. It could be hard on you if you're tone deaf and your baby is keen on sounds. Don't worry. They don't need symphonies just yet – talking and humming will do just fine.

Cuddle Care: The Best Way to Comfort

A baby of this age loves to be picked up, caressed, and cuddled.
You can never give them too much of a good thing.

Brain Changes

At approximately seven to eight weeks, a baby's head circumference dramatically increases. Researchers have recorded changes in the brain waves of babies six to eight weeks old.

The Magical Leap Forward

About this age, your baby no longer experiences the world and themselves as one universe. They will start to recognize recurring shapes, patterns, and structures. For instance, your baby might now discover that their hands belong to them. At this age, your baby will look at them in wonder and wave them around. Once they realize that they are their hands, your baby may also try to use them to close them around a toy, for instance. Not only do they begin to see patterns in the world around them, at this time your baby might begin to distinguish patterns in sounds, smells, tastes, and textures, too. In other words, your little one now perceives patterns with all of their senses. This new awareness is not just confined to what is going on outside their body – it also includes an enhanced perception of what is happening inside their body. For instance, now your baby may realize that holding their arm in the air feels different than letting it hang down. At the same time, they might also gain more control from within. Your baby may be able to maintain certain positions, not only with their head, body, arms and legs, but also with smaller areas of their body. For example, they might start to make all kinds of faces, now that they have more control over their facial muscles. They might make explosive sounds because they can keep their vocal cords in a certain position. They may focus more sharply on an object because they have more control over their eye muscles than before.

Many of the reflexes your baby had at birth will start to disappear at this age. They will be replaced by something similar to voluntary movements. They no longer need the gripping reflex, for example, because your baby is now able to learn how to close their hand around a toy or other object. Your baby doesn't use the sucking reflex anymore because they are able to latch onto a nipple in one single movement, instead of finding it by what appears to be sheer coincidence after nuzzling for a while. By now, your infant is no longer completely dependent on reflexes. In general, babies will only resort to their old reflexes if they are hungry or upset.

(continued on page 71)

My Diary

How My Baby Explores the New World of Patterns

Check off the boxes below as you notice your baby changing. Stop filling this out once the next stormy period begins, heralding the coming of the next leap. A new world of possibilities opens up to your baby when they're eight weeks old. Your baby cannot possibly discover everything there is to explore in this new world at once – although some babies will try to sample everything. Exactly when your baby starts to do what will depend on their preferences and the opportunities offered to them.

Each chapter from now on will list behaviors that your baby might be doing that signal that they have entered their new world. Look for the sections like this one called "How My Baby Explores The New World." Each list is divided up into activity areas, such as "body control" and "looking and seeing." As you go through the book, you may notice a pattern emerging. Every baby has a completely distinctive profile and you should be aware that right now your baby will not demonstrate many of the skills listed here – some will appear later and some will be skipped altogether. Don't forget: All babies have different talents.

BODY CONTROL

☐ Holds their head upright when they are very alert

☐ Consciously turns their head toward something interesting

☐ Consciously rolls from their side onto their stomach

☐ Consciously rolls from their side onto their back

☐ Kicks their legs and waves their arms

☐ Kicks at plaything, with jerking movements

☐ Allows themselves to be pulled into a sitting position

☐ Allows themselves to be pulled into a standing position

☐ Tries to lift their head and body when lying facedown

☐ Shows an increased desire to sit

☐ Is able to look left and right when lying on their stomach

☐ Makes faces

HAND CONTROL

☐ Swipes at toys

☐ Attempts to grab objects within reach but does not succeed

☐ Closes their hand around objects within easy reach

☐ Holds a plaything and moves it jerkily up and down

☐ Touches and feels objects without holding them

LOOKING AND SEEING

☐ Discovers hands

☐ Discovers feet

☐ Discovers knees

☐ Watches people moving or working

☐ Is fascinated by children playing close by

☐ Enjoys watching fast-moving images on TV

☐ Watches pets eating or moving

☐ Is fascinated by waving curtains

☐ Discovers luminous object, such as a flickering candle

☐ Watches treetops outdoors and is particularly fascinated by movements such as rustling leaves

☐ Looks at items on grocery store shelves

- ☐ Looks at complex shapes and colors, such as abstract art, especially while being rocked
- ☐ Is fascinated by shiny clothing or jewelry
- ☐ Enjoys watching people chewing food
- ☐ Enjoys watching and listening to people talk
- ☐ Watches facial gestures

LISTENING AND CHATTING

- ☐ Enjoys listening to voices, singing, and high-pitched sounds
- ☐ Makes short bursts of sounds, such as ah, uh, eh, mmm, and listens to themselves
- ☐ Makes a series of sounds, mumbles, and gurgles, as if they are telling a story
- ☐ Repeats these sounds if you encourage them
- ☐ Sings along when you dance and sing with them
- ☐ "Chats" to and smiles at cuddly toys
- ☐ Consciously makes eh sounds to attract attention
- ☐ Interrupts while others are talking

OTHER CHANGES YOU NOTICE

Your baby's first intentional movements are still very different from those of an adult. Their movements will be quite jerky, rigid, and stiff, like those of a puppet, and they will stay like this until the next big change occurs.

Your Baby's Choices: A Key to Their Personality

Why are all babies unique? They have all undergone the same changes and entered the same new world with new discoveries to make and new skills to learn. But every baby decides for themselves what they want to learn, when, and how. They will choose what they consider the most appealing. Some babies will try to learn a variety of new skills, using one or more of their senses. Some will seem particularly interested in exploring this new world with their eyes. Some will prefer to try out their talking and listening skills. Others will try to become more adept with their bodies. This explains why a friend's baby may be doing something that your baby can't, or doesn't enjoy, and vice versa. A baby's likes and dislikes are determined by their unique makeup — their build, weight, temperament, inclination, and interests.

Babies love anything new. It's so very important that you respond when you notice any new skills or interests. Your baby will enjoy it if you share these new discoveries with them, and their learning will progress quickly.

What you Can Do to Help

The best way to help your baby make this leap is to encourage them to develop the skills that they find most interesting. When you notice them working on a new skill, show them that you're enthusiastic about every attempt they make to learn something new. If you praise them, you'll make them feel good, and this will encourage them to continue. Try to find a balance between providing enough challenges and demanding too much of them. Try to discover what they enjoy doing most. Most importantly, stop as soon as you feel they have had enough of a game or toy.

Your baby may want or need to practice some games or activities on their own. As long as you show some enthusiasm, this will be sufficient to reassure them that they are doing well.

How to Tell When They've Had Enough

Practicing a new skill is fun, but it can also be tiring for a baby. When they've had enough, they will usually let you know with very clear body signals. For example, they may look away, or if they are physically strong enough, they may turn their body away from you.

Stop the game or activity as soon as you notice that your baby has had enough. Sometimes they will only want a short break before resuming the game or activity with renewed enthusiasm, but don't push them. They need time to let it all sink in. Always let your baby's responses guide you.

Help Them Explore the New World through Sight

If your baby loves to explore their world with their eyes, you can help them by offering them all sorts of visual "patterns," for instance by showing them brightly colored objects. Make sure you move the object slowly across their line of vision, since this will draw their attention quicker and hold their interest longer than a fast moving object. You can also try moving the object slowly backward and then forward, but make sure they are still able to see it move, otherwise they will lose interest.

When your baby is in a playful mood, they may become bored if they always see, hear, or feel the same objects in the same old surroundings. It's very normal for babies of this age to show boredom, as their new awareness of patterns also means that they understand when things are repetitious. For the first time in their life, your baby may get fed up with the same plaything, the same view, the same sound, the same feel of an object, and the same taste. They will crave variety and learn from it. If they seem bored, keep them stimulated. Carry them around in your arms or provide them with different objects to look at.

At this time, toys may not be as interesting to your baby as the myriad of interesting "real things" in their world. Your home is full of items that may fascinate your baby, such as books, photographs, pets, cooking utensils, and even your eyeglasses. If your baby suddenly prefers the "real thing" to their toys, they will need your help. At this age, they cannot get close enough to objects on their own. They need you to either take them to the object or for you to pick it up and show it to them. If you notice that they like looking at "real things," help them do this.

> "My baby likes looking at everything: paintings, books on shelves, items in the kitchen cupboard. I have to take her everywhere. I even carry her in my arms when I go outside or when I go shopping."
>
> **Hannah's mom, 11th week**

At this age, your baby may notice that familiar objects keep waving across their line of vision. If they investigate, they'll discover their hands or feet. They may gaze at them in wonder and begin to study them in detail. Every baby has their own way of investigating this new phenomenon. Some babies will need a lot of time to complete their explorations, while other babies won't. Most babies have a particular fondness for hands. Perhaps this is because their tiny hands pass by more often.

Help Your Baby Explore the New World through Touch

Hands and arms can be placed in a myriad of different postures. Each posture is another pattern to be seen and felt. Allow your baby to study their hands as long and as often as they want to. A baby has to learn what their hands are for before they can learn to use them properly. Therefore, it is very important for them to get to know all about these "touching devices."

"My little darling studies every detail of how his hands move. He plays quite delicately with his fingers. When he's lying down, he holds his hand in the air then spreads his fingers. Sometimes he opens and closes his fingers, one at a time. Or he clasps his hands together or lets them touch. It's one continuous flowing movement."

Bob's mom, 9th week

Have you noticed your baby attempting to use their hands by trying to clasp a rattle, for instance? Holding a plaything involves a feeling pattern related to the position of the hand plus the object touching the palm of the hand. A baby's first attempts at grasping an object are generally far from successful. Show them that you are enthusiastic about the effort they are making and encourage each serious attempt. Praise from you will encourage them to continue.

"My son is trying to grab things! His little hand gropes in the direction of his rattle, or he tries to hit it. A moment later he tries to grab the rattle, using a proper clasping motion. He puts a lot of effort into it. When he thinks he's got it, he clenches his fist, but the rattle is still a few inches away. The poor darling realizes his mistake, gets frustrated, and starts to cry."

Paul's mom, 11th week

Try to bear in mind that at this age your baby is definitely not yet able to reach out and touch the things that they want to grab. They are only capable of closing their hands around an object. Make sure that you always place easy-to-grab toys near their waving hands. Your baby will then be able to touch the object and practice closing and opening their hands whenever they want.

Help Your Baby Explore the New World through Sound

A baby's greatest passion is the latest sounds that they make themselves. This is why you should try to respond to every sound your young infant makes. Your baby might be totally enthralled with making explosive sounds, because from this leap onward they can keep their vocal cords in a certain position. Just like a hand position, a vocal cord position is a feeling pattern. Try to imitate your baby's sounds so that they can hear them from someone else. Respond when they use sounds to attract your attention. These "conversations" are essential for their learning process, and they will teach them to take turns, listen, and imitate – skills which form the basis of communication. These chats will also teach them that their voice is an important tool, just like their hands are.

"My baby chats away, trying to attract my attention all day long. She listens to my voice as well. It's wonderful."
Hannah's mom, 11th week

Every parent tries to encourage their baby to "chat." Some mothers and fathers talk to their babies throughout their waking hours as a matter of course, whereas others do this only at certain times, such as when their babies are on their laps. The disadvantage of planned chat times is that the baby may not always be in the right mood to listen and respond. It appears that babies whose parents "plan" chat times do not always understand what is expected of them, and their mothers and fathers become easily discouraged because they think their babies are not responding properly yet.

Help Your Baby Explore the New World through Body Postures

Your baby may be ready for pull-up games. A little one who is able to lift their head on their own may love being pulled up by their arms from a half-sitting position to an upright position or being pulled from a sitting position to standing. Be careful to support their heavy head. If they are very strong, they may even actively participate. This game teaches the baby how different postures feel and how to maintain them. Each of those postures is another "pattern" that your baby can perceive inside their body. If they cooperate in the pull-up game, they will jerk rather unsteadily from one position to the next. Once they have jerked into a certain position, they will want to retain it for a moment. Although their movements are still far from supple, they will love being in a certain position for a short while. They may even become very upset when you decide it's time to end the game.

"Suddenly, my son is jerking all over the place when I pull him onto his feet. He also makes jerky, spastic movements when he's lying naked on his changing mat. I don't know if this is normal. It worries me a bit."

Kevin's mom, 11th week

"If my baby had her way, she'd be on her feet all day, listening to me telling her how strong she is. If I don't rush in with compliments, she starts complaining."

Ashley's mom, 10th week

Fathers are usually the first to discover that babies enjoy these pull-up games, then mothers will follow, although fathers tend to be slightly more enthusiastic with baby boys than with baby girls.

Some Things to Keep in Mind

Your baby will be very eager to learn when they are discovering a new world. They will learn quickly, easily, and it will be a lot of fun when you give them the things that suit their personality. Very demanding babies will automatically get more attention, as their parents strive to keep them amused and satisfied. These high-interest babies may become the best students of tomorrow if they are given the right help and encouragement in their early years.

Quiet babies are easily forgotten, because they don't demand as much attention from their parents. Try to give a quiet baby just that little bit more encouragement and stimulation to get the best out of them.

You may think that your infant should be able to be a little bit more independent now, because you notice the great pleasure they take in their surroundings, their playthings, their own hands and feet, and because they enjoy lying flat on their back on the floor. You could start using the playpen for the first time at this stage. It's a good place to hang toys within easy reach of your baby's hands, allowing them to swipe at them or watch them swinging backward and forward. You could also try to let your baby amuse themselves for as long as possible, presenting them with new playthings when they get bored. With your help, your baby may be able to amuse themselves for about 15 minutes at this age.

Top Games for this Wonder Week

These games and activities can be used when your baby enters the world of patterns. Before you start working your way down the list, look back at "How My Baby Explores the New World of Patterns" on page 68 to remind yourself of what your baby likes to do. And remember that the games that don't work for your baby right now may do later on when they're ready.

HANDS OR FEET, A FAVORITE TOY

Give your baby ample opportunity and room to watch their hands and feet. They will need to move freely to be able take in every detail. The best thing to do is to put them on a large towel or blanket. If it is warm enough, let them play without their clothes on, since they will really enjoy the freedom of their naked body. If you want, you can tie a colorful ribbon around their hand or foot as an added attraction. If you do this, however, be sure it is securely attached and watch the baby closely so that they do not accidentally choke on the ribbon should it come loose.

COZY CHATS

When your baby is in a talking mood, sit down and make yourself comfortable, making sure that you have enough support in your back, draw up your knees, and lie your baby on their back on your thighs. They can see you properly from this position, and you'll be able to follow all their reactions. Chat to them about anything: their beauty, their soft skin, their eyes, the events of the day, or your plans for later. The most important things are the rhythm of your voice and your facial expressions. Be sure you give them enough time to respond. This means being patient, waiting, smiling, nodding at them so that they realize it takes two to have a conversation. Watch your baby's reactions to discover what they find interesting. Remember that a talking mouth, together with a face that shifts from one expression to another, is usually a smash hit!

THE GREAT INDOORS

At this age, an inquisitive baby is still unable to grab objects that catch their eye to take a closer look. Until they are able to do this themselves, they will have to rely on you to bring interesting objects to them. Remember, there are many interesting things in the house that will arouse their curiosity. Explain to them what they are seeing. They will enjoy listening to the intonation in your voice. Let them touch and feel whatever they seem to like.

THE PULL-UP GAME

You can only play this game if your baby is able to lift their head on their own. Sit down and make yourself comfortable. Make sure that you have enough support in your back. Draw up your knees and put your baby on your legs and tummy so that they are virtually in a half-sitting position. They will feel more comfortable like this. Now, hold their arms and pull them up slowly, until they are sitting upright, giving them words of encouragement at the same time, such as telling them what a clever little baby they are. Watch their reactions carefully, and only continue if you're sure they are cooperating and enjoying themselves.

TAKING A BATH TOGETHER

Water is a wonderful toy in itself. At this age, "water babies" in particular will enjoy watching water move. Place the baby on your stomach and show them drops and little streams of water running off your body onto theirs. Babies will also enjoy having small waves washed over their bodies. Lay them on their back on your stomach, and play "Row, Row, Row Your Boat" together. Move back and forth slowly to the rhythm of the song, and make small waves. They will enjoy the feel of the waves running over their skin. After the freedom of the bath, they are likely to love being wrapped up snugly and securely in a warm towel and given a good cuddle!

A Word of Consolation: A Demanding Baby Could Be Gifted

Some babies catch on to new games and toys quickly, soon growing tired of doing the same things, day in and day out. They want new challenges, continual action, complicated games, and lots of variety. It can be extremely exhausting for mothers and fathers of these "bubbly" babies, because they run out of imagination, and their infants scream if they are not presented with one new challenge after another.

It is a proven fact that many highly-gifted children were demanding, discontented babies. They were usually only happy as long as they were being offered new and exciting challenges.

A new awareness or new world will offer new opportunities to learn additional skills. Some babies will explore their new world and make discoveries with great enthusiasm, but they demand constant attention and help in doing this. They have an endless thirst for knowledge. They discover their new world with tremendous speed. They try out and acquire almost every skill the new world has to offer, then experiment a little before growing bored again. For parents of babies like this, there is little more they can do than to wait for the next big change to occur.

Top Toys for this Wonder Week

Here are some toys and things that babies like as they explore the world of patterns.

- Playthings that dangle overhead
- A moving or musical mobile
- A musical box with moving figures
- Playthings to swipe at or to touch
- Cuddly toys to talk to or laugh at
- Mommy and daddy – you still top the chart as their favorite toy!

After the Leap

Around ten weeks, another period of comparative ease sets in. Most mothers and fathers seem to put the concerns and anxieties of recent weeks quickly behind them. They sing their babies' praises and talk about them as if they had always been easygoing and cheerful babies. What changes can you see in your baby at this stage? At approximately 10 weeks, your baby may not require as much attention as they did in the past. They are more independent. They are interested in their surroundings, in people, animals, and objects. It seems as if they suddenly understand and clearly recognize a whole range of new things. Their need to be with you constantly may also diminish at this time. If you pick them up, they may squirm and wriggle in discomfort and attempt to sit up in your arms as much as possible. The only time they might seem to need you now is when you are willing to show them things of interest. Your baby may have become so cheerful and busy amusing themselves that life is much easier for you now. You may feel a surge of energy. At this age, lots of parents regularly put babies in their playpens, as they feel their children are ready for it now.

"My daughter suddenly seems much brighter. She's lost that newborn dependency. I'm not the only who's noticed. Everyone talks properly to her now, instead of making funny cooing noises."

Emily's mom, 10th week

"My baby seems wiser. She's become more friendly, happier, and even roars with laughter once in a while. Thank goodness she's stopped that incessant crying! Life has changed drastically from thinking 'How can I cope with her screaming?' to enjoying having her around now. Even her father looks forward to seeing her in the evening nowadays. He used to come home dragging his feet, dreading the probable torment of her non-stop crying. Now he loves being around her. He feeds and bathes her every evening."

Jenny's mom, 10th week

"My son no longer seems so vulnerable. I see a definite change in him now. He has progressed from just sitting on my lap to gaining a bit of independence and playing."

Steven's mom, 10th week

"I think my baby is really starting to develop into a real little person with a life of her own. At first, all she did was eat and sleep. Now she has a good stretch when I take her out of bed, just like grown-ups do."

Nina's mom, 10th week

"I don't know if there's any connection, but I certainly have noticed that I had a lot more energy this past week, and this coincided with my little boy's newfound independence. I must say I really enjoy watching the progress he's making. It's fascinating the way he laughs, enjoys himself, and plays. We seem to communicate better now. I can let my imagination run wild with his stuffed toys, sing him songs, and invent different games. Now that I'm getting some feedback from him, he's turning into a little friend. I find this age much easier than when he just nursed, cried, and slept."

Bob's mom, 10th week

Wonder Week 12

The World of Smooth Transitions

**ONE THING CAN FLOW
SMOOTHLY INTO THE NEXT**

At around 11 or 12 weeks, your baby will enter yet another new world as they undergo the third major developmental leap since their birth. You may recall that one of the significant physical developments that occurred at eight weeks was your baby's ability to swipe and kick at objects with their arms and legs. These early flailing movements often looked comically puppetlike. At 12 weeks, these jerky actions are about to change. Like Pinocchio, your baby is ready to change from a puppet into a real person.

Of course, this transformation will not happen overnight, and when it does it will entail more than just physical movement, although that's usually what parents notice most. It will also affect your baby's ability to perceive the way things change around them with their other senses – such as a voice shifting from one register to another, the cat slinking across the floor, and the light in a room becoming dimmer as the sun dips behind the clouds. Your baby's world is becoming a more organized place as they discover the constant, flowing changes around them.

Discovering these subtleties will enable your baby to enjoy life in new ways. But it's not easy entering a world that's shifting beneath your feet. Overnight, your baby's world has changed. Nothing seems to stand still anymore.

Keep in mind that if your baby is suddenly fussier now, they're probably getting ready to master new skills. Watch them closely during this exciting time. In this changing world, the one constant is you, the boat on the rolling seas. Is it any wonder they want to hang on to you for dear life as they enter this next major developmental leap in their life? Fortunately, this fussy period will not last quite as long as the previous one. Some babies will behave normally again after just a day, while others may need a whole week before they feel themselves again.

Note: *This leap into the perceptual world of "smooth transitions" is age-linked and predictable. It sets in motion the development of a whole range of skills and activities. However, the age at which these skills and activities appear for the first time varies greatly and depends on your baby's preferences, experimentation and physical development. For example, the ability to perceive smooth transitions emerges at about 12 weeks, and is a necessary precondition for "trying to sit up while helped by an adult," but this skill normally appears anywhere from three to eight months. The skills and activities in this chapter are stated at the earliest possible age they could appear so you can watch for and recognize them. (They may be rudimentary at first.) This way you can respond to and facilitate your baby's development.*

Is it any wonder they want to hang on to you for dear life as they enter this next major developmental leap in their life? Fortunately, this fussy period will not last quite as long as the previous one. Some babies will behave normally again after just a day, while others may need a whole week before they feel themselves again.

This Week's Fussy Signs

When a change happens, all babies will cry more often and for longer periods than before, although some will cry more than others. Some babies will be inconsolable, while others may be fretful, cranky, moody, or listless. One baby may be especially difficult at night, while another may tend to get upset during the day. Usually, all babies will usually be a little less tearful if they are carried around or if they are just given extra attention or cuddles. But even under these circumstances, anybody who knows the baby well will suspect that they will cry or fret again at the least opportunity.

How you Know it's Time to Grow

Here are the major signs that your baby is about to make this developmental leap.

They May Demand More Attention

Just when you thought that your baby had learned to amuse themselves, they don't seem to do so well at it anymore. It may seem as if they want you to play with them more now and keep them entertained all the time. Just sitting with them may not be enough; they might want you to look at them and talk to them, too. This change in their behavior will be all the more obvious if they had already shown you that they could be independent after the last leap forward. If anything, you may think that they've suffered a setback. You may feel that if your baby previously took three steps forward, here come the two steps back.

They May Become Shy With Strangers

Some babies will be shy with everyone except their parents at this time. If your baby is shy, you will notice that they cling to you whenever you have company. They may start to cry when a stranger talks to them or even looks at them. Sometimes, they may refuse to sit on anyone's lap but yours. If they are safely snuggled up to you, they may give someone else a reluctant smile, but if they are particularly shy, they will quickly bury their head in your shoulder afterwards.

They May Cling to You More Tightly Now

Your baby may cling to you so tightly when you carry them that it seems as if they are afraid of being dropped. Babies who do this may sometimes even pinch their mothers or fathers very hard in the process.

They May Lose Their Appetite

At this time, your baby might drag out each feeding session. Babies who are breastfed on demand might start behaving as if they want to eat all day long. Bottle-fed babies take longer to finish their bottles, if they manage to get that far. These unruly drinkers spend their time chewing and gnawing at the nipples without actually drinking. They do this as a form of comfort and so they hang on for dear life, afraid to let go. Often, they will drift off to sleep with the nipple still in their mouths. Your baby may try to hold on to you or grab your breast during nursing, even if they are being bottle-fed, as if they are afraid of relinquishing their only source of comfort.

They May Sleep Poorly

Your baby will probably sleep less well now than before. Many babies wake several times a night demanding to be fed. And other babies wake up very early in the morning. Still other babies refuse to take naps during the day. For many families, the normal routine has turned into absolute chaos because the baby's regular feeding and sleeping patterns have changed so drastically.

They May Suck Their Thumb More Often

Your infant may now discover their thumb for the first time, or they might suck their thumb longer and more regularly than before. Like sucking at the breast or bottle, this is a comfort and can avert another crying session. Some parents introduce a pacifier to help soothe the baby at this time.

They May Be Listless

Your baby may be quieter or seem less lively than usual. They may also lie still for quite some time, gazing around or just staring in front of them. This is only a temporary event. Their previous sounds and movements will soon be replaced by new ones.

How This Leap May Affect You

Obviously, your baby will not be the only one affected by the changes occurring within them. Their whole family suffers too, especially their mother. Here are some of the feelings you may experience during this turbulent time.

My Diary

Signs My Baby Is Growing Again

Between 11 and 12 weeks, you might notice your baby showing any of the following behaviors. They are probably signs that they are ready to make the next leap, into the world of smooth transitions. Check off the signs your baby shows.

THEIR INTEREST IN THEIR SURROUNDINGS

☐ Cries more often

☐ Wants you to keep them busy

☐ Loses appetite

☐ Is more shy with strangers

☐ Clings more

☐ Wants more physical contact during nursing

☐ Sleeps poorly

☐ Sucks their thumb, or does so more often than before

☐ Is less lively

☐ Is quieter, less vocal

OTHER CHANGES YOU NOTICE

You May Feel Worried

It's normal to feel anxious when you notice that your once-lively infant has become fussier, is crying more often, is sleeping poorly, or is not nursing as well as they were. You may be worried because it seems that your baby has suffered a setback in producing sounds and movements or seems to have lost the independence that they had so recently acquired. Parents usually expect to see progress, and if this doesn't seem to be happening, even for just a short while, they get concerned. They feel insecure, and they wonder what's the matter. "Is something wrong with the baby? Could they be ill? Could they be abnormal after all?" are the most common worries. Generally, it is none of the above. (When in doubt, always consult your family doctor.) On the contrary, your baby is showing signs of progress. A whole new world is there for them to discover, but when this world reveals itself, the baby first has to deal with the upheaval it brings. It's not easy for them, and they will need your support. You can do this by showing that you understand that they are going through a difficult time.

"When my baby is crying incessantly and wants to be carried around all the time, I feel pressured. I can't seem to accomplish even the simplest things. It makes me feel insecure, and it saps all my energy."

Juliette's mom, 12th week

"I'm trying to find out why my baby cries so much. I want to know what's troubling her so that I can fix it. Then I'll have some peace of mind again."

Laura's mom, 12th week

"There's no way I can cope with my son's crying. I just can't take it anymore. I'd even prefer getting out of bed four times a night to deal with a baby who is not crying than twice a night to deal with a tiny screamer."

Paul's mom, 11th week

You May Become Irritated

During this period, many mothers and fathers get annoyed with their babies' irregular eating and sleeping routines. They find it impossible to plan ahead. Their entire schedule is thrown off balance. They often feel under pressure from family or friends, too. The parents' instincts tell them to focus all their attention on their unhappy infant, but other people often seem to disapprove of too much babying. The mother and father may feel trapped in the middle.

"I get irritated every time my son starts fretting, because he can't seem to amuse himself for even just a short while. He wants me to keep him occupied all day long. Of course, everybody loves giving me advice on how to deal with him, especially my husband."

Kevin's mom, 12th week

"I seem to cope better with my baby's erratic behavior if I don't make plans in advance. In the past, when my plans went completely haywire, I felt irritated. So I've changed my attitude. And would you believe it —I sometimes find I even have a few hours to spare!"

Laura's mom, 12th week

You May Reach Your Wit's End

Sometimes parents are unable, or unwilling, to suppress their anger any longer, and they let their demanding little creatures know they're fed up.

"My boy was so fretful. I kept worrying about what the neighbors would think of the noise. Sunday afternoon was the last straw. I'd tried everything to make him settle, but nothing helped. At first I felt helpless, but then I became furious because I just couldn't cope, so I left him in his room. I had a good cry myself, which calmed me down a bit."

Bob's mom, 12th week

"We had company, and my son was being terribly trying. Everyone gave me their two cents' worth of advice, which always makes me really upset. When I went upstairs to put him to bed, I lost my self-control, grabbed him, and gave him a good shake."

Matt's mom, 11th week

Baby Care

Shaking Can Be Harmful

While it is normal to feel frustrated and angry with your baby at times, never shake a baby. Shaking a young child can easily cause internal bleeding just below the skull, which can result in brain damage that may lead to learning difficulties later on or even death.

You May Feel Tremendous Pressure

If a mother or father worries too much about their noisy little grump, and if they are not given enough support from family and friends, they may become exhausted. If they are suffering from a lack of sleep as well, they could easily lose control of the situation, both mentally and physically.

Unwelcome advice, on top of panic and exhaustion, could make any parent feel even more irritable and snappish – and their partner often becomes the target. At times, however, the distressed infant will bear the brunt of a parent's pent-up frustration, and they may be a little rougher with them than necessary. When a mother or father admits to having slapped their baby, this has nearly always occured during one of these fussy periods. It's certainly not because they dislike the poor infant, but simply because they long to see them happy, and feel threatened by other people's criticism. They feel they have no one to turn to with their problems; they feel alone. However understandable these feeling of frustration may be, one should never act on them. Slapping, or hurting a baby in any other way, is not acceptable.

"Every time my baby stopped crying, I felt as if a load had been lifted from my shoulders. I hadn't noticed how tense I was until then."

Emily's mom, 11th week

Matt's mom, 12th week

When it all gets to be too much, just remember: It can only get better. At this stage, some parents fear that these dreadful crying fits may never stop. This is a logical assumption because until now the fussy periods followed each other in rapid succession with only two to three weeks in between. This barely left enough time for mothers and fathers to catch their breaths. But don't despair – from now on, the intervals between the fussy periods will be longer. The fussy periods themselves will also seem less intense than before.

How Your Baby's New Skills Emerge

When your baby is upset, you will generally want to keep an extra close eye on them because you want to know what's wrong. In doing so, you may suddenly notice that your baby has actually mastered new skills or is trying to do so. In fact, you'll discover that your baby is making their next big leap – into the world of smooth transitions.

At approximately 12 weeks, your baby will be able to perceive the many subtle ways that things change around them, not abruptly but smoothly and gradually. They will be ready to experiment with making such smooth transitions themselves.

Your baby will make many new discoveries in this new world. They will select the things that appeal to them and that they are ready to attempt, physically and mentally. You should, as always, be careful not to push them but do help them with the things they show they are ready to do. In many ways, however, they will still rely on your help. They will need you to show them things in their world, to put their toys where they can see and reach for them, and to respond to their increasing attempts at communication.

Brain Changes

At approximately 10 to 11 weeks, a baby's head circumference dramatically increases.

The Magical Leap Forward

As they enter the world of smooth transitions, for the first time your baby is able to recognize continuous changes in sights, sounds, tastes, smells, and touch. For example, they may now notice how a voice shifts from one tone to the next or how a body shifts from one position to another. Not only can they register these smooth transitions in the outside world, your infant is now able to learn to make them on their own. This will enable your baby to work on several important skills.

You will see that now your baby's movements become much smoother, more flowing, and more like an adult's. This new control applies to their whole body as well as to the parts that they can move consciously – their hands, feet, head, eyes, and even their vocal cords. You will probably notice that when they stretch out towards a toy, the movement is smoother than it was just a few weeks ago. When they bend their knees to sit or pull themselves to stand, the whole exercise looks more deliberate and mature.

Their head movements also become smoother than before, and they can now vary their speed. They can look around the room in the way that older children do and follow a continuous movement. Their eyes are able to focus more sharply now on what they see, and their vision will soon be as good as an adult's. When your baby was first born, they came ready equipped with a reflex that moved their gaze in the direction of any new sound. This disappeared somewhere between four and eight weeks after birth, but now

(continued on page 96)

My Diary

How My Baby Explores the New World of Smooth Transitions

Check off the boxes below as you notice your baby changing.

BODY CONTROL

- ☐ Barely needs support to keep their head upright
- ☐ Smooth head movement when turning to one side
- ☐ Smooth eye movement when following a moving object
- ☐ Is generally more lively and energetic than before
- ☐ Playfully lifts their bottom when their diaper is being changed
- ☐ Rolls independently from back to stomach or vice versa while holding on to your fingers
- ☐ Sticks their toes in their mouth and twists them around
- ☐ Sits up straight when leaning against you
- ☐ Pull themselves into sitting position while holding on to your fingers
- ☐ Is able to move into a standing position when seated on your lap, by holding on to two of your fingers
- ☐ Uses both feet to push off when seated in a bouncing chair or lying in a playpen

HAND CONTROL

- ☐ Grabs and clutches at objects with both hands
- ☐ Shakes a rattle once or twice
- ☐ Studies and plays with your hands
- ☐ Studies and touches your face, eyes, mouth, and hair
- ☐ Studies and plays with your clothes
- ☐ Puts everything into their mouth
- ☐ Strokes their head, from neck to eyes
- ☐ Rubs a toy along their head or cheek

LISTENING AND TALKING

- ☐ Discovers shrieking and gurgling; can easily shift between loud and soft tones, low notes and high ones
- ☐ Produces new sounds that resemble the vowels of real speech: ee, ooh, ehh, oh, aah, ay
- ☐ Uses these sounds to "chat"
- ☐ Is able to blow saliva bubbles, and laughs as if they find this very amusing

LOOKING AND SEEING

- ☐ Turns hands over, studies both sides
- ☐ Studies their own feet moving
- ☐ Studies a face, eyes, mouth, and hair
- ☐ Studies someone's clothing

OTHER SKILLS

- ☐ Expresses enjoyment by watching, looking, listening, grabbing, or by "talking," then waiting for your response
- ☐ Uses different behavior with different people
- ☐ Expresses boredom if they see, hear, taste, feel, or do the same things too often; variety suddenly becomes important

OTHER CHANGES YOU NOTICE

they can do the same thing consciously, and the response will be quicker than before. They will be able to follow something or somebody with their eyes in a controlled, well-coordinated manner. They may even begin to do this without turning their head. They will be able to follow people or objects approaching them or moving away. In fact, they will become capable of surveying the whole room. You may feel for the first time that they are really a part of the family as they notice everybody's comings and goings.

This new responsiveness is enhanced by new vocal possibilities as they begin to recognize changes in pitch and in volume of sounds and to experiment with these by gurgling and shrieking. Their improved coordination even helps them to swallow more smoothly than previously.

Although some remarkable developments have occurred in your baby's mind and body, they can't cope with quick changes in succession. Don't expect them to be able to follow an object that is moving up and down as well as from left to right or a toy that rapidly reverses its direction of movement. And when they move their own hand, there will be a noticeable pause before any change of direction, almost like a tiny conductor waving a baton.

Parents are generally less concerned if their babies show a reluctance to amuse themselves at this stage. They are too proud of their babies' achievements and efforts on so many levels. There are so many new discoveries to be made and so many new things to be learned and practiced, and for the moment that is what matters the most.

Your Baby's Choices: A Key to Their Personality

If you watch your baby closely, you will be able to determine where their interests lie. As you mark off the things they are showing you that they can do in this world, be aware of your child's uniqueness.

Some babies are very aware of the world around them, and they prefer looking, listening, and experiencing sensations to being physically active themselves. Most of the time, professionals, as well as friends and family, assess a baby's development by looking at the physical milestones, such as grasping, rolling over, crawling, sitting, standing, and walking. This can give a one-sided view of progress as it makes the "watch-listen-feel" baby seem slower than other babies. These babies usually take longer to begin grasping objects, but once they start, they will examine them very closely. Given a new item, a watch-listen-feel baby will turn it around, look at it, listen to it, rub it, and even smell it. These babies are actually doing something very complicated that will give them a broad base for their later learning skills. In contrast, babies who are more physically active often become engrossed in the action of grabbing itself, and once they have attained possession of the object, they quickly lose interest and drop it in favor of looking for another challenge. Babies love anything new, and it is important that you respond when you notice any new skills or interests. Your baby will enjoy it if you share these new discoveries, and their learning will progress quickly.

What you Can Do to Help

The more your baby plays or experiments with a new skill, the more adept they will become. Practice makes perfect as far as babies are concerned, too. Your baby might want to try out a new skill over and over again. Although they will play and practice on their own, your participation and encouragement are vital. As well as cheering them on when they do well, you can help when the going gets tough and they feel like giving up. At this point, you can make the task easier for them – usually by rearranging the world so that it is a bit more accommodating. This might mean turning a toy around so that it's easier to grab, propping them up so that they can see the cat through the window, or maybe imitating the sounds they are trying to make.

You can also help by making an activity more complex or vary it a bit so that they stay with it longer and are challenged just a little more. Be careful to watch for signs that your baby has had enough. Remember that they will go at their own pace. Just as babies are all different, so are their mothers. Some mothers have more imagination than others in certain areas. It may be a particular challenge for you if your baby is the physical type but you prefer talking, singing, and storytelling. Gather new ideas from books, your friends, and family members. The baby's father and older siblings can help – most children will be able to go on long after the baby's desire for repetition has exhausted you. But whatever type of baby you have and whatever type of mother you are, your child will always benefit from some help from you.

The Gender Gap

Baby boys seem to take up more of their parents' time than baby girls do during the first months. This is probably because boys generally cry more and don't sleep as well as girls.

Also, mothers of baby girls are much quicker to respond to the sounds produced by their daughters than are mothers of baby boys. Mothers also tend to "chat" more to their babies when they are girls.

Help Your Baby Explore the New World through Sound

If your baby has a special love for sound, encourage them to use their voice. They may now begin to shriek, gurgle, or make vowel-like sounds themselves. These may range from highto low-pitched sounds and from soft to loud ones. If they also start to blow saliva bubbles, don't discourage them. By doing these things, they are playing with "smooth transitions" and in the process, they are exercising the muscles of their vocal cords, lips, tongue, and palate as well.

Your baby may often practice when they are alone, sounding like somebody who is chattering away just for fun. They do this because the range of notes, with all the high and low vowel sounds and little shrieks in between, sound a lot like talking. Sometimes a baby will even chuckle at their own sounds.

Most babies love to have cozy chats with their parents. Of course, a baby has to be in the mood. The best time to chat is when they attract your attention with their voice. You will probably find yourself speaking in a slightly higher-pitched tone than usual, which is just right for your baby's ear. It is very important that you stick to the rules of conversation – your baby says something, then you say something back. Make sure you let them finish. Because if you don't give them time to reply, they will feel that you aren't listening to them, and they won't learn the rhythm of conversation. If that happens – if you do not give them enough time to reply – they may become confused or despondent because you are not listening to them. The subjects of your conversation don't matter very much at this age, but it is better to stick to familiar territory and shared experiences. Occasionally, try imitating the sounds they are making. Some babies find this so funny they will break into laughter. This is all-important groundwork for later language skills.

It is very important to talk to your baby frequently. Voices on the radio or television, or people talking in the same room, are no substitute for a one-on-one conversation. Your baby is prompted to talk because there is someone who is listening and responding to them. Your enthusiasm will play an important role here.

"I always talk back whenever my son makes sounds. Then he waits a little, realizes it's his turn, and replies with a smile or by wriggling around. If he's in the right mood, he'll gurgle back at me again. If I reply once more, he gets so excited that he waves his arms and legs all over the place and sometimes shrieks with laughter as well. When he's had enough, he turns away and looks at something else."

John's mom, 13th week

"When my son saw that I was about to feed him, he shrieked with excitement and grabbed my breast, while my blouse was still only half undone."

Matt's mom, 13th week

Your baby might use one of their latest sounds when they want something. This is often a special "attention!" shriek. If they do this, always answer them. This is important since it will give them the sense that you understand what they are trying to communicate, even if you don't have time to stop and play with them at that moment. They will begin to use their voice to attract your attention. That's a significant step towards language.

When they're happy, a baby will often use a special "cry for joy" sound. They will use it when they see something they find amusing. It's natural to respond to these cries for joy with a kiss, a cuddle, or words of encouragement. The more you are able to do this, the better. It shows your baby that you share their pleasure and that you understand them.

When Your Baby Laughs, They're On Top of the World

When you make your baby laugh, you have struck the right chord with them. You have stimulated them in exactly the right way. Don't overdo it because you may frighten them. On the other hand, half-hearted attempts on your part could lead to boredom on theirs. You must find the comfortable middle ground for your baby.

Help Your Baby Explore the New World through Touch

As your baby now lives in the world of smooth transitions, you may notice that they stretch out toward a toy with a smoother action than before. Help them. They have just entered this new world and reaching is still very difficult. Hold a toy within easy reach of your baby's hands and watch to see if they are able to reach for it. Hold the object right in front of them, keeping in mind that at this age they are only able to make a controlled movement with their arm in one direction at a time. Now pay close attention to what they do. If they are only just starting to master this skill, they will probably react something like this baby.

"My son is really starting to reach out to grab things! He reached for a toy dangling in front of him with both hands. He put out his right hand on one side of the toy and his left hand on the other side of the toy. Then, when both hands were just in front of the toy, he clasped them together... and missed! He'd tried really hard, so it wasn't at all surprising that he got very upset when he found himself empty-handed."

Paul's mom, 12th week

When your child reaches for objects and misses, encourage them to try again, or make the game a little easier for them so that they get a taste of success. At this age, they are not yet able to make an accurate estimate of the distance between their hands and the plaything they are trying to grab. They will not be able to learn this properly until they are between 23 and 26 weeks old.

As your baby becomes more adept at grabbing objects, they will want to play the "grabbing game." Because they can turn their head smoothly and look around the room, they can choose what they want from the entire world of things that is now waiting to be grabbed, felt, and touched. After the last developmental leap, most babies spent about one-third of their waking hours playing and experimenting with their hands. After about 12 weeks, this suddenly doubles to two-thirds of their waking hours.

(continued on page 104)

Top Games for this Wonder Week

Here are some games and activities that work for babies at this point in their development. At this age, your baby will particularly enjoy games where you move their whole body around. Try to do this gently, with slow and even movements, remembering that these are the only kind that your baby can properly understand. It is better to play several different games in a row, rather than continue the same game for too long.

THE AIRPLANE

Lift your baby up slowly, while making a sound that increases in volume or changes from a low-pitched to a high-pitched sound. They will stretch out their body automatically as you raise them above your head. Then start the descent, making the appropriate airplane sounds. When they are in line with your face, welcome them by burying your face in their neck and giving them a nibble with your lips. You will soon notice that your baby expects you to do this and will open their mouth and nibble back. You will also see your baby opening their mouth again, as if anticipating the nibble, when they want you to repeat this flying game.

THE SLIDE

Sit down on the floor or a sofa, lean back, and make your body as straight as possible. Place your baby as high up on your chest as you can and let them slide gently down to the floor, while you make the appropriate sliding sound.

THE PENDULUM

Place the baby on your knees so that they are facing you and slowly sway them from side to side. Try to make all kinds of clock sounds, such as a high-pitched, fast tick-tock, or a low-pitched, slow bing-bong. Try to make sounds that range from high to low and from fast to slow, or whatever clock sound you notice that your baby enjoys the most. Make sure you hold them firmly and that their head and neck muscles are strong enough to move with the rhythm.

THE ROCKING HORSE

Place the baby on your knees so that they are facing you and make stepping movements with your legs, so your baby sways up and down as if they were sitting on a horse. You can also make the accompanying clip-clop noises or "schlupping" sounds that babies love at this age.

THE NIBBLING GAME

Sit in front of your baby and make sure they are looking at you. Move your face slowly toward their tummy or nose. Meanwhile, make a drawn-out sound, increasing in volume, or changing in tone, for instance "chooooomp" or "aaaaaah-boom" or sounds similar to those the baby makes themselves.

FEELING FABRICS

Here's a way to play and get chores done! Fold your laundry with your baby nearby, and let them feel different types of fabrics, such as wool, cotton, terry cloth, or nylon. Run their hand over the fabrics to allow them to feel the different textures, too. Babies like touching materials with their fingers and mouths. Try something unusual such as chamois, leather, or felt.

JUMPING AND BOUNCING

A physically active baby loves repeating the same flowing movements over and over again when they are on your lap. Let them stand up and sit down again at their own pace. They will want to repeat this "stand up, sit down, stand up, sit down" game endlessly. It will probably make them laugh too, but, again, hold them tightly and watch their head.

If you notice that your baby enjoys stroking things with their hands, encourage this activity as much as you can. Not only the stroking movement involves a "smooth transition," but also the feeling in their hand caused by the moving contact with the object. Carry your baby around the house and garden, letting them feel all kinds of objects and experience their properties – hard, soft, rough, smooth, sticky, firm, flexible, prickly, cold, wet, and warm. Tell them what the items are, and describe the sensations. Help to get your meaning across by using your tone of voice to express the feeling an object or surface arouses. They really will be able to understand more than they are able to tell you.

"I washed my baby's hands under running water, which made her laugh out loud. She couldn't seem to get enough of it."

Jenny's mom, 15th week

Many babies like to examine their parents' faces. As your little one runs their hands over your face, they may linger slightly longer by your eyes, nose, and mouth. They might tug on your hair or pull at your nose, simply because they are easy to grasp. Items of clothing are interesting as well. Babies like to stroke and feel fabrics. Watch out for your earrings, too!

Some babies are interested in their parents' hands and they will study, touch, and stroke them. If your baby enjoys playing with your hands, help them with this. Slowly turn your hand over, and show them the palm and then the back of your hand. Let them watch while you move your hand or pick up a toy. Try not to make your movements too fast or to change

direction too quickly, or you will lose their attention. Simple movements are all they can cope with in this world. Your baby won't be able to deal with more complicated movements until after another big change in their nervous system, which is the start of the next developmental leap.

Help Your Baby Explore the New World through Body Movement

At this age, all babies are getting livelier than before. They are playing with smooth transitions felt inside their bodies, while they kick and wave their arms about. Some babies perform acrobatics; for example, they might stuff their toes in their mouths and almost spin around on their backs in the process. Obviously, some babies are much livelier and stronger than others. Some babies are not really interested in gymnastic feats, while others will get frustrated if their physical strength is not yet up to the task.

"My son moves his body, arms, and legs around like mad, grunting and groaning in the process. He's obviously trying to do something, but whatever it is he's not succeeding because he usually ends up having an angry screaming fit."

Frankie's mom, 14th week

Whatever your baby's temperament, they will benefit from a little time spent without their clothes on in a warm environment. You may already have noticed that they are lively when you are changing them, enjoying the opportunity to move freely without being hampered by the diaper and clothes. It's easier to bend the little limbs, to wave, kick, and roll over when naked. Success comes more easily, and the baby will get to know their

body better and control it more precisely without the restriction of clothes. Some babies attempt to roll over at this age, but nearly all of them will need a bit of help with it. If your little squirmer tries to roll over, let them hold on to one of your fingers as they practice. A very persistent baby who is also physically strong may manage to roll from their tummy to back. Some can do it the other way around and go from their back to tummy. However persistent the infant, they won't manage it unless their physical development has progressed far enough. So give help and support, but also be ready to help your baby deal with their frustration if they just can't manage something that they would clearly like to do.

Many babies love pushing themselves up with their legs. If your baby enjoys doing this, they will practice pushing off in their playpen, in their bouncing chair, on their changing table (watch out for this one!), or while sitting on your lap. You need to hold on tight to an active squirmer. If your baby is able to do these push-ups unaided, give them lots of opportunities to practice. If your baby is physically strong, they may also try to pull themselves up into a sitting position when they are on your lap. If they like doing this, you can help them by making a game out of it.

Top Toys for this Wonder Week

Here are some toys and things that babies like best as they explore the world of smooth transitions:

- Wobbly toys that bounce back when the baby swipes them
- The clapper inside a bell
- A rocking chair
- Toys that emit a slow squeak, chime, or other simple sound
- Rattles
- Dolls with realistic faces

After the Leap

Between 12 and 13 weeks, another period of comparative calm settles in. Parents, family, and friends will notice what a cheerful little person your baby has become and admire the wonderful progress they have made. You may find your baby is much smarter now than before. When they are carried around or sit on your lap, they act like a little person. They immediately turn their head in the direction of something they want to see or hear. They laugh at everyone, and answer them when they are talked to. They shift their position to get a better look at things they want to see, and they keep an eye on everything going on around them. They are cheerful and active. It may strike you that other family members now show a lot more interest in them as a person. It appears that they have gained their own place in the family. They belong!

"My daughter is developing an interest in a whole variety of things now. She talks or shrieks at different objects, and when we watch her more closely, we think, 'My goodness, can you do that already?' Or 'Aren't you clever noticing all of those things?'"

Jenny's mom, 13th week

"My little one is definitely wiser. She's all eyes these days. She responds to everything and immediately turns her little head in response to sounds. She's suddenly gained her own little place in the family."

Hannah's mom, 14th week

"It's wonderful watching my baby enjoying herself so much and chatting affectionately to her cuddly toys and to people."

Juliette's mom, 14th week

"We have a lot more interaction with my child now because she responds to everything. After I've played a game with her, I can tell when she's waiting for me to play again. She also 'replies' a lot more now."

Ashley's mom, 13th week

"My daughter used to be so easy going and quiet, but she's turned into a real little chatterbox now. She laughs and gurgles a lot more often. I really enjoy getting her out of bed to see what she'll do next."

Eve's mom, 14th week

"My son is much more interesting to watch now because the progress he's made is so obvious. He responds immediately with a smile or a gurgle, and he can turn his head in the right direction, too. I love giving him a good cuddle because he's so soft and chubby now."

Frankie's mom, 14th week

LEAP 4

Wonder Week 19

The World of Events

**THE MOST TROUBLESOME
LEAP OF ALL…**

The realization that our experience is split up into familiar events is something that we as adults take for granted. For example, if we see someone drop a rubber ball, we know that it will bounce back up and will probably continue to bounce several times. If someone jumps up into the air, we know that they will come down. We recognize the initial movements of a golf swing and a tennis serve, and we know what follows. But to your baby, everything is new, and nothing is predictable.

After the last leap forward, your baby was able to perceive smooth transitions in sound, movement, light, taste, smell, and texture. But all of these transitions had to be simple for them to perceive them. As soon as the transitions became more complicated, they were no longer able to follow them.

At around 19 weeks (or between 18 and 20 weeks), their ability to understand the world around them becomes far more developed and a little more like our own. They will begin to experiment with events. The word "event" has a special meaning here and has nothing to do with special occasions. In fact, here it means a short, familiar sequence of smooth transitions from one pattern to the next. Sound like a mouthful? Let's try to explain what it means.

While at 12 weeks it may have taken all your baby's cross-eyed concentration simply to grasp an object with both hands that you held in front of them, they'll now begin to understand they can reach out to a toy, grab it with one hand, shake it, turn it around to inspect it, and put it in their mouth. This kind of physical activity is much more complicated than it seems and far more than just the physical mastery of their arms and hands. It actually depends

----

Note: *The first phase (fussy period) of this leap into the perceptual world of "events" is age-linked and predictable, and starts between 14 and 17 weeks. Most babies start the second phase (see box "Quality Time: An Unnatural Whim" on page 17) of this leap 19 weeks after full-term birth. The first perception of the world of events sets in motion the development of a whole range of skills and activities. However, the age at which these skills and activities appear for the first time varies greatly and depends on your baby's preferences, experimentation and physical development. For example, the ability to perceive events is a necessary precondition for "grasping a cube with partial opposition of the thumb," but this skill normally appears anywhere from four to eight months. The skills and activities in this chapter are stated at the earliest possible age they could appear so you can watch for and recognize them. (They may be rudimentary at first.) This way you can respond to and facilitate your baby's development.*

upon a high degree of neurological development. This change will enable your baby to develop a whole new set of skills. Although the subtleties of these skills may escape you at first, they will gradually become more obvious. The sounds your infant emits may still just seem like baby babble to you for a while, but they are actually becoming much more complicated. No doubt you'll notice when they string their consonants and vowels together to say "Mama" and "Dada." You also will be very aware of their attempts to roll over and their first attempts to crawl. In all of these activities, they are now capable of learning how single patterns and transitions string together like beads to become what we as adults recognize as events.

This process is also vital for your baby to understand something that adults take completely for granted – that the world is made up of objects that continue to exist, whether or not we can completely see them at the time. You can see just how hard your baby is working in this first year of life to make sense of their world.

Your baby's awareness of the new changes that accompany this leap in their development actually begins at approximately 15 weeks (or between 14 and 17 weeks). These changes affect the way they see, hear, smell, taste, and feel. They need time to come to terms with all of these new impressions, preferably in a place where they feel safe and secure. They will once again show a pronounced need to be with their mommy, cling to her for comfort, and they will grow into their new world at their own pace. From this age on, the fussy periods will last longer than before. This particular one will often last five weeks, although it may be as short as one week or as long as six. If your baby is fussy, watch them closely to see if they are attempting to master new skills.

This Week's Fussy Signs

Because your baby is upset by what is happening to them, they will be much quicker to cry at this time. A very demanding little one, in particular, will cry, whine, and grumble noticeably more often than they did in the past. They will make no bones about the fact that they want to be with their mommy. Your baby will generally cry less when they are with you, although they may insist you give them your undivided attention. They may not only want to be carried around constantly but also expect to be amused all through their waking hours. If they are not kept busy, they may continue to be extra cranky even when sitting on your lap.

How you know it's Time to Grow

Watch for these sometimes subtle, sometimes obvious, clues that your baby is changing and about to leap into the world of events.

They May Have Trouble Sleeping

Your baby may not settle down well at night now. It may be more difficult than before to get them to go to bed in the evenings, or they may lie awake at night. They may want a night feeding again, or they might even demand to be fed several times a night. They might also wake up much earlier in the morning than usual.

They May Become Shy with Strangers

Your baby might refuse to sit on anyone else's lap but yours, or they may get upset if a stranger looks at or talks to them. They may even seem frightened of their own father if they are not around them for much of the day. Generally, their shyness will be more apparent with people who look very different from you.

> "When my daughter sees my sister, she gets extremely upset and starts screaming at the top of her lungs and buries her face in my clothes, as if she's afraid to even look at my sister. My sister has dark eyes and wears black eye makeup, which tends to give her a rather hard look. I'm blonde and wear hardly any makeup at all. Perhaps that has something to do with it."
>
> **Nina's mom, 16th week**

They May Demand More Attention

Your baby might want you to amuse them by doing things with them, or at the very least, they may want you to look at them all the time. They may even start to cry the moment you walk away.

LEAP 4

Their Head May Need More Support

When you carry your fussy baby around, you may notice you have to support their head and body more often now. They may slump down a little in your arms when you hold them, particularly during crying fits. When you carry them, it may strike you that they feel more like the tiny newborn they used to be.

They May Always Want to Be with You

Your baby may refuse to be set down, although they may agree to sitting in their bouncing chair as long as you stay near by and touch them frequently.

They May Lose Their Appetite

Both breastfed and bottle-fed babies can temporarily have smaller appetites than usual as they approach this leap. Don't worry if your little one is more easily distracted than they used to be by the things they see or hear around them, or if they are quick to start playing with the nipple. Occasionally, babies may even turn away from the bottle or breast and refuse to drink completely. Sometimes, a fussy eater might eat their fruit but refuse their milk, for example. Nearly all mothers who breastfeed see this refusal as a sign they should switch to other forms of nourishment. Some mothers feel as if their babies are rejecting them personally. This is not the case at all. Your baby is simply upset. You don't need to stop breastfeeding at this point; on the contrary, it would be a bad time to decide to wean your baby.

"Around 15 weeks, my daughter suddenly started nursing less. After five minutes, she would start playing around with my nipple. After that had gone on for two weeks, I decided to start supplementing my milk with formula, but she wouldn't have any of that either. This phase lasted four weeks. During that time, I worried she would suffer from some kind of nutrition deficiency, especially when I saw my milk supply starting to diminish. But now she is drinking like she used to again, and my milk supply is as plentiful as ever. In fact, I seem to have more."
Hannah's mom, 19th week

They May Be Moody

Some babies' moods swing wildly at this time. One day they are all smiles, but the next they do nothing but cry. These mood swings may even occur from one moment to the next. One minute they're shrieking with laughter, and the next they burst into tears. Sometimes, they even start to cry in the middle of laughing. Some parents say that both the laughter and the tears seem to be dramatic and exaggerated, almost unreal.

My Diary

Signs My Baby is Growing Again

Between 14 and 17 weeks, you may notice your baby starting to show any of the following behaviors, signs that they are ready to make the next leap into the world of events. Cross off the signs your baby shows on the list below, in comparison to how they were before.

☐ Cries more often; is often bad-tempered, cranky, or fretful.

☐ Wants you to keep them busy

☐ Needs more support for their head

☐ Wants more physical contact

☐ Sleeps poorly

☐ Loses their appetite

☐ Is shyer with strangers than they were before

☐ Is quieter, less vocal

☐ Is less lively

☐ Has pronounced mood swings

☐ Wants more physical contact during nursing

☐ Sucks their thumb, or sucks more often than before

OTHER CHANGES YOU NOTICE

They May Be Listless

Your baby may stop making their familiar sounds for a brief period or might occasionally lie motionless, staring into thin air or fidgeting with their ears, for example. It's very common for babies at this age to seem listless and preoccupied. Many parents find their infants' behavior peculiar and alarming. But actually, this apathy is just a lull before the storm. This interlude is a sign that your baby is on the brink of making many discoveries in a new world where they will learn to acquire many new skills.

How This Leap May Affect You

On one hand, you may find it hard to believe your baby is 19 weeks old, but on the other, you may have felt every hour of those 19 weeks, having been up for so many of them, comforting a wailing baby. Here are some ways this latest leap may be affecting you.

You May (Still) Be Exhausted

During a fussy period, most mothers and fathers complain increasingly of fatigue, headaches, nausea, backaches, or emotional problems. Some less fortunate parents contend with more than one of these problems at the same time. They blame their symptoms on a lack of sleep, having to constantly carry their little screamers, or worrying about their unhappy infants. The real cause of these symptoms, though, is the stress of constantly coping with a cranky baby. Some parents visit their family doctor and are prescribed an iron supplement, or go to a physiotherapist for their back troubles, but the real problem is that they are nearing the end of their tether. Especially now, make time for yourself, and give yourself a treat now and then. But remember that your baby will eventually come to your aid by learning the skills they need to deal with their new world, and then the sun will shine again.

"If my daughter won't settle down for a few nights in a row and wants to be walked around all the time, I get a terrible backache. At times like these, I wish she was gone for just one night. I'm a total wreck."

Emily's mom, 17th week

You May Feel Trapped

Toward the end of a fussy period, parents sometimes feel so confined by their baby's demands they almost feel they're in prison. It seems as if the baby is calling all the shots, and the parents feel irritated by their "selfishness." It's no wonder that mothers and fathers sometimes wish their babies would just disappear for a while. Some even daydream about how wonderful it would be if they could put the baby out of their minds for just one night.

"This week, there were moments when I would have liked to forget that I had a son altogether. Aren't human beings weird creatures? At times, I felt so closed in. I just had to get away from it all, and so that's what I did."

Bob's mom, 18th week

LEAP 4

"When I'm at the store with my baby and he wakes up and starts crying, everybody stares at me. I get all hot and bothered. Sometimes I think, 'Why don't you shut up, you stupid kid!'"

Steven's mom, 18th week

You May Feel Resentful

After a few weeks of living with a fussy baby, you may be shocked to find you are beginning to resent this demanding little person who disrupts your life so much. Don't blame yourself. This is an understandable and surprisingly common reaction. Many mothers and fathers grow more irritated toward the end of a fussy period. They are convinced their baby has no valid reason for making such a fuss, and they are inclined to let their babies cry a little longer than they used to. Some begin to wonder what "spoiling" actually means, and think they may be giving in to their whims too much. They might also begin to wonder if they should be teaching their little ones to consider that parents have feelings, too. Now and then, a parent may feel a surge of aggression toward their persistent little screamer, especially when the baby won't stop crying, and the parents are at their wit's end. Having these feelings is not abnormal or dangerous, but acting on them is. Get help long before you lose control. Shaking, in particular, can be harmful. Remember, while it is normal to feel frustrated and angry with your baby at times, never shake a baby. Shaking a young child can easily cause internal bleeding of the spine just below the skull which can result in brain damage that may lead to learning difficulties later on or even death.

"My son refused to continue with his feeding and started having an incredible crying tantrum, while I just kept trying to get his milk down his throat. When the same thing happened with the next bottle, I felt myself becoming terribly angry because none of my little distraction tricks were working. I felt as if I were going around in circles. So I put him on the floor where he would be safe and let him scream his lungs out. When he finally stopped, I went back into the room, and he finished his bottle."

Bob's mom, 19th week

"I started to feel my temper rise every time my daughter launched into one of her crying fits because I'd left her on her own for just a second. So I let her get on with it and ignored her."

Ashley's mom, 17th week

"The last four evenings, my son started screaming at 8:00 P.M. After consoling him for two nights in a row, I'd had enough. So I let him cry until 10:30 P.M. He's certainly persistent, I'll give him that!"

Kevin's mom, 16th week

How Your Baby's New Skills Emerge

Because this fussy phase lasts longer than the previous ones, most parents immediately sense that this period is different. They are concerned about their baby's seemingly slower progress and the fact that their baby seems to have a sudden aversion to the things they liked in the past. But don't worry. From this age on, the new skills are much more complicated to learn. Your little one needs more time.

"My baby seems to be making such slow progress. Before he was 15 weeks old, he developed much faster. It's almost as if he's come to a standstill these past few weeks. At times, I find this to be very upsetting."

Matt's mom, 17th week

"It's almost as if my son is on the verge of making new discoveries, but something seems to be holding him back. When I play with him, I can sense there's something missing, but I don't know what it is. So I'm playing the waiting game, too."

Steven's mom, 17th week

"My daughter has been trying to do lots of new things this week. All of a sudden, it hit me how much she can do at just four months, and to tell you the truth, I feel very proud of her."

Jenny's mom, 18th week

At approximately 19 weeks, you will notice that your baby is once again trying to learn new skills, because this is the age when babies will generally begin to explore the world of events. This world offers them a huge repertoire of event skills. Your baby will choose the skills best suited to them – the ones they want to explore. You can help them with what they are actually ready to do, rather than trying to push them in any and every direction.

The Magical Leap Forward

After the last leap forward, your baby was able to see, hear, smell, taste, and feel smooth and continuous transitions. But all these transitions had to be relatively simple, such as a toy moving steadily across the floor in

The World of Events   119

front of them. As soon as they became more complicated, they were no longer able to follow them. In the new world that babies begin to explore at approximately 19 weeks, most babies will start to perceive and experiment with short, familiar sequences. This new ability will affect a baby's entire behavior.

As soon as a baby is able to make several flowing movements in sequence, this will give them more opportunities with objects within their grasp. They might, for instance, be able to repeat the same flowing movement several times in succession. You may now see them trying to shake playthings from side to side or up and down. They may also attempt to press, push, bang, or beat a toy repeatedly. Besides repeating the same movement, they might now learn to perform a short sequence of different movements smoothly. For instance, they may grab an object with one hand, then try to pass it to the other hand. Or they may grab a plaything and immediately attempt to put it in their mouth. They are capable of turning a plaything around and looking at it from every possible angle. From now on, they are able to carry out a thorough examination of any object within reach.

In addition, your baby might now learn how to adjust the movements of their body, especially their upper arms, lower arms, hands, and fingers, to reach the exact spot where the plaything is, and they can learn to correct their movements as they go along. For instance, if a toy is farther to the left, their arm will move to the left in one flowing movement. If it is more to the right, their arm will immediately move to the correct spot. The same applies to an object near at hand, one that is farther away, or a toy hanging high up or low down. They will see it, reach for it, grab it, and pull it towards them, all in one smooth movement. As long as an object is within arm's length, your little one will now actually be able to reach out and grasp the object of their choice.

When your baby is toying with these movements, you may see them twist and turn. They might now learn to roll over or spin on their back easily. They may also make their first attempts at crawling, because they are now capable of pulling their knees up, pushing off, and stretching. They might also learn to make a short series of sounds now. If they do, they will develop

Brain Changes

Recordings of babies' brain waves show that dramatic changes occur at approximately four months. Also, babies' head circumferences suddenly increase between 15 and 18 weeks.

their chatter, which started after the previous leap, to include alternating vowel and consonant sounds. They will gradually use all of these sounds to speak in "sentences." This abba baba tata is what adults fondly call "baby talk." You could say they are now able to become just as flexible with their voice as they are with the rest of their body.

LEAP 4

All over the world, babies start making these short sentences when they reach this age. For example, Russian, Chinese, and American babies all babble the same language initially. Eventually, the babies will start to develop their babble-sounds into proper words of their native language, and they will stop using the universal babble sounds. Each baby will then become more proficient at imitating the language they hear being spoken around them because they will get the most response and praise when they produce something close to home.

Apparently, everyone's ancestors must have felt as if they were being addressed personally when they heard their offspring say "Dada" or "Mammam," because the words for mommy and daddy are very similar in many different languages. The truth, though, is that the little babbler is carrying out a number of technical experiments with short, familiar sequences of the same sound element: "da" or "ma."

Your baby may now begin to recognize a short series of flowing sounds. They may be fascinated by a series of notes running smoothly up and down a musical scale. They may now respond to all voices that express approval, and they may be startled by voices that scold. It doesn't matter what language is used to express these feelings, since they will be able to

(continued on page 126)

The World of Events   121

My Diary

How My Baby Explores the New World of Events

Check off the boxes below as you notice your baby changing. Stop filling this out once the next stormy period begins, heralding the coming of the next leap. The big change that eventually allows your baby to make sense of the world of events begins at around 15 weeks. The leap into this world is a pretty big one, and the skills that come with it only start to take wing around 19 weeks. Even then, it may be a while before you see any of the skills listed here. It's most likely they will not acquire many of these skills until months later.

BODY CONTROL

Your baby:

☐ Starts moving virtually every part of their body as soon as they are put on the floor

☐ Rolls over from their back onto their tummy

☐ Rolls over from their tummy onto their back

☐ Is able to fully stretch their arms when lying on their tummy

☐ Lifts their bottom and attempts to push off; does not succeed

☐ Raises themselves onto their hands and feet when lying on their tummy, then tries to move forward; does not succeed

☐ Attempts to crawl; manages to slide forwards or backwards

☐ Supports themselves with forearms, and raises upper half of their body

☐ Sits up straight (all by themselves) when leaning against you

☐ Attempts to sit up straight when they're by themselves and briefly succeeds by leaning on their forearms and bringing their head forward

☐ Remains upright in the high chair with cushions for support

☐ Enjoys moving their mouth – puckers their lips in a variety of ways, sticks their tongue out

GRABBING, TOUCHING, AND FEELING

☐ Succeeds in grabbing objects

☐ Grabs things with either hand

☐ Is able to grab an object with either hand if it comes into contact with the object, even if they are not looking at it

☐ Is able to pass objects between their hands

☐ Sticks your hand in their mouth

☐ Touches or sticks their hands in your mouth as you talk

☐ Sticks objects in their mouth to feel and bite them

☐ Is able to pull a cloth from their face by themselves, slowly at first

☐ Recognizes a toy or other familiar object, even if it is partially covered by something; will soon give up with unsuccessful attempts to retrieve the toy

☐ Tries shaking a plaything

☐ Tries banging a plaything on a tabletop

☐ Deliberately throws a plaything on the floor

☐ Tries grabbing things just out of reach

☐ Tries to play with an activity center

☐ Understands the purpose of a particular toy; for example, they push buttons on a toy telephone

☐ Studies objects closely; they are especially interested in the minute details of toys, hands, and mouths

WATCHING

- ☐ Stares in fascination at repetitive activities, such as jumping up and down, slicing bread, or brushing hair
- ☐ Stares in fascination at the movements of your lips and tongue when you are talking
- ☐ Searches for you and is able to turn around to do this
- ☐ Looks for a plaything that is partially hidden
- ☐ Reacts to their own reflection in a mirror; they are either scared or laugh
- ☐ Holds a book in their hands and stares at the pictures

LISTENING

- ☐ Listens intently to sounds coming from your lips
- ☐ Responds to their own name
- ☐ Is now able to distinguish one particular sound in a medley of different sounds, so responds to their own name even if there are background noises
- ☐ Genuinely understands one or more words; for example, they look at their teddy bear if asked "Where's your teddy bear?" (Won't respond correctly if the toy isn't in its usual place.)
- ☐ Will respond appropriately to an approving or scolding voice
- ☐ Recognizes the opening bars of a song

TALKING

☐ Makes new sounds, using their lips and tongue: ffft-ffft-ffft, vvvvvv, zzz, sss, brrr, arrr, rrr, grrr, prrr. This rrr is known as the "lip r."

Your baby may particularly like to do this with food in their mouth!

☐ Uses consonants: d, b, l, m

☐ Babbles. Utters first "words": mommom/mammam, dada, abba, hadahada, baba, tata

☐ Makes noises when yawning and is aware of these noises

BODY LANGUAGE

☐ Stretches their arms out to be picked up

☐ Smacks their lips when hungry; waves arms and legs

☐ Opens their mouth and moves their face toward food and drink

☐ "Spits" when they've had enough to eat

☐ Pushes the bottle or breast away when they have had enough

☐ Turns away from the feeding of their own accord when full

OTHER SKILLS

☐ May exaggerate their actions; for example, when you respond to their coughing, they will cough again, then laugh

☐ Gets grumpy when becoming impatient

☐ Screams if they fail to do what they seem to be trying to do

☐ Has one special cuddly toy, such as a blanket

OTHER CHANGES YOU NOTICE

perceive the differences in tones of voice. For the first time, they are now able to pick out one specific voice in the middle of a commotion. Your baby may also start to recognize short, familiar tunes. At 19 weeks, babies are even capable of hearing whether interruptions in a piece of music being played are genuine or do not belong to that particular piece of music, even if they have never heard the music before. In an unusual experiment, researchers found that if a part of a minuet by Mozart was played to babies, they showed a definite response if the music was interrupted by random pauses. Babies may also start recognizing words for the very first time.

Your baby may now learn to see a short, familiar sequence of images. For instance, they may be fascinated by the up-and-down motion of a bouncing ball. There are endless examples to be seen, all disguised as normal, everyday activities or events, such as someone shaking their bottle up and down, stirring a saucepan, hammering a nail, opening and closing a door, slicing bread, filing nails, brushing hair, the dog scratching itself, somebody pacing back and forth in the room, and a whole range of other events and activities.

Two more basic characteristics of the world of events should be mentioned here. First, as adults, we usually experience an event as an inseparable whole. We do not see a falling-rising-falling ball – we see a bouncing ball. Even when the event has only just begun, we already know it's a bouncing ball. As long as it continues, this remains one and the same event – an event for which we have a name. Second, most events are defined by the observer. For instance, when we speak, we don't separate the words clearly, but run one into the next without a pause. The listener creates the boundaries between words, giving the impression that they are heard one at a time. It is exactly this special power of perception that will begin to be available to your baby between 14 and 17 weeks.

Your Baby's Choices: A Key to Their Personality

The world of events offers a wide range of new skills to your baby. From the opportunities available to them, your little one will make their own selections, based on their own inclinations, interests, and physical characteristics. Some babies will want to concentrate on feeling skills, while others might choose the watching skills, and yet another group will specialize in physical activities. Obviously, there are also babies who like to learn a variety of different skills without specializing in any one of them. Every baby makes their own choices, because every baby is unique.

Watch your baby closely to determine their particular interests. If you respect their choices, you will discover the special pattern that makes your baby unique. All babies love anything new. It's important that you respond when you notice any new skills or interests. Your baby will enjoy it if you share these new discoveries, and it will accelerate their learning progress.

What you Can Do to Help

The more your baby comes in contact with events and the more they play with them, the greater their understanding of them will be and the more proficient they will become. It doesn't matter which discoveries they choose to make in this new world. They may pay close attention to music, sounds, and words. Or they may choose looking and observing, or physical activities. Later on, it will be easy for them to put the knowledge and experience they have gained learning one skill to good use when learning another. Besides wanting to experiment with the discoveries they make in their world of events, your baby will also become tremendously interested in everything going on around them. This may now occupy most of their waking hours, because they will want to look at and listen to everything they possibly can. Even better (or worse!), every toy, household item, and gardening or kitchen utensil within a small arm's length is theirs for the taking. You are no longer their only toy. They may try to become involved in the world around them by pushing themselves forward with their hands and feet, toward something new, and away from their parents. They may now have less time to spare for their old cuddling games. Some parents feel a little rejected by this.

Even so, they still need your help just as much as ever. Your baby's fascination with the whole world around them is typical at this age. You have probably started to sense these new needs, and your main contribution can be supplying your baby with enough playthings and then waiting to see how they respond. Only give them a hand if you notice they are having real difficulties in fully understanding a toy. You'll also want to keep an eye on your baby to make sure they use their hands, feet, limbs, and body properly when reaching out to grab objects. If you see they have a particular problem, you can help them to practice activities like rolling over, turning, and sometimes even crawling, sitting, or standing up.

Help Your Baby Explore the New World through Body Movement

Perhaps you have seen your baby spin on their back and squirm in an attempt to roll over from their tummy onto their back. If you did, you saw your little one toying with a short series of flowing movements of several body parts. They can make these now because they are living in the world of events. However, being able to make several flowing movements in succession does not automatically mean they are successful in rolling over or crawling. It usually takes quite some trial and error to get there.

"My little one is trying to roll over from her back onto her tummy. She's not having much success yet, and it's making her awfully upset. She really gets exasperated."

Ashley's mom, 20th week

Here's a playful way to help your baby practice rolling from their back onto their tummy. Lay your baby on their back, and hold a colorful plaything next to them. To reach it, they will be forced to stretch their body and turn so they can't help but roll over. Of course, you have to encourage them in their efforts and praise them for trying.

You can also make a game out of helping them to roll from their tummy onto their back. One way is to lay your baby on their stomach and hold a colorful toy behind them, either to their left or to their right. When they turn to reach for it, move the plaything farther behind their back. At a certain point, they will roll over, simply from turning a little too much when reaching for the toy. Their heavy head will automatically help them in the process.

Babies often try to crawl around this age. The problem with crawling is the moving forward part. Most babies would love to move forward, and they do try. Some babies get into the right starting position – they tuck their knees under their bodies, stick their bottoms in the air, and push off – but they don't succeed. Other babies get into the crawling position but bounce up and down without moving forward. There are also little squirmers who slide backwards, because they push off with their hands. Others push off with one foot, thus going around in circles. Some lucky babies fumble around for a while and hit on a forward motion seemingly by accident. This is the exception rather than the rule at this age.

LEAP 4

Many parents try to help their babies crawl. They carefully push their wriggling infants' bottoms forward, or they put all kinds of attractive objects just out of baby's reach in an attempt to coax them forward. Sometimes these maneuvers will do the trick, and the baby somehow manages to move a little. Some babies do this by throwing themselves forward with a thud. Others lie on their tummies and push themselves forward with their legs, while using their arms to steer themselves in the right direction.

If you imitate your baby's attempts, they may find it absolutely hilarious. They may also really enjoy watching you show them how to crawl properly. Nearly every child who is having crawling problems will be fascinated by your attempts. Just try it and see!

Let Them Wriggle Around Naked

Your baby has to practice if they want to learn how to roll over, turn, and crawl properly. It will be a lot more fun, and much easier for them, if they are not wearing their clothes and diaper. Lots of physical exercise will give them the opportunity to get to know their body and help them to increase their control over it.

Help Your Baby Explore the New World through Manipulation and Examination

In the world of events, your baby's arms, hands, and fingers are just like the rest of their body – able to make several flowing movements in succession. As a result, they are able to practice reaching for, grabbing, and pulling a toy towards them in one smooth movement and manipulate it in all sorts of ways such as shaking, banging, or poking. Thus, they can examine the objects they can lay their hands on. And that is just what they want to do at this age, though again they need a lot of practice to become perfect. Let them explore as many objects as they want to. They might turn them around, shake them, bang them, slide them up and down, and stick an interesting part in their mouth to feel and taste it. An activity center offers a variety of these hand and finger exercises all on one board. It usually has an element that can be turned. It may have a knob that also makes a noise when pressed. There could be animals to slide up and down and revolving cylinders and balls to turn, and so on. Each separate activity will emit a different sound when your baby handles it. Lots of babies love their activity centers. But don't expect your little one to understand and use all these features properly at first. They're just a beginner! When you see that your baby is trying to do something without much success, you can help them by holding their hand to show them how to do it properly. Or if your baby has a preference for observing how things are done, let them watch how your hand does it. Either way, you will encourage them to be playful and clever with their little hands.

"We had an activity center hanging in the playpen for weeks. My son looked at it from time to time, but he wouldn't do anything with it. But this week, he suddenly started grabbing it. Now he just loves touching and turning all those knobs. You can tell he's really exploring the whole board. He does get tired quickly, though, because he has to push himself up with one hand all the time."

Paul's mom, 18th week

If your baby gets tired because they have to constantly push themselves up with one hand, support them so they can use their hands freely. For instance, put them on your lap and examine a toy together. They will love being able to play while sitting comfortably. Besides, when they are sitting up, they will be able to look at playthings from a completely different angle. Just watch them to see if they do different things with toys when they are sitting comfortably. Perhaps you may even see new activities.

"I put my baby in his high chair for the first time and propped him up with a cushion. He immediately discovered that you can do certain things with toys while sitting up that you can't do on the floor. When I gave him his plastic key ring, he first started banging it on the tabletop, and then he kept throwing it on the floor. He did that about 20 times in a row. He thought it was great fun and couldn't stop laughing."

Paul's mom, 19th week

If your baby is a keen explorer, you can enrich their environment by offering them playthings and other objects of different shapes, such as round or square things, or made of different materials, such as wood and plastic. Give them fabrics with different textures or soft, rough, and smooth paper to play with. Many babies love empty crisp bags, because they slowly change shape and make wonderful crackling sounds when crumpled. Give your baby objects with rough edges or dents. Most babies have a weakness for weird shapes. The shape of a plastic key, for instance, will challenge them to make a closer inspection. Many babies find the jagged edge particularly intriguing and will want to touch it, look at it, and taste it.

Some babies are drawn to the smallest details. If you have such a tiny researcher, they will probably look at an object from all sides, examining it very carefully. They will really take their time and closely inspect the object. They will fuss with the smallest of protrusions. It may take ages before they've finished stroking, feeling, and rubbing textures and examining shapes and colors. Nothing seems to escape their inquisitive eyes and probing mind. If they decide to examine you, they will do this meticulously, too. If they study your hand, they will usually begin with one finger, stroke the nail, and then look and feel how it moves, before they proceed to the next finger. If they're examining your mouth, they will usually inspect every single tooth. Stimulate their eye for detail by giving them toys and objects that will interest them.

"My daughter is definitely going to be a dentist. I almost choke every time she inspects my mouth. She probes around and practically shoves her whole fist inside my mouth. She makes it very clear she doesn't appreciate being interrupted while she's working when I try to close my mouth to give her a kiss on the hand."
Emily's mom, 21st week

Does your baby want to grab everything you are eating or drinking? Most babies do. So, take care not to drink hot tea or coffee with a wriggly baby on your lap. In an unguarded moment, they may suddenly decide to grab your cup and tip the hot contents all over their hands and face.

"My son will try to grab my sandwich with his mouth already open in anticipation. Whatever he manages to grab, he swallows immediately. The funny thing is, he seems to enjoy everything."
Kevin's mom, 19th week

Baby Care

Make Your Home Baby-Proof

You probably began this process a long time ago, but since your baby is now becoming increasingly mobile, it's time to do a quick safety check to make sure they are safe.

- Never leave small objects, such as buttons, pins, or coins, near your baby.

- When your baby is on your lap during feeding, make sure they can't suddenly grab a cup or mug containing a hot drink.

- Never leave hot drinks on a table within your baby's reach. Don't even leave them on a high table. If the baby tries to reach it by pulling at the leg of the table – or, even worse, the tablecloth – they could spill the drink over themselves.

- Use a guard or fence around stoves and fireplaces.

- Keep poisonous substances such as turpentine, bleach, and medicines out of your baby's reach and in childproof containers when possible.

- Make sure electrical outlets are secured with socket covers and that there are no trailing wires anywhere.

Help Your Baby Explore the New World through Sight

Is your baby a real observer? The daily routine in every household is full of events that your baby might enjoy watching. Many babies love to watch their mothers or fathers preparing food, setting the table, getting dressed, or working in the garden. They are now capable of understanding the different actions or events involved in various activities, such as putting plates on the table, slicing bread, making sandwiches, brushing hair, filing nails, and mowing the lawn. If your baby enjoys observing things, let them watch your daily activities. All you have to do is make sure they are in a perfect position to observe what you are doing. It's really no extra trouble for you, but it will be an enjoyable learning experience for them.

> *"My little one smacks her lips, kicks her legs, and reaches out with her hands as soon as she sees me making sandwiches. She's obviously aware of what I'm doing, and she's asking to be fed."*
> **Hannah's mom, 20th week**

Some babies at this age already enjoy looking at picture books that show events. If your baby enjoys this, they may want to hold the book themselves, using both hands, and gaze at the illustrations in wonder. They may make a real effort to hold the book and concentrate on the pictures, but after a while the book will usually end up in their mouth.

You can start to play the first peek-a-boo and hide-and-seek games at this age. As soon as your baby becomes familiar with the world of events, they can recognize a plaything, even when they can see only part of it. If you see them looking quizzically at a partially hidden toy, or if you want to turn their attempts to retrieve a toy into a game of hide-and-seek, move the object about a bit to make it easier for them to recognize it. At this age, they are still quick to give up. The idea that an object continues to exist all the time, wherever it is, is not yet within their mental grasp.

Top Games for This Wonder Week

Here are games and activities that most babies like best now. Remember, all babies are different. See what your baby responds to best.

HAPPY TALK

Talk as often as you can to your baby about the things they see, hear, taste, and feel. Talk about the things they do. Keep your sentences short and simple. Emphasize the important words. For instance: "Feel this–grass," "Daddy's coming," "Listen–the doorbell," or "Open your mouth."

WHAT HAPPENS NEXT?

First you say, "I'm going to (dramatic pause) pinch your nose." Then grab their nose and gently wiggle it about. You can do the same with their ears, hands, and feet. Find out what they enjoy most. If you play this game regularly, they will know exactly what you are going to do next. Then they will watch your hands with increasing excitement and shriek with laughter when you grab their nose. This game will familiarize them with both their body and the words for the body parts as you play together.

LOOKING AT PICTURES

Show your baby a brightly colored picture in a book. They might even want to look at several pictures. Make sure the pictures are bright, clear, and include things they recognize. Talk about the pictures together, and point out the real object if it's in the room.

SING SONGS

Many babies really love songs, particularly when they are accompanied by movements, such as "Pat-a-cake, pat-a-cake, baker's man." But they also enjoy being rocked to the rhythm of a song or nursery rhyme. Babies recognize songs by their melody, rhythm, and intonation.

TICKLING GAME

This familiar song encourages tickling, which your baby may love.

This little piggy went to market...
And this little piggy stayed at home...
This little piggy ate roast beef...
And this little piggy had none...
This little piggy went...
Weeweeweewee all the way home.

While saying this, wiggle each of your baby's toes in turn, before finally running your fingers up their body and tickling them in the neck.

PEEK-A-BOO

Cover your baby's face with a blanket, and ask: "Where's...?" Watch them to see if they can remove the blanket from their face on their own. If they can't do this yet, help them by holding their hand and slowly pulling the cloth away with them. Each time that they can see you again, say "Boo" – this helps to mark the event for them. Keep the game simple at this age; otherwise, it will be too difficult for them.

MIRROR GAME

Look in a mirror together. Usually, a baby will prefer looking and smiling at their own reflection first. But then, they will look at your reflection, and then back to the real you. This normally bewilders them, and they will usually look back and forth at you and your reflection, as if they can't make up their mind which one is their real parent. If you start talking to them, they will be even more amazed, because no one but their real mother or father talks like that. This might reassure them that they're with the right person, so they may start laughing before they snuggle up to you.

Top Toys for This Wonder Week

Here are toys and other objects that most babies like best as they explore the world of events. Nearly all everyday household items will appeal to your baby. Try to find out what your baby likes best. Be careful, though, to screen out any that may be harmful to them.

- Bath toys. Your baby will enjoy playing with a variety of household items in the bath, such as measuring cups, plastic colanders, plant spray bottles, watering cans, soap dishes, and plastic shampoo bottles.

- Activity center

- Balls with gripping notches, preferably with a bell inside

- Plastic or inflatable rattles

- A screw-top container with some rice in it

- Crackly paper

- Mirrors

- Photographs or pictures of other babies

- Photographs or pictures of objects or animals they recognize by name

- Children's songs

- Wheels that really turn, such as those on a toy cars

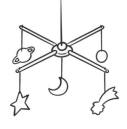

Help Your Baby Explore the New World through Language and Music

Does your baby make "babbling sentences"? Sometimes it may sound as if your little one is really telling you a story. This is because in the world of events your baby becomes just as flexible with their voice as with the rest of their body. They start to repeat whatever syllables they already know and string them together to form a "sentence," such as dadadada and bababababa. They might also experiment with intonation and volume. When they hear themselves making a new sound, they may stop for a while and laugh before resuming the conversation.

It's still important to talk to your baby as often as possible. Try to respond to what they say, imitate their new sounds, and reply when they "ask" or "tell" you something. Your reactions encourage them to practice using their voice.

You might notice that your baby understands a word or short sentence, although they cannot say the word or words themselves. Try asking in familiar surroundings "Where's your teddy?" and you may see they actually look at their teddy bear.

In the world of events, babies are able to understand a short, familiar series of sounds such as "Want to go for a ride?" This doesn't mean that they understand a sentence in the same way that an older child or an adult does. Your baby is hearing a familiar pattern of syllables along with the intonation of your voice as a single sound event. This is just the kind of simple string of patterns and changes that forms an event for them in this world.

Being able to recognize the teddy-bear-sentence event doesn't mean that your baby can recognize sound events under all circumstances. If you were looking in a toy store window with your baby and saw a teddy identical to their own, for example, you might try "Where's your teddy?" with absolutely no success, since they really won't be able to understand meaning in a context so far removed from their own familiar surroundings.

Because parents naturally repeat the same or similar sentences over and over again as they go about their daily routines, babies gradually come to recognize them. This is the only way they can begin to learn about speech, and all babies understand words and phrases long before they can say them.

> 'In our living room, there's a painting of flowers on one wall and a photo of my son on another. When I ask him 'Where are the flowers?' or 'Where's Paul?' he always looks at the correct picture. I'm not imagining it, because the pictures are on opposite sides of the room.'
>
> **Paul's mom, 23rd week**

You will be really enthusiastic and proud when you discover that your baby understands their first short sentence. Initially, you may not believe what has happened. You may keep repeating the sentence until you are convinced it wasn't just a coincidence. Next, you could create a new situation to practice the little sentence your baby already recognizes. For instance, you could put the teddy bear in every conceivable spot in a room to test if your baby knows where it is. You could even show them photographs of their teddy bear to see if they recognize it. Many parents change the way they talk to their babies at this age. They will slow down their sentences when talking to their baby, and often, they will use just single words instead of whole sentences.

Is your baby a budding music lover? In the world of events they may be fascinated by a series of notes running smoothly up and down the musical scale, and they are able to recognize a short, familiar sequence such as the opening tune of a commercial on TV. Help them with their musical talents. Let them hear the music they like best. Your music lover may also appreciate all kinds of sounds. If so, it's worth stimulating and encouraging this interest. Some babies grab toys and objects primarily to find out if they

will make a noise of any kind. They turn around sound-producing objects, not for inspection, but to see if the sound changes when the object is turned quickly or slowly. These babies will squeeze a toy in a variety of ways to see if it produces different sounds. Give them sound-producing objects to play with and help them to use them properly.

The Virtue of Patience

When your baby is learning new skills, they may sometimes try your patience. Both you and your baby have to adjust to their progress and renegotiate the rules to restore peace and harmony. Remember, from now on your baby will no longer be completely dependent on you for their enjoyment, since they are now in touch with the world around them. They can do and understand a lot more than they did in the past, and, of course, they think they know it all. You may think they are a handful. They think *you* are! If you recognize this behavior, you could say you are experiencing your infant's first struggle for independence.

"Every time my daughter sits with me on my favorite chair, she tries to grab the tassels on the lamp shade. I don't like her doing that, so I pull her away and say 'No.'"

Jenny's mom, 20th week

What irritates many parents more than anything else is a baby's obsession for grabbing everything within reach or anything they see in passing – especially when they seem to prefer doing this over playing with their mother or father. Some see it as antisocial – sometimes even slightly selfish – on the part of their little ones. Others feel that the baby is still too young

to be touching everything in sight – plants, coffee cups, books, stereo equipment, eyeglasses – nothing is safe from their exploring hands. Most parents try to curb this urge for independence by stopping their babies in every way possible when they again push away from them and towards the things that take their fancy now. Often, a mother or father may try to distract their infant with cuddling games or a tight embrace as their baby wriggles and squirms in their arms to get at something. But both methods will nearly always have the opposite effect. The baby will squirm and wriggle with even more determination as they struggle to free themselves from their long-suffering parent. Other mothers and fathers try to discourage this grabbing mania by firmly saying "No." This sometimes works.

Impatience can be a nuisance. Most parents think their babies should learn a little patience at this age. They don't always respond to their babies as quickly as they used to. When the baby wants something, or wants to do something, a mother or father may now make them wait for a few brief moments. The child may insist on sitting up straight, on being where the action is, and staying somewhere as long as they like. The same goes for eating and sleeping. Grabbing food impatiently is particularly irritating to most parents. Some put an immediate stop to it.

Baby Care

Don't Lose Control

Now and again, a mother or father may feel a surge of aggression toward their little troublemaker. Remember that having these feelings is not abnormal or dangerous, but acting on them is. Try to calm yourself, and if you can't, be sure to get help long before you lose control.

There is nothing funny or amusing about hurting someone. Now that the baby is stronger and understands the world of events, they are also capable of causing physical pain. They might bite, chew, and pull at your face, arms, ears, and hair. They may pinch and twist your skin. Sometimes they will do this hard enough that it really hurts. Most parents feel their baby could easily show a little more consideration and respect for others. They're no longer amused by biting, pulling, and pinching.

Some parents rebuke their babies if they get too excited. They do this by immediately letting them know that they have gone too far. Usually they do this verbally by saying "Ouch," loudly and sternly. If they notice that their baby is preparing to launch a new attack, they warn them with "Careful." At this age, babies are perfectly capable of understanding a cautioning voice. Occasionally, a mother or father will really lose their temper.

Matt's mother is very honest about her feelings. Fortunately, she doesn't act on them. Although your baby might inflict physical pain on you during this difficult period, they are not doing this "on purpose." Giving your baby "an eye for an eye" is not acceptable and it certainly doesn't teach them that they shouldn't hurt their mother or father.

LEAP 4

After the Leap

Between 20 and 22 weeks, another period of comparative calm begins. Many parents praise their baby's' initiative and love of enterprise. Babies seem to have boundless energy now. You are no longer your baby's only toy. They explore their surroundings with great determination and enjoyment. They grow increasingly impatient with only mother or father to play with. They want action. They may try to wriggle off of your lap at the least opportunity if they spot anything of interest. They are obviously a lot more independent now.

"I put away my son's first baby clothes today and felt a pang of regret. Doesn't time fly? Letting go isn't easy. It's a very painful experience. He suddenly seems so grown up. I have a different kind of relationship with him now. He has become more of his own little person."

Bob's mom, 23rd week

"My baby drinks her bottle with her back toward me now, sitting up straight, not wanting to miss any of the world around her. She even wants to hold the bottle herself."

Laura's mom, 22nd week

"When my son is on my lap, he tries to lie almost flat so he doesn't miss anything going on behind him."

Frankie's mom, 23rd week

"I hardly ever put my baby in the playpen now. I think that he's too restricted in such a small space."

Bob's mom, 22nd week

> "My son is starting to resent being carried around in the sling. At first, I thought he wanted more room because he's so active. But then I put him facing forward, and he's happy now that he's able to see everything."
>
> **Steven's mom, 21st week**

Babies who like to be physically active no longer need to be handed the objects they want, because they will twist and turn in every direction to get them themselves.

> "My daughter rolls from her tummy onto her back and wriggles and squirms all over the place to get to a plaything, or she'll crawl over to it. She's as busy as a bee all day long. She doesn't even have time to cry. I must say she seems happier than ever, and so are we."
>
> **Jenny's mom, 21st week**

> "My baby crawls and rolls in every direction. I can't stop her. She tries getting out of her bouncing chair, and she wants to crawl up onto the sofa. The other day we found her halfway into the dog basket. She's also very busy in the bath. There's hardly any water left in it once she's practically kicked it all out."
>
> **Emily's mom, 22nd week**

During this time, the calm before the next storm, most babies are more cheerful than before. Even demanding, trying babies are happier now at this stage. Perhaps this is because they are able to do more so they are less bored. Parents delight in this less-troubled, well-deserved time.

> "My little one is in such a cheerful mood now. She laughs and 'tells stories.' It's wonderful to watch her."
>
> **Juliette's mom, 23rd week**

"I'm enjoying every minute I spend with my daughter again. She's such a cutie, really easygoing."

Ashley's mom, 22nd week

"My son is suddenly easier. He's back in a regular routine, and he's sleeping better."

Frankie's mom, 23rd week

"My son is surprisingly sweet and cheerful. He goes to sleep without any complaining, which is an achievement in itself. He sleeps much longer now in the afternoons, compared to these past weeks. He's so different from how he was several months ago when he cried all day. Apart from a few ups and downs now and again, things are steadily improving."

Paul's mom, 22nd week

LEAP 5

Wonder Week 26

The World of Relationships

**SEPARATION ANXIETY
NOW REARS ITS HEAD**

At about 26 weeks, your baby will start showing the signs of yet another significant leap in their development. If you watch closely, you will see them doing, or attempting to do, many new things. Whether or not they are crawling at this stage, they will have become significantly more mobile by now as they increasingly learn to coordinate the action of their arms and legs and the rest of their body. Building on their knowledge of events, they are now able to begin understanding the many kinds of relationships among the things that make up their world.

One of the most significant relationships your baby can now perceive is the distance between one thing and another. We take this for granted as adults, but for a baby it is an alarming discovery, a very radical change in their world. The world is suddenly a very big place in which they are but a tiny, if very vocal, speck. Something they want can be on a high shelf or outside the range of their crib, and they have no way of getting to it. Their mother can walk away, even if only into the next room, and they might as well have gone to China if they can't get to her because they're stuck in their crib or haven't yet mastered crawling. Even if they are adept at crawling, they realize that she moves much faster than they do and can get away from them.

This discovery can be very frightening for a baby, and it may make these few weeks quite taxing for their parents. But when you understand the source of this fear and uneasiness, there are many things you will be able to do to help. Naturally, once your baby learns to negotiate the space around them and control the distance between themselves and the things they want, they will be able to do much more on their own than they used to. But there will be a period during which they will need a lot of support.

Note: *The first phase (fussy period) of this leap into the perceptual world of "relationships" is age-linked and predictable, emerging about 23 weeks. Most babies start the second phase (see box "Quality Time: An Unnatural Whim" on page 17) of this leap 26 weeks after full-term birth. It sets in motion the development of a whole range of skills and activities. However, the age at which these skills and activities appear for the first time varies greatly and depends on your baby's preferences, experimentation and physical development. For example, the ability to perceive spatial relationships is a necessary precondition for "crawling inside or under things," but this skill normally appears anywhere from six to 11 months. The skills and activities in this chapter are stated at the earliest possible age they could appear so you can watch for and recognize them. (They may be rudimentary at first.) This way you can respond to and facilitate your baby's development.*

Entering the world of relationships will affect everything your baby perceives and does. They sense these changes taking place at around 23 weeks, and that's when the disturbances begin. Caught up in a tangle of new impressions, they need to touch base, return to their parents, and cling to them for comfort. The familiar feeling of security and warmth the parents provide will help them to relax, let the newness sink in, and enable them to grow into the new world at their own pace. This fussy period often lasts about four weeks, although it may be as short as one week or as long as five. Since one of the important skills they have to learn during this leap is how to handle the distance between their parents and themselves, your baby may actually become fussy again for a while around 29 weeks, after their new skills have started to take wing. Do remember that if your baby is fussy, watch them closely to see if they are attempting to master new skills.

This Week's Fussy Signs

When your baby becomes aware that their world is changing, they will usually cry more easily than before. At this point, many parents might call their babies cranky, bad-tempered, whiny, or discontented. If your baby is already strong willed, they may come across as being even more restless, impatient, or troublesome than ever. Almost all babies will cry less when they are picked up and cuddled, nestled up against mother or father, or at least when they are kept company while they're playing.

"My baby is starting to stand up for herself more and more. She makes demands, angrily ordering me to come to her or stay with her. In this way, she makes sure I am there to help reach her toys."

Hannah's mom, 25th week

How You Know it's Time to Grow

Here are some of the signals that your baby may give you to let you know they're approaching this leap into the world of relationships.

They May Sleep Poorly

Your baby might sleep less than you are used to. Most babies have difficulty falling asleep or wake up sooner compared to before. Some don't want to nap during the day, and others don't want to go to bed at night. There are even those who refuse to do either.

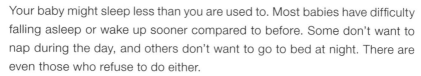

"Bedtime and naptime are accompanied by terrible screaming fits. My son yells furiously and practically climbs the walls. He'll shout at the top of his voice and practically wind himself. I just can't handle it. It seems as if I never see him lying peacefully in his crib anymore. I just pray it doesn't last forever."
Bob's mom, 26th week

"My baby's rhythm is totally off because he keeps waking up a little earlier each day. But apart from that, his sleep is normal."
Frankie's mom, 25th week

They May Have "Nightmares"

Your baby might sleep uneasily at this time. Sometimes, babies can toss and turn and thrash about so much during their sleep that it looks as if they're having nightmares.

"My daughter is a very restless sleeper. Sometimes, she'll let out a scream with her eyes closed, as if she's having a nightmare. So I'll lift her up for a minute to comfort her. These days, I usually let her play in the bathtub in the evening. I'm hoping it will calm her down and make her sleepier."
Emily's mom, 23rd week

They May Become Shyer Than Before

Your baby may not want other people to look at them, talk to them, or touch them, and they certainly won't want to sit on their laps. They might even start to want you in plain sight more often from this age on, even when there aren't any strangers around. Almost every parent will notice this now. At this age, shyness is especially obvious, for a very good reason – your baby is now able to understand that you can walk away and leave them behind.

"My baby gets shyer every day now. I need to be where he can see me at all times, and it has to be close to him. If I walk away, he'll try to crawl right after me."

Matt's mom, 26th week

"Even when I sit down, I can hardly move without my daughter crying out in fear."

Ashley's mom, 23rd week

They May Demand More Attention Than Usual

Your baby might want you to stay with them longer and play with them more than before, or just look at them and them alone.

"My daughter is easily discontented and has to be kept busy. When she wakes up in her crib, for instance, she's really eager to see one of us right away. Also, she's quick to react. She doesn't just cry; she gets really mad. She's developing a will of her own."

Hannah's mom, 26th week

"All my baby wants is to get out of his playpen. I really have to keep him occupied on my lap or walk around with him."

Frankie's mom, 27th week

They May Always Want to Be With You

Your baby may insist on remaining in your arms. Many babies don't want to be put down very much. But some are not completely satisfied with the peaceful rest on mommy's lap that they cried for. As soon as they reach their goal, they start to push off and reach out for interesting things in the world around them.

The Gender Gap

Girls who want physical contact usually agree to play with their parents, but boys who want physical contact insist on exploring the world around them at the same time.

They May Lose Their Appetite

Both babies who are breastfed and those who are bottle-fed sometimes drink less milk at this stage or refuse to drink at all. Other food and drink may be rejected, too. Often, babies also take longer to finish their meals now. Somehow they seem to prefer the comfort of sucking or playing with the nipple over the contents of the bottle or breast.

"My baby always refuses to nurse in the morning and at night. He just pushes my breast away, and it really hurts. Then, when he's in bed and can't get to sleep, he does want to nurse. He'll drink a little and doze off in the middle of it."

Matt's mom, 26th week

They May Be Listless

Your baby might stop making their familiar sounds. Or they may lie motionless, gazing around or staring in front of them. Parents always find this behavior odd and alarming.

LEAF 5

"Sometimes, all of a sudden, my little one will stare or gaze around silently. On days when she does it more than once, it makes me feel insecure. I start to wonder whether perhaps there's something wrong. I'm not accustomed to seeing her that way. So lifeless. As if she's sick or mentally challenged."

Juliette's mom, 24th week

They May Refuse to Have Their Diaper Changed

Your baby might cry, kick, toss, and turn when they are set down to be changed or dressed. Many babies do. They just don't want their parents to fiddle with their clothes.

My Diary

Signs My Baby Is Growing Again

Between 22 and 26 weeks, you may notice your baby starting to show any of these behaviors. They are probably signs that they are ready to make the next leap into the world of relationships. Check off the signs you see on the list below.

THEIR INTEREST IN THEIR SURROUNDINGS

- ☐ Cries more and is bad-tempered, cranky, or whiny more often than they were
- ☐ Wants you to keep them busy
- ☐ Wants more physical contact than before
- ☐ Sleeps poorly
- ☐ Loses appetite
- ☐ Doesn't want to be changed
- ☐ Is shyer with strangers than they used to be
- ☐ Is quieter, less vocal than they were
- ☐ Is less lively than before
- ☐ Sucks their thumb, or sucks more often than before
- ☐ Reaches for a cuddly toy, or does so more often than before

OTHER CHANGES YOU NOTICE

"When I put my baby on her back for a clean diaper, she'll cry every time. Usually not for very long, but it's always the same old story. Sometimes I wonder if there could be something wrong with her back."

Juliette's mom, 23rd week

They May Reach For a Cuddly Object More Often Now

Some babies reach for a teddy, slipper, blanket, or towel more often than before. For most babies, anything soft will do, but some babies will accept only that one special thing. Sometimes, they'll cuddle it while sucking a thumb or twiddling an ear. It seems that a cuddly object spells safety, especially when mommy or daddy is busy.

How This Leap May Affect You

Your baby certainly lets you know how these changes make them feel. This is bound to affect you. Here are some emotions you may feel this time around.

You May Be (Even More) Exhausted (Than Before)

Fussy periods can be nerve-racking. Mothers and fathers of especially demanding babies may feel like complete wrecks toward the end. They complain of stomachaches, backaches, headaches, and tension.

> "My son's crying gets on my nerves so much that I'm totally obsessed with keeping myself from crying. The tension it creates swallows up all my energy."

Steven's mom, 25th week

> "One night, I had to keep walking back and forth to put the pacifier in my daughter's mouth. Suddenly, at 12:30 A.M., she was wide awake. She stayed awake until 2:30 A.M. I'd already had a busy day, with a lot of headaches and backaches from walking her up and down. I just collapsed."

Emily's mom, 27th week

You May Be Concerned

It's natural that you might feel troubled or nervous every time something seems to be the matter, and you can't figure out what it is. When very young babies are involved, parents generally rationalize that they must be suffering from colic because nothing else seems to be wrong. At this age, however, mothers and fathers are quick to put two and two together and embrace the thought that their babies are fussy because they're teething. After all, most babies start cutting their teeth around this age. Still, there is no connection between clinginess due to a big change in the baby's mental development and teething. Just as many babies start teething during fussy periods as in between them. Of course, if your baby starts teething at the same time as they undergo a big change in their mental development, they can become super troublesome.

> "My daughter right now is extremely bad-tempered, only wanting to sit on my lap. Perhaps it's her teeth. They've been bothering her for three weeks now. She seems pretty uncomfortable, but they still haven't come through."

Jenny's mom, 25th week

> "My little guy became very weepy. According to the doctor, he has a whole bunch of teeth waiting to come through."

Paul's mom, 27th week (His first tooth didn't emerge until seven weeks later.)

Being Fussy Doesn't Necessarily Mean Teething

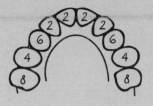

The illustration to the left shows the general order in which teeth emerge. Just remember that babies are not machines. Your baby will cut their first tooth whenever they are ready. How quickly teeth are cut in succession has nothing to do with the state of health or mental or physical development of the baby either. All babies can cut their teeth early or late, fast or slow.

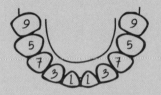

Generally speaking, the lower front teeth are cut when the baby reaches six months. By their first birthday, a baby generally has six teeth. At about age 2½, the last molars come through, completing the full set of baby teeth. The toddler then has 20 teeth. Despite the old wives' tale, a high temperature or diarrhea has nothing to do with teething. If your baby shows one of these symptoms, call their pediatrician.

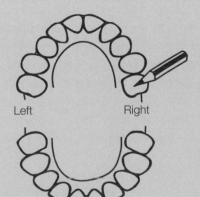

Left   Right

Date

L1	R1 ....
L2	R2 ....
L3	R3 ....
L4	R4 ....
L5	R5 ....
L6	R6 ....
L7	R7 ....
L8	R8 ....
L9	R9 ....
L10	R10 ....

You May Become Annoyed

Many parents get angry as soon as they are convinced their baby has no good reason for being so troublesome and fussy. This feeling tends to get stronger towards the end of the fussy period. Some mothers and fathers, especially those with very demanding babies, just can't take it anymore.

"It was a terribly trying week. My son would cry over anything. He demanded attention constantly. He was up until 10:00 P.M., and agitated. I carried him around an awful lot in the infant carrier. He liked that. But I felt tired, tired, tired from all that schlepping and the continuous crying. Whenever he started throwing one of his temper tantrums in bed at night, it was as if I'd crossed a line. I could feel myself getting really angry. This has happened frequently this past week."

Bob's mom, 25th week

Don't lose control. Remember that having feelings of anger and frustration at times is not abnormal or dangerous, but acting on them is. Try to get help long before you lose control.

You May Start to Argue

Arguments might develop around mealtimes. Most parents hate it when their babies won't eat and they continue to try and feed them. They try doing it playfully, or they try to pressure them into eating. Whatever the approach, it's usually to no avail.

At this age, strong-willed babies can be extremely stubborn in their refusal. This sometimes makes mothers and fathers, who are also being stubborn (but out of concern!) very angry. And so mealtimes can mean war. When this happens to you, try to stay calm. Don't turn it into a fight. You can't force them to eat, anyway. During this fussy phase, many babies are poor eaters. It's a temporary thing. If you make an issue out of it, the chances are your baby will continue to refuse food even after the fussy period is over. They will have made a habit of it.

At the end of the fussy phase, you may correctly sense that your baby is capable of a lot more than you thought possible. Many mothers and fathers do. That is why an increasing number of parents now get fed up with the annoying clinginess and decide that it's time to put a stop to it.

"My little girl keeps whining for attention or to be picked up. It's really aggravating and, what's worse, she has no excuse whatsoever! I have enough to do as it is. So when I'm fed up now, it's off to bed with her."
Juliette's mom, 26th week

How Your Baby's New Skills Emerge

At about 26 weeks, you'll discover that your baby is once again trying to learn one or more new skills. This is the age at which babies will generally begin to explore the world of relationships. This world offers them many opportunities to develop skills that depend upon understanding the relationships among objects, people, sounds, and feelings. Your baby, depending on their own temperament, inclinations, preferences, and physical makeup, will focus on the sorts of relationships that appeal to them the most. They will use this understanding to develop the skills best suited to them personally. You can help them best by encouraging them to do what they are ready to do, rather than trying to push them in directions that don't interest them. You will find that increasingly hard to do, anyway, as their personality begins to emerge and their own ideas start to dominate.

"I keep seeing this pattern of a difficult, sometimes extremely trying period that peaks at the end, and which is then followed by a peaceful stage. Every time I think I can't take it anymore, my little boy changes course and suddenly does all these new things."
Bob's mom, 26th week

My Diary

How My Baby Explores the New World of Relationships

The world of relationships opens up so many possibilities that your baby could not explore them all, even if they wanted to. The aspects of this world they decide to explore depend entirely on what sort of child they are growing up to be and what their talents are. A very physical baby will use the distance perception to improve balance and to crawl after you if they are able. The watching-listening baby will find plenty to occupy themselves as they try to figure out just how this world works. As you read the following list of possibilities, check off the ones that apply to your baby right now. You might want to do this two or three times before the next leap happens, since not all of the skills your baby will develop are going to appear at once. In fact, some won't appear at all until much later.

BALANCE

Your baby:

☐ Sits up by themselves from lying down

☐ Stands up by themselves; pulls themselves up

☐ Sits down again by themselves after standing

☐ Stands without support

☐ Walks with support

☐ Makes a jumping movement without leaving the ground

☐ Grabs a toy from an overhead shelf or table

BODY CONTROL

☐ Walks around the edge of the crib, table, or playpen while holding on

☐ Walks around, pushing a box in front of them

☐ Lunges from one piece of furniture to another

- ☐ Crawls inside or under things, such as chairs and boxes
- ☐ Crawls back and forth over small steps
- ☐ Crawls in and out of rooms
- ☐ Crawls around the table
- ☐ Bends over or lies flat on their stomach to get something from under the couch or chair

GRABBING, TOUCHING, AND FEELING

- ☐ Opposes their thumb and index finger to grasp small objects
- ☐ Can play with something using both hands
- ☐ Lifts rugs to look under them
- ☐ Holds toys upside down to hear the sound inside
- ☐ Rolls balls across the floor
- ☐ Invariably grabs a ball rolled toward them
- ☐ Knocks over the wastepaper basket to empty out its contents
- ☐ Throws things away
- ☐ Puts toys in and next to a basket, in and out of a box, or under and on a chair, or pushes them out of the playpen
- ☐ Tries to fit one toy inside another
- ☐ Tries prying something out of a toy, like a bell's clapper
- ☐ Pulls own socks off
- ☐ Pries your shoelaces loose
- ☐ Empties cupboards and shelves
- ☐ Drops objects from high chair to test how something falls
- ☐ Puts food in the mouth of the dog, mommy, or daddy
- ☐ Pushes doors closed

WATCHING

☐ Observes adult activities, such as putting things into, on, or through something

☐ Looks from one animal to another in different picture books

☐ Looks from one person to another in different photographs

☐ Looks from one toy, object, or food to another in their hands

☐ Observes the movements of an animal, particularly when it's an unusual action, such as a dog pattering across a wooden floor

☐ Observes the movements of a person behaving unusually, such as daddy standing on his head

☐ Explores their own body – particularly the penis or vagina

☐ Pays a lot of attention to smaller details or parts of toys and other objects, such as labels on towels

☐ Selects books to look at

☐ Selects toys to play with

LISTENING

☐ Makes connections between actions and words; comprehends short commands, such as "No, don't do that" and "Come on, let's go"

☐ Listens to explanations intently and seems to understand

☐ Likes to hear animal sounds when looking at animal pictures

☐ Listens intently to voices on the telephone

☐ Pays attention to sounds that are related to a certain activity, such as chopping vegetables. Listens to sounds they make themselves, such as splashing bathwater

TALKING

☐ Understands the link between actions and words. Says their first words in the correct context. For instance, says oo (for "Oops") when they fall and a-choo when you sneeze

☐ Puffs and blows

PARENT-BABY DISTANCE

☐ Protests when their mother or father walks away

☐ Crawls after their mother or father

☐ Repeatedly makes contact with their mother or father although busy playing on their own

MIMICKING GESTURES

☐ Imitates waving good-bye

☐ Claps their hands on request

☐ Mimics clicking with their tongue

☐ Mimics shaking and nodding their head, although often only nods with their eyes

MISCELLANEOUS

☐ Dances to the sound of music (sways their tummy)

OTHER CHANGES YOU NOTICE

The Magical Leap Forward

For the first time, your baby can perceive all kinds of relationships and act on them. They can now discover that there is always a physical distance between two objects or two people. And of course, their distance from you is one of the first things they will notice and react to. While observing this phenomenon, they discover that you can increase the distance too much for their liking, and it dawns on them that they can't do anything about it. Now they know that they have lost control over that distance, and they get frightened. So, they will start to cry.

"We have a problem. My girl doesn't want to be put in her playpen any more. Her lips start to tremble if I even hover her anywhere above it. If I put her in it, she starts screaming. It's fine, though, if I put her on the floor, just outside of the 'cage.' Immediately, she rolls, swivels, and squirms in my direction."

Nina's mom, 25th week

The juxtaposition of objects comes as a real revelation to your baby when the idea first dawns of them. They begin to understand that something can be inside, outside, on top, above, next to, underneath or in between something else. They will love to toy with these notions.

"All day long, my son takes toys out of his toy box and puts them back in again. Sometimes, he'll toss everything over the side of the playpen. Another time, he'll carefully fit each item through the bars. He clears cupboards and shelves and is thrilled by pouring water from bottles and containers into the tub. But the best thing yet was while I was feeding him. He let go of my nipple, studied it with a serious look on his face, shook my breast up and down, sucked once, took another look, and continued this way for a while. He's never done this before. It's as if he was trying to figure out how anything could come from there."

Matt's mom, 30th week

Next, your baby can begin to understand that they can cause certain things to happen. For example, they can flip a switch that causes music to play or a light to come on. They become attracted to objects such as stereo equipment, television sets, remote controls, light switches, and toy pianos. They can now start to comprehend that people, objects, sounds, or situations can be related to each other. Or that a sound is related to an object or a particular situation. They know, for example, that bustling in the kitchen means that someone is preparing their dinner, the key in the front door means "daddy's home," the dog has its own food and toys, and that they have a mommy and daddy who belong together. Your baby's understanding of "family" won't be anywhere near as sophisticated as your own, but they do have their own understanding of what it means to belong together.

Next, your baby can begin to understand that animals and people coordinate their movements. Even if two people are walking separately, they still notice that they are taking each other's movements into consideration. That is a "relationship" as well. They can also tell when something goes wrong. If you drop something, let out a yell, and bend down quickly to catch it, if two people accidentally bump into each other, or if the dog falls off the couch, they understand that these things are out of the ordinary. Some babies find this highly amusing; others are scared out of their wits. And others become curious or take things very seriously. After all, they are seeing something that is not meant to happen. Each brand-new observation or skill can, incidentally, make your baby feel wary until these things prove themselves harmless.

"I've noticed my son is scared of the slicing machine at the bakery. As soon as the bread goes into it, he glances at me as if to ask, 'Are you sure that it's okay?' Then he looks frightened, then he looks at me, then frightened again, then at me again. After a while, he calms down."

Paul's mom, 29th week

Your baby may also begin to discover that they can coordinate the movements of their body, limbs, and hands and that they work together as one. Once they understand this, they can learn to crawl more efficiently. Or they may try to sit up by themselves or pull themselves up to stand and sit down again. Some babies now take their first steps with a little help. And the exceptional baby will even do it without help, just before the next leap begins. All this physical exercise can also be frightening to a baby. They fully realize that they could lose control of their body. They still need to learn how to keep their balance. And keeping one's balance has a lot to do with being familiar with the idea of distances.

When your baby starts to be active in the world of relationships, they will do it in their unique way. They will use the skills and concepts they have acquired from previous leaps in their mental development. So they will only be able to perceive and experiment with relationships that involve things they already understand – things they have learned from the worlds of patterns, smooth transitions, and events.

Your Baby's Choices: A Key to Their Personality

Between 26 and 34 weeks, you can discover what your baby likes best in the world of relationships. Take a good look at what your baby is doing. Use the "My Diary" list to help you determine where their interests lie, and respect your baby's choices. It's only natural to make comparisons with other parents' observations of their babies, but don't expect all babies to be the same. The only thing you can be certain of is that they won't be the same! Keep in mind that babies love anything new. Whenever you notice your baby showing any new skills or interests, be sure to respond. Your baby will enjoy it if you share these new discoveries. Your interest will accelerate their learning progress more quickly. That's just how babies are.

The Gender Gap

Are boys different from girls after all?

Mothers of boys sometimes seem to have a harder time with their babies than mothers of girls. They often don't understand their sons. Does he or doesn't he want to play with his mom?

> "My son often whines for contact and attention. I always respond. But when I pick him up to play a game, it's obviously not what he had in mind. Then he'll spot something, and all of a sudden that's what he wants, and he reaches and whines to get at it. He seems to want two things – me and exploring. But he always makes a mess of these adventures. He'll grab something pretty roughly and hurl it aside. He likes to go through the entire house this way. I would have liked him to be a bit cuddlier. We could talk, play games – just do new things together and have some fun. Whereas now, I'm constantly trying to prevent accidents from happening. Sometimes I feel dissatisfied myself."
>
> **Matt's mom, 32nd week**

Mothers with both boys and girls usually find they can do more with their girls. They feel they are better at sensing what a girl wants. They share more of the same interests, which they call sociable and fun.

> "I'm able to play mother with my daughter more. We do all kinds of things together. When I talk, she really listens. She enjoys my games and asks for more. Her brother was much more his own man."
>
> **Eve's mom, 33rd week**

What You Can Do to Help

Every baby needs time, support, and lots of opportunities to practice and experiment with new skills. You can help them by encouraging them when they succeed and by comforting them when they fail (by their own baby standards). If they persist too long with trying something they're not able to master yet, you may be able to distract them by coming up with something they can do. Most of your activities as an adult are firmly rooted in the world of relationships – loading the car, getting dressed, putting cards in envelopes, holding conversations, following exercise videos, to name a few. Let your baby watch these activities and join in where they can. Let them share your experience of sights, sounds, sensations, smells, and tastes whenever they want to. You are still their guide in this complex world.

Always keep in mind that they will almost certainly be specializing in some kinds of activities at the expense of others. It really doesn't matter whether your baby learns about relationships from the watching or listening areas only. Later on, they will quickly and easily be able to put this understanding to use in other areas.

Show Them That You Are Not Deserting Them

When they are in the world of relationships, almost every baby begins to realize that their parents can increase the distance between them and can walk away and leave them. Previously, their eyes could see it, but they didn't fully grasp what leaving means. Now that they do, it poses a problem. They get frightened when it hits them that their mommy and daddy are unpredictable and beyond their control – they can leave them behind at any time! Even if they're already crawling, their mommy and daddy can easily outdistance them. They feel they have no control over the distance between themselves and their parents, and this makes them feel helpless. It's hard to accept at first that this state of affairs is progress, but it is a clear sign of a mental leap forward. Your baby has to learn how to deal with this development and make it a part of their new world so that it is no longer frightening. Your task is to help them achieve this. It takes understanding, compassion, practice, and above all, time.

If your baby shows fear, accept that fear. They will soon realize that there is nothing to be afraid of, since their mother or father is not deserting them. Generally, babies panic the most around 29 weeks. Then it improves somewhat, until the next leap begins.

"My son has his moods when he screams until he's picked up. When I do, he'll laugh, utterly pleased with himself."

Frankie's mom, 31st week

"Everything's fine as long as my daughter can see me. If not, she starts crying out in fear."

Eve's mom, 29th week

"My little girl had been with the babysitter, as is usual. She wouldn't eat, wouldn't sleep, wouldn't do anything. She just cried and cried. I've never seen anything like it with her. I feel guilty leaving her behind like that. I'm considering working shorter hours, but I don't know how to arrange it."

Laura's mom, 28th week

"If my daughter even suspects I'll be setting her down on the floor to play, she starts whining and clinging with intense passion. So now, I carry her around on my hip all day long. She has also stopped smiling the way she used to. Just last week, she had a smile for everyone. Now it's definitely less. She's been through this once before, but in the past, she'd always end up with a tiny grin on her face. Now, it's out of the question."

Nina's mom, 29th week

LEAP 5

"This was a week of torment. So many tears. Even five minutes on his own was already too much for my guy. If I so much as stepped out of the room, there'd be a crying fit. I've had him in the infant carrier a lot. But at bedtime, all hell would break loose. After three days, I was beat. It was too much. I started feeling extremely angry. It looked like it was starting to become a vicious circle. I was really pushing myself, feeling lonely and completely exhausted. I kept breaking things, too – they would just drop from my hands. That's when I took him to the day care center for the first time. Just so I could catch my breath. But it didn't work out, so I quickly went to get him. I felt really bad about dumping him somewhere, while at the same time, I had given it a lot of thought and felt it was the best solution. I push myself too far too often, and it only makes me feel lonely, aggressive, and confined. I also keep wondering whether it's me, whether I'm to blame for being inconsistent or for spoiling him too much."

Bob's mom, 29th week

To ease your baby's anxiety, make sure they feel you near them in case they really need you. Give them the opportunity to grow accustomed to the new situation at their own pace. You can help them by carrying them more often or staying a bit closer to them than usual. Give them some warning before you walk away, and keep talking to them as you walk away and when you're in the other room. This way, they will learn that you are still there, even if they can't see you. You can also practice "leaving" by playing peek-a-boo games. For example, you can hide behind a newspaper while sitting next to your baby, then you can hide behind the couch close to your baby, then behind the cupboard a little farther away, and finally behind the door. If your baby is already somewhat mobile, you can reassure them with their feeling of desertion by helping them to follow you. First try telling them you are leaving – this way, your baby will learn they do not have to keep an eye on you and that they can continue to play at ease. Then slowly walk away, so that they can follow you. Always adjust your pace to your baby's. Soon, your baby will learn they can control the distance between the two of you. They will also come to trust that you will not completely disappear when you have to get something from another room, and they won't bother you as much.

Often, the desire to be near you is so strong that even the inexperienced crawler is willing to put in some extra effort and ends up improving their crawling. The desire to keep up with mommy and daddy, along with the coordination they're able to utilize at this point, might provide just the extra incentive they need.

If your baby was already a bit mobile after the last leap, you will see a big difference now. Their laborious journeys used to take them farther away from you, and they would stay away longer than they do now. Suddenly, they're circling you and making short dashes backward and forward, making contact with you each time.

Offer your baby the chance to experiment with coming and going, with you as the center point. If you sit on the floor, you'll notice they will interrupt their excursions to crawl over you.

Over the weeks, parents grow more and more irritated if they don't get the opportunity to continue their everyday activities. Once their baby has reached 29 weeks, most mothers and fathers call it a day. They start to gradually break the old habit ("I am always here for you to cling to") and lay down a new rule ("I need some time and space to move as well"). They generally do this by distracting their baby, sometimes by ignoring their whines for a while, or by putting the baby to bed if they are really fed up with their behavior.

LEAP 5

Whatever you decide to do, consider how much your baby can handle before they get really afraid. Knowing that you can leave them whenever you choose can be very frightening for them and very difficult to deal with.

"It's so annoying the way he keeps clinging to my legs when I'm trying to do the cooking. It's almost as if he chooses to be extra difficult because I am busy. So I put him to bed."

Kevin's mom, 30th week

Help Your Baby Explorethe New World through Roaming Their Surroundings

If your baby loves to crawl, allow them to roam freely around a room where they can do no harm. Watch them just to see what they do. When they enter the world of relationships, an early crawler begins to understand that they can crawl into, out of, under, over, in between, on top of, and through something. They will love to toy with these various relationships between themselves and the objects in their surroundings.

"I like to watch my son play in the living room. He crawls up to the couch, looks under it, sits down, quickly crawls over to the closet, crawls into it, rushes off again, crawls to the rug, lifts it up, looks under it, heads toward a chair that he crawls under, whoosh, he's off to another cupboard, crawls into that one, gets stuck, cries a little, figures out how to get out and closes the door."

Steven's mom, 30th week

If your baby takes pleasure in doing these things, leave some objects around that will encourage them to continue their explorations. For instance, you can make hills for them to crawl over using blankets, quilts, or pillows. Of course, you should adjust this soft play circuit to suit what your baby can do.

You can also build a tunnel from boxes or chairs that they can crawl through. You can make a tent out of a sheet, which they can crawl into, out of, and under. Many babies enjoy opening and closing doors. If your baby likes this, too, you can include a door or two. Just watch out for their fingers. If you crawl along with them, it will double the fun. Try adding some variety with peek-a-boo and hide-and-seek games, too.

If your baby enjoys moving their toys around, make this into a game. Give them the opportunity to put playthings inside, on top of, next to, or under objects. Allow them to throw their toys – it's important in getting to understand how the world works. Let them pull toys through something, such as the legs of a chair or a box made into a tunnel. To the outsider, it may seem as if they are flying like a whirlwind from one object to the next, but this frenzied activity is providing precisely the input their brain needs to understand this new world of relationships.

Give your baby a shelf or cupboard of their own, which they can empty *out* and you can easily tidy up again. Give them a box they can put their things *in*. Turn a box upside down, so they can put things *on top of it*. Allow them to push things *out of* the playpen *through* the bars, or throw them out over the top. This is an ideal way for babies who aren't yet interested in crawling to explore relationships like i*nside, outside, underneath,* and *on top of.*

Another way your baby can toy with relationships is by throwing, dropping and overturning objects. It is one way of seeing and hearing what happens. Maybe they want to find out just how a particular object breaks into several pieces. You can watch them enjoy knocking over towers of blocks, which you have to keep building up again. But they will gain just as much pleasure from tipping over the wastepaper basket, overturning the cat's water bowl, dropping a glass of milk or a bowl of cereal from their high chair, or any other activity that is bound to make a mess.

"My daughter loves experimenting with the way things fall. She's been trying it with all kinds of things — her pacifier, her blocks, and her cup. Then, I gave her a feather from Big Bird, the parakeet. This took her by surprise. She prefers things that make a lot of noise!"

Nina's mom, 28th week

"Boy, did my son laugh when I dropped a plate, and it shattered into a million pieces. I've never seen him laugh so hard."

John's mom, 30th week

In the world of relationships your baby may discover that things can be taken apart. Give them a few items that are designed for exactly that purpose – nesting cups or bright laces tied into bows. They will tug and pull at things that are attached to objects or toys, such as labels, stickers, the eyes and noses of cuddly toys, wheels, latches, and doors of toy cars.

Baby Care

Make Your Home Baby-Proof

Remember that your baby can be fascinated by things that are harmful to them. They can stick a finger or tongue into anything with holes or slots, including things such as electrical outlets, electronic equipment, drains, and the dog's mouth. Or they can pick up and eat little things they find on the floor. Always stay near your baby whenever you let them explore the house freely.

But take care: Buttons on clothing, switches and wires trailing from electrical equipment, and bottle caps are equally attractive and just as liable to be taken apart whenever possible. To your baby, there is no such thing as off limits in this new and exciting world.

"My son keeps pulling his socks off."
Frankie's mom, 31st week

If your baby dearly loves watching things disappear into something else, invite them to watch your activities. You may think cooking is ordinary, but to them it's magic to watch all the ingredients disappear into the same pot. But do keep an eye on them because they may try out their own disappearing acts in ways that could be hazardous.

"My daughter likes to watch the dog emptying his bowl. The closer she can get, the better. It seems pretty dangerous to me, because with all that attention, the dog gulps it down faster and faster. On the other hand, the dog suddenly seems to be paying more attention to my daughter as well when she's eating. She'll be sitting at the table in her high chair, with the dog right next to her. So what do you know? It turned out she was dropping little pieces of bread and watching him wolf them down."
Laura's mom, 31st week

Sometimes babies like putting one thing inside another. But this only happens by coincidence. They can't yet distinguish between different shapes and sizes.

"My girl tries fitting all kinds of things together. A lot of the time, the size is right, but the shape never is. Also, she isn't accurate enough. But if it doesn't work, she gets mad."

Jenny's mom, 29th week

"My son discovered his nostrils. He stuck an inquisitive finger in one. I hope he doesn't try the same with a bead!"

John's mom, 32nd week

"I held a toy bear upside down so that it growled. Then I put the bear on the floor, and my son crawled right over and rolled it around, until it made that sound. He was so fascinated that he kept turning the bear over and over, faster and faster."

Paul's mom, 33rd week

Is your baby intrigued by a toy that squeaks when pushed, or a toy piano that produces a musical tone when they hit a key? Let them explore these things. They concern relationships between an action and an effect. But beware, they can also turn over a bottle filled with nail polish or perfume or some other dangerous substance.

Help Your Baby Explore the New World through Using Their Body

In your baby's body, there are numerous relationships between the various body parts. Without the efforts of all the muscles we would lose the relationships that exist between the various parts of the skeleton and we would collapse like a sack of bones. About this time, your baby may start to try to sit up by themselves, depending on their balance skills.

If your baby is not sitting steadily enough to feel confident on their own, help them. See if you can help them gain confidence by playing balancing games in which they have to regain their balance every time the wobble sets In. Look for favorite balancing games under "Top Games for This Wonder Week" on page 184.

Some babies try to stand up at this stage. If your baby does, how is their balance? Help your baby when they're not standing firmly, or if they're afraid of tumbling down. Play balancing games with them – these will make them familiar with being in a vertical position. But never try to rush your baby into sitting or standing. If you try too early for their liking, they could become afraid and you may even slow their development.

LEAP 5

"My daughter is beginning to stand up, but she doesn't know how to sit back down. It's tiring. Today, I found her standing in her crib for the first time, wailing. That irritates me. She's supposed to go to sleep when she's in bed. I just hope it doesn't take too long and that she works out how to sit back down sometime soon."

Juliette's mom, 31st week

"My baby insists on me sitting her back down after she's stood up. Her sister isn't allowed to help her, even though there are many things she will let her do. She's obviously scared that she won't be able to do it well enough."

Ashley's mom, 32nd week

"My baby kept trying to pull herself up this week, and at a certain point she succeeded. She had pulled herself up in bed, stood up right away, and stayed standing up, too. Now she can really do it. She pulls herself up using the bed, playpen, table, chair, or someone's legs. She also stands by the playpen and takes toys from it with one hand."

Jenny's mom, 28th week

If and only if you notice that your baby has great fun walking, give them a hand. Hold on to them tightly, because their balance is usually unstable. Play games with them that will familiarize them with keeping their balance, especially when they shift their weight from one leg to the other. Never go on hour-long walks with them. They really won't learn any faster that way. Your baby won't start walking until they are ready to.

"When I hold both my baby's hands, she walks in perfect balance. She crosses the small gap between the chair and the television while standing. She walks alongside the table, around the bends. She'll walk through the room pushing a Pampers box. Yesterday, the box slid away, and she took three steps by herself."

Jenny's mom, 34th week

"I'm irritated by my son's slow coordination. He doesn't crawl, he won't pull himself up. He just sits there and fiddles with his playthings."

Frankie's mom, 29th week

Remember that your baby has no motive for learning to walk or crawl just yet. Plenty of other activities will teach them things worth knowing. For them, these things are more important right now.

Babies who have entered the world of relationships can also begin to understand the connection between what their two hands are doing, and they can get better control over them. This way, they can cope with two things at once. If you see your baby trying to use both hands at the same time, encourage them to go on. Get them to hold a toy in either hand and clash them together. Or help them make this clashing movement without toys, so that they clap their hands. Let them knock toys against the floor or the wall. Encourage them to pass toys from one hand to the other. And see if they can put two toys down at the same time, and pick them up again.

> *"My daughter has the hitting syndrome. She beats anything she can lay her hands on."*
> **Jenny's mom, 29th week**

First Steps

Once your baby has acquired the knack of perceiving and experimenting with relationships, they can understand what walking is, but understanding doesn't mean they will actually do it. They will only really start walking when they choose to. And even if they do, they might not succeed because their body is not ready. Your baby won't learn how to walk at this age unless the proportions between the weight of their bones, their muscles, and the length of their limbs compared to their torso meet certain specifications. If your baby is occupied with something else – for instance, speech, sounds, and music – they may simply have no time left to spend on walking. They can't do everything at once.

If your baby tries to master the concerted action between two fingers – for instance their thumb and forefinger – once again they are toying with relationships between the two. In the process, they are also busy inventing a new tool, the pincer grip, that they can put to use immediately. They can learn how to pluck extremely small objects, such as threads, from the carpet. They can learn to pick blades of grass, or they may take pleasure in touching and stroking all kinds of surfaces with their finger. And they may have great fun examining every detail of very small objects.

"My baby goes through the entire room and spots the smallest irregularities or crumbs on the floor, picks them up between her thumb and her index finger, and sticks them in her mouth. I really have to pay attention so she doesn't eat anything peculiar. I let her eat small pieces of bread by herself now. At first, she kept sticking her thumb in her mouth instead of the bread she was holding between her fingers. But she's starting to improve now."

Hannah's mom, 32nd week

Help Your Baby Explore the New World through Language And Music

Babies who were extra sensitive to sounds and gestures in the past may start to grasp the connection between short sentences and their meaning or particular gestures and their meaning as soon as they have entered the world of relationships. In fact, they may even make the connection between words and gestures that go with them. But you will still find that these babies can only understand these things when they are in their own surroundings and as a part of a familiar routine. If you were to play the same sentences from a tape recorder in a strange place, they wouldn't have a clue. That skill doesn't develop until much later.

If your baby likes playing with words and gestures, use this to their advantage. There are several things you can do to help your baby to understand what you're saying. Use short sentences with clear and obvious gestures. Explain the things you are doing. Let them see, feel, smell, and taste the things you are talking about. They understand more than you think.

"Once, I told my son to watch the rabbit, and he understood what I meant. He listens very closely."

Paul's mom, 26th week

"I get the feeling that my son knows what I mean when I explain something or make a suggestion, such as, 'Shall we go for a nice little walk?' or 'I think it's bedtime!' It's so cute – he doesn't like hearing the word 'bed'!"

Bob's mom, 30th week

"When we say, 'Clap your hands,' my daughter does. And when we say, 'Jump up and down,' she bends her knees and bounces up and down, but her feet don't leave the ground."

Jenny's mom, 32nd week

"When I say 'Bye, say bye, bye' while waving at her daddy who is leaving, my daughter waves while keeping a steady eye on my waving hand."

Nina's mom, 32nd week

Their First Word

Once your baby has gained the ability to perceive and experiment with relationships, they may discover their first word. It doesn't mean that they will start to talk, though. The age at which babies begin to use words differs greatly. So don't worry if they put it off for a few more months. Most babies produce their first real word during the 10th or 11th month.

If your baby is obsessed with something else, such as crawling and standing, they may simply have no time left to spend on words. They can't do everything at once.

If your baby attempts to say or ask something with a sound or gestures, make sure you let them know that you are thrilled with their potential. Talk and signal back to them. The best way to teach your baby to talk is by talking to them a lot yourself. Call everyday items by their names. Ask questions, such as, "Would you like a sandwich?" when you put their plate down. Let them hear nursery rhymes, and play singing games with them. In short, make speech appealing.

"Whenever my son wants to do something, he'll put his hand on it and look at me. It's as if he's trying to ask, 'May I?' He also understands, 'No.' Of course, it doesn't stop him from trying, but he knows what it means."

Bob's mom, 32nd week

"Last week, my daughter said 'Oo' (oops) for the first time when she fell. We also noticed that she was starting to copy sounds from us, so we've started teaching her to talk."

Jenny's mom, 29th week

"My daughter is a real chatterbox. She's especially talkative while crawling, when she recognizes someone or something. She talks to her stuffed toys and to us when she's on our laps. It's as if she's telling entire stories. She uses all kinds of vowels and consonants. The variations seem endless."

Hannah's mom, 29th week

"My son nods his head and makes a certain sound. When I imitate him, he starts giggling uncontrollably."

Paul's mom, 28th week

If your baby loves music, make sure you do a lot of singing, dancing, and clapping songs with them. This way, your baby can practice using words and gestures. If you don't know many children's songs... Google is your best friend!

Promoting Progress by Raising Expectations

You can't demand more of your baby than the things they can comprehend, but also, you shouldn't demand less. Breaking old habits and setting new rules are also part of developing new skills. When your baby is busy learning new skills, they can be very irritating in the process. This is because old ways of doing things and established rules of behavior may no longer suit the baby's current progress. Both parents and baby have to renegotiate new rules to restore peace and harmony.

At first parents worry when their baby enters a new fussy phase. They get annoyed when they discover that nothing is wrong with their baby and, to the contrary, they are in fact ready to be more independent. It is then that they start demanding that their baby do the things they feel their baby is able to do. As a consequence, they promote progress.

LEAP 5

(continued on page 190)

Top Games for This Wonder Week

Here are some games and activities that work best for babies exploring the world of relationships. Whatever kind of game you choose, language can now begin to play a big part in your games.

PEEK-A-BOO AND HIDE-AND-SEEK GAMES

These are very popular games at this age. The variations are endless.

PEEK-A-BOO WITH A HANDKERCHIEF

Put a handkerchief over your head and see if your baby will pull it away. Ask "Where's Mommy? or Where's Daddy?" Your baby will know you're still there, because they can hear you. If they don't make any attempts to pull away the handkerchief, take their hand and pull it away together. Say "Peek-a-boo" when you reappear.

VARIATIONS ON PEEK-A-BOO

Cover your face with your hands and then take them away, or pop up from behind a newspaper or book held between you and the baby. Babies also like it when you appear from behind a plant or under a table. After all, they can still see parts of you. Or hide in a conspicuous place, such as behind a curtain. This way, they can follow the movements of the curtain. Make sure your baby sees you disappear. For example, announce that you're going to hide (for non-crawlers), or that they have to come look for you (for crawlers). If they didn't watch you or were distracted for a moment by something else, call their name. Give in a try in the door opening too. This will teach them that leaving is followed by returning. Reward them every time they manage to find you. Lift them up in the air or cuddle them – whatever they like best.

WHERE'S THE BABY?

A lot of babies discover they can hide themselves behind or under something. They usually start with a cloth or an item of clothing while being changed. Take advantage of any opportunity to develop a game that the baby has started. This way, they'll learn that they can take the lead.

HIDING TOYS

Try hiding toys under a blanket. Make sure you use something your baby likes or that they're attached to. Show them how and where you hide it. Make it easy for them the first time around. Make sure they can still see a tiny part of the toy.

HIDING TOYS IN THE BATHTUB

Put bath foam in the bathtub and allow your baby to play with it. Try hiding toys under the foam some time and invite them to look for them. If they can blow, try blowing at the foam. Or give them a straw and encourage them to blow through it.

TALKING GAMES

You can make talking appealing by talking to your baby frequently, by listening to them, by reading books together, and by playing whispering, singing, and word games.

LOOK AT PICTURE BOOKS TOGETHER

Take your baby on your lap – they usually like that best. Let them choose a book to look at together. Whatever your baby looks at, call it by its name. If it's a book with animals in it, mimic the sounds the animals make. Babies generally love hearing and making sounds like bark, moo, and quack. Let them turn the pages by themselves, if they want to.

WHISPERING GAME

Most babies love it when sounds or words are whispered in their ears. Making little puffs of air that tickle their ear is interesting, too, perhaps because a baby can now understand what blowing is.

SONG AND MOVEMENT GAMES

These games can be used to encourage both singing and talking. They also exercise the baby's sense of balance.

GIDDY-UP, GIDDY-UP, LITTLE ROCKING HORSE

Take your baby on your knee, upright and facing you. Support them under their arms and jog them up and down gently, singing:

Giddy-up, giddy-up, little rocking horse
Giddy-up, giddy-up, little rocking horse
Giddy-up, giddy-up, little rocking horse
Ride away, away to Candy Land.

THIS IS THE WAY THE LADY RIDES

Take your baby on your knee, upright and facing you. Support them under their arms, and sing the following song:

This is the way the lady rides,
The lady rides,
The lady rides,
This is the way the lady rides,
So early in the morning.
(Sing slowly and seriously, and jog them neatly up and down
on your knee.)

This is the way the gentleman rides,

The gentleman rides,

The gentleman rides,

This is the way the gentleman rides,

So early in the morning.

(Sing faster, and jog them faster.)

This is the way the farmer rides,

The farmer rides,

The farmer rides,

This is the way the farmer rides,

So early in the morning.

(Sing wearily and jog them up, down, and sideways.)

CLIP CLOP CLIP CLOP

AND DOWN INTO THE DITCH!

("DOWN" comes as a surprise. Pull your knees apart and let them "fall" between your knees.)

BALANCING GAMES

A lot of singing games, like those above, are also balancing games. Here are some others.

SITTING GAME

Sit down comfortably. Take your baby on your knee. Hold their hands, and move them gently from left to right, so that they shift their weight from buttock to buttock. Also try making them lean forwards or backwards carefully. Babies find the latter the most exciting. You can also move them in small or large circles, to the left, backward, to the right, and forward. Adjust yourself to what your baby is doing. The movement has to challenge them just enough to make them want to find their balance themselves. You can also let them swing like a pendulum of a clock while you sing: tick tock, tick tock in time with the movement.

STANDING GAME

Kneel comfortably on the floor and have them stand in front of you while you hold their hips or hands and move them gently from left to right, so that they transfer their weight from one leg to the other. Do the same thing in a different plane so that their body weight shifts from back to front. Adjust yourself to what your baby is doing. It has to challenge them just enough to make them want to find their balance themselves.

FLYING GAME

Grasp your baby firmly, lift them, and "fly" them through the room, making them rise and descend. Turn left and right. Fly in small circles, in a straight line, and backwards. Vary the movement and speed as much as possible. If your baby enjoys this, then try making them land carefully upside down, head first. Naturally, you'll accompany the entire flight with different zooming, humming, or screeching sounds. The more alert you are to their reactions, the easier it will be for you to adjust this game so it's just right for them.

STANDING THEM ON THEIR HEAD

Most physically active babies love horsing around and being stood on their heads. However, others find standing on their heads frightening or over-exciting. Only play this game if your baby likes playing rough. It's a healthy exercise for them. Remember to support their body completely as you hold them upside down.

GAMES WITH TOYS

For now, the best "toys" are all the things babies can find to get into around the house. The best games are emptying cupboards and shelves, dropping things, and throwing things away.

BABY'S OWN CUPBOARD GAME

Organize a cupboard for the baby and fill it with things that they really like. Usually this will include empty boxes, empty egg cartons, empty toilet paper rolls, plastic plates, and plastic bottles with lids and filled with something that rattles. But also include things they can make a lot of noise with, such as pans, wooden spoons, and old sets of keys.

FALLING GAME

Some babies like hearing a lot of noise when they drop something. If your baby does, you could make a game of it by putting them in their high chair and placing a metal serving tray on the floor. Hand them blocks, and show them how to let them go so that they fall on the tray and make a big bang.

OUTDOOR GAMES

Babies love riding in a baby seat on a bicycle, in a baby jogger, or in a baby backpack. Stop frequently to point out things along the way and talk to your baby about what they are seeing.

SWIMMING FOR BABIES

Many babies love playing in the water. Some swimming pools have specially heated pools for small children and special hours when a group of babies can play games with parents in the water.

PETTING FARMS

A visit to a petting farm or duck pond can be extremely exciting for your baby. They can see the animals from their picture book. They'll enjoy looking at their wobbly, pattering, or leaping motions. And they'll particularly like feeding the animals and watching them eat.

Just like parents get annoyed when their babies keep insisting on being rocked to sleep, there are at least three other situations where you may feel the urge to make demands on your child: with mealtime aggravations, when having to forbid things, and when they are displaying impatience.

At this age, many babies get fussy over food, while before they enjoyed whatever they grabbed from your mouth. In the world of relationships many babies come to realize that certain foods taste better than others. So why not pick the tastier one? Many mothers and fathers think it's funny at first. Soon, however, almost every parent becomes irritated when their baby gets fussy. They wonder whether the baby is getting enough nutrition. They try to distract the fussy eater so they can stick the spoon in their mouth at an unsuspected moment. Or they run after them with food the whole day.

Don't do these things. Strong-willed babies will resist something that is being forced upon them even more. And a worried parent will in turn react to that. This makes meals a battleground. Stop fighting it. You can't force a baby to swallow, so don't even try to. If you do, you might only increase their dislike of anything that has to do with food. Resort to different tactics and make use of other new skills your baby is able to learn now. At this stage, they can try holding something between their thumb and forefinger, but they will still need a lot of practice and feeding themselves is good for their coordination. A baby this age also loves to make their own decisions, and the freedom to eat by themselves will make eating more enjoyable. Use these new skills to their advantage. Allowing them to finger-feed themselves could put them in a better mood so they let you feed them as well. It can be messy, but encourage them anyway. Keep putting two pieces of food on

their plate, so that they are kept occupied. Generally, it will be easy to feed them in between. You can also make eating more pleasurable for your baby by feeding them in front of a mirror. This way, they can watch as you put a spoonful of food in their mouth or in your own. Don't worry if it doesn't work first time. Many babies go through eating problems, and they also get over them.

Finally, certain eating habits are perceived as irritating by some parents, while others find them perfectly normal.

"What really gets to me is that she wants to stick her thumb in her mouth after every bite. I won't allow it! Minor disagreement!"

Ashley's mom, 29th week

Now that the baby is in the middle of learning new skills, many mothers and fathers constantly find themselves having to forbid things. A crawling baby especially is liable to inspect all your possessions. After all, their pleasures are by no means the same as yours. So anything you can do to make life easier for both of you will be worthwhile. Try to stay a step ahead and prevent the things you can't allow from happening in the first place and help them with the activities they are interested in. Above all, remember that you are not the only mother or father with this problem.

"I constantly have to forbid things. My daughter rampages from one thing to the next. Her favorite targets are the wine rack, the video, my needlepoint kit, cupboards, and shoes. Another one of her hobbies is knocking down plants, digging up plants, and eating cat food. I can't warn her enough. So sometimes, I slap her hand when I feel it's gone far enough."

Jenny's mom, 31st week

Top Toys for This Wonder Week

These are toys and things to play with that suit the new skills your baby is developing as they explore the world of relationships.

- Their very own cupboard or shelf
- Doors (watch their fingers)
- Cardboard boxes in different sizes; also, empty egg cartons
- Wooden spoons
- Round nesting or stacking cups
- Wooden blocks
- Balls (light enough to roll)
- Picture books
- Photo books
- Children's songs
- Bath toys: things to fill and empty out, such as plastic bottles, plastic cups, plastic colanders, funnels, watering cans
- Toy cars with rotating wheels and doors that can be opened
- Cuddly toys that make noise when turned upside down
- Squeaky toys
- Drums
- Toy pianos
- Toy telephones

It's important to put away or take precautions with electrical outlets, plugs, wires, keys, drains, stairs, bottles (such as perfume and nail polish and remover), tubes (such as toothpaste and antiseptics), stereo equipment, remote controls, television sets, plants, wastepaper baskets, trash cans, alarm clocks, and watches.

Your baby does not learn anything from a "correcting" slap on the hand. And more importantly, hitting a baby is never not acceptable, even if it is "only" a correcting slap on the hand. It's better to remove your baby from things they are not allowed to touch. And to clearly say "No" when they are doing something that is against your rules. After this leap, babies can be very impatient. This may have several reasons. They don't want to wait for their food. They get mad if a toy refuses to behave as they want it to, or if something is not allowed, or if mommy or daddy doesn't pay attention to them quickly enough. Babies do have an idea of what they want to have or achieve, but unfortunately, they don't understand why their mommies or daddies don't allow it or why they can't have it in a flash. This frustrates them, so be understanding but see what you can do to stop the "I want it now" problem.

After the Leap

Between 30 and 35 weeks, another comparatively easy period begins. For anywhere from one to three weeks, the baby is admired for their cheerfulness, independence, and progress.

"My girl is becoming less and less shy. She laughs a lot. And she's good at keeping herself occupied. She has become very agile and active again. Actually, I started to see this change last week, but it seems to be progressing."

Nina's mom, 33rd week

"Because she was so sweet, my baby seemed like a totally different child. She used to cry and whine a lot. The way she tells stories is also delightful. She's actually already like a little toddler, the way she trots through the room."

Jenny's mom, 35th week

"My son was extremely cheerful, so it wasn't hard to have fun with him. It also pleases me to see him a little more active and lively in the physical sense. But he's at his best when he can observe people. He's very talkative, too, a great kid."

Frankie's mom, 30th week

"My daughter's obviously gotten bigger and older. She reacts to everything we do. She watches everything. And she wants to have whatever we have. I'd almost say that she wants to be a part of it."

Ashley's mom, 34th week

"Finally, some rest after a long period of constant changes. A wonderful week. He's gone through another change. He cries less, sleeps more. I can see a certain pattern starting to develop again, for the umpteenth time. I talk to him much more. I've noticed myself explaining everything I do. When I go to prepare his bottle, I tell him. When it's time for him to go to bed, I tell him. I explain why he has to take a nap. And these talks seem to do me good. The daycare center is going well now, too."

Bob's mom, 30th week

"We seem to have a different kind of contact now. It's as if the umbilical cord has finally been cut. The feeling of complete dependency is also gone. I'm quicker to rely on a babysitter. I also notice that I've been giving my son a lot more freedom. I don't have to be on top of him all the time."

Bob's mom, 31st week

"This was a really nice week. My baby is cheerful, and he can occupy himself pretty well on his own with his toys. Everything's still going fine at day care. He reacts in a friendly way to other children. He is a cute little guy, and he's much more his own little person."

Bob's mom, 32nd week

LEAP 6

Wonder Week 37

The World of Categories

**DIVIDING THE WORLD
INTO GROUPS**

about 37 (or between 36 and 40) weeks, you may notice your baby attempting to do new things. At this age, a baby's explorations can often seem very methodical. For example, you may notice your little one picking up specks from the floor and examining them studiously between their thumb and forefinger. Or a budding little chef may explore the food on their plate by testing the way a banana squashes or spinach squishes through tiny fingers.

They will assume the most serious, absorbed expression while carrying out these investigations. In fact, that is just what they are – investigations that will help the little researcher begin to categorize their world. Your baby is now able to recognize that certain objects, sensations, animals, and people belong together in groups or categories. For example, a banana looks, feels, and tastes different than spinach, but they are both foods. These are important distinctions and similarities to sort out. The leap into the world of categories will affect every sense – sight, hearing, smell, taste, and touch. Your baby will learn more about other people and their own emotions, too. Language skills will be developing. Your baby may not yet use words themselves, but they will understand much more than they did before.

Like all of the previous worlds, the arrival of these new perceptions begins by turning your baby's world inside out. Babies' brain waves show drastic changes again around this time. These changes will begin to alter the way your baby perceives their world, which will be disturbing to them at first. You can expect a fussy period to begin around 34 weeks, or between 32 and

---

Note: *The first phase (fussy period) of this leap into the perceptual world of "categories" is age-linked and predictable, emerging at about 34 weeks. Most babies start the second phase (see box "Quality Time: An Unnatural Whim" on page 17) of this leap 37 weeks after full-term birth. The initial perception of the world of categories sets in motion the development of a whole range of global concepts such as "animal," for instance. However, the first categories are acquired through real-time, corrective feedback and trial and error experiences through comparing things and learning the within-category similarities and the between-category differences. Consequently, there may be a difference of many weeks or even months between two babies in mastering a particular concept. The skills and activities in this chapter are stated at the earliest possible age they could appear so you can watch for and recognize them. (They may be rudimentary at first.) This way you can respond to and facilitate your baby's development.*

37 weeks. This fussy period will often last for four weeks, but it may last anywhere from three to six weeks. As your baby enters this fussy phase, play close attention to see if they are attempting to master new skills.

This Week's Fussy Signs

As they prepare to leap into the world of categories, all babies will cry more easily than they did during the past few weeks. To their parents, they may seem cranky, whiny, fidgety, grumpy, bad-tempered, discontented, unmanageable, restless, or impatient. All of this is very understandable. Your little one is now under extra pressure because from their last leap they know that you can go away from them whenever you please and leave them behind. At first, most babies were temporarily distressed by this discovery, but over the past few weeks they have learned to deal with it in their own way. It all seemed to be going much more smoothly than it was – and then the next big change came along and ruined everything. Now the little worrier wants to stay with their mommy and daddy again, as they realize perfectly well that their parents can walk away whenever they choose. This makes the baby feel even more insecure and increases their tension.

LEAP 6

"These past few days, my daughter insists on sitting on my lap constantly. For no apparent reason, I might add. When I don't carry her around, she screams. When I take her for walks in her stroller, the moment she even thinks I've stopped, she demands to be lifted out."
Ashley's mom, 34th week

"My baby acts cranky and seems to be bored. She picks up everything and just tosses it away again."
Laura's mom, 35th week

> *"Everything's fine, as long as my little girl can sit on someone's lap. Otherwise, she whimpers and wails. I'm not used to this behavior from her. She seems to grow bored quickly wherever she is – in the playpen, in her high chair, or on the floor."*
>
> **Eve's mom, 34th week**

A fussy baby will usually cry less when they are with their mother or father, especially when they have their mother or father all to themselves.

> *"My son kept screaming and grumping and acting horribly. Everything was fine as long as I stayed with him or took him on my lap. I put him to bed several times when I got fed up with his demands."*
>
> **Frankie's mom, 36th week**

How You Know it's Time to Grow

Here are some giveaways that your little one is about to make another developmental leap.

They May Cling to Your Clothes

Your baby may become anxious when you walk around. Non-crawlers can do nothing but cry. For some, every step their parents take is reason for genuine panic. Crawling babies are able to follow their mothers and fathers, and sometimes they cling to them so tightly that the parents can hardly move.

> *"It was another difficult week with a lot of crying. My son literally clings to my skirt. When I leave the room, he starts crying and crawling after me. When I'm cooking, he'll crawl behind me, grab hold of my legs, and hold on in such a way that I can't move. He'll only play if I play with him. A few times, it just got to be too much. Putting him to bed is a struggle all over again. He falls asleep very late."*
>
> **Bob's mom, 38th week**

They May Be Shy

Your baby may want to keep other people at a greater distance now than they usually do. The desire to be close to you may become even more apparent in the presence of other people – sometimes even when that other person is their father or a brother or sister. Often, mother is the only one allowed to look at them and talk to them. And they are almost always the only one allowed to touch them.

LEAP 6

The World of Categories   201

They May Hold on to You Tightly

When they are sitting on your lap or being carried, your baby may hold on to you as tightly as they can. They may even react furiously if you dare to put them down unexpectedly.

"My baby gets mad if I put her down even for a second. Then, when I lift her up again, she always pinches me. When our poor old dog happens to be within the reach of her hand, she'll pinch him even before I can lift her up."
Emily's mom, 35th week

"My son wants to be carried all of the time, and he clings to my neck or hair really tightly in the process."
Matt's mom, 36th week

"It's almost as if there's something about my baby's bed. I'll take her upstairs, sound asleep, and as soon as she feels the mattress, her eyes pop open. And boy, does she start screaming!"
Laura's mom, 33rd week

They May Demand Attention

Most babies start asking for more attention at this stage, and even easy ones are not always content at being left alone. Some of the more demanding little ones are not satisfied until their parents' attention is focused completely on them. Some may become super troublesome as soon as their mothers or fathers dare to shift their attention to someone or something else, as if they are jealous.

"When I'm talking to other people, my son always starts screaming really loudly for attention."
Paul's mom, 36th week

"My baby is having more difficulty staying in the playpen on his own. He's clearly starting to demand attention. He likes having us close."
Frankie's mom, 34th week

They May Sleep Poorly

Your baby may start sleeping less well than before. Most babies do. They may refuse to go to bed, don't fall asleep as easily, and wake up sooner than usual. Some are especially hard to get to sleep during the day, others at night. And some stay up longer now both during the day and at night.

> "My son keeps waking up at night. Sometimes, he'll be up playing in his crib for an hour and a half at 3:00 A.M."
> **Matt's mom, 33rd week**

> "My daughter stays up late in the evenings and doesn't want to go to bed. She doesn't sleep much."
> **Hannah's mom, 35th week**

> "My baby cries herself to sleep."
> **Juliette's mom, 33rd week**

They May Have "Nightmares"

A fussy baby can also be a very restless sleeper. Sometimes, they may yell, toss, and turn so much that you think they are having a nightmare.

> "My son wakes up often during the night. One time, he seemed to be dreaming."
> **Paul's mom, 37th week**

> "My daughter keeps waking up in the middle of the night screaming. When I lift her from her crib, she quiets down again. Then, I put her back, and she'll go back to sleep."
> **Emily's mom, 35th week**

They May Act Unusually Sweet

At this age, your baby may employ entirely new tactics to stay close to you. Instead of whining and complaining, they may opt for something entirely different and kiss and cuddle up to you. Often, they will switch back and forth between troublesome and sweet behavior, trying out what works best to get the most attention. Parents of an independent baby are often pleasantly surprised when their baby finally starts cuddling up to them!

"Sometimes, my baby didn't want anything. At other times, she became very cuddly."

Ashley's mom, 36th week

"My son is more affectionate than he's ever been. Whenever I get near him, he grabs and hugs me tightly. My neck is full of red blotches from nuzzling and snuggling. He's also not as quick to push me away any more. Sometimes, he'll sit still so I can read a book with him. I love it! He finally wants to play with me, too."

Matt's mom, 35th week

"My baby expresses his clinginess by acting sweeter and more affectionate, coming to lie down with me and snuggling up against me. I enjoy being with him."

Steven's mom, 36th week

They May Be Listless

Your baby may become altogether quieter now. You may hear them babbling less often, or you may see them moving around and playing less than before. At other times, they might briefly stop doing anything and just lie there, gazing into the distance. Don't worry, it's only temporary.

"My son's quieter and often lies there staring into nothingness. I wonder if something's bothering him or he's starting to get sick."

Steven's mom, 36th week

They May Refuse to Have Their Diaper Changed

When you set your baby down to be dressed, undressed, or changed, they may protest, scream, wriggle, act impatient, and be unmanageable. Most babies do this now.

My Diary

Signs My Baby Is Growing Again

Between 32 and 37 weeks, you may notice your baby starting to show any of these behaviors. They may be signs that they are ready to make the next leap. Check off the signs that your baby shows below.

- ☐ Cries more often than usual and is frequently bad-tempered or cranky
- ☐ Is cheerful one moment and cries the next
- ☐ Wants you to keep them busy, or does so more often than before
- ☐ Clings to your clothes, or clings more often than they used to
- ☐ Acts unusually sweet
- ☐ Throws temper tantrums, or does so more often than before
- ☐ Is shyer than they were
- ☐ Wants physical contact to be tighter or closer now
- ☐ Sleeps poorly
- ☐ Seems to have nightmares, or more frequently than before
- ☐ Loses appetite
- ☐ Babbles less than usual
- ☐ Is less lively than they were
- ☐ Sometimes just sits there, quietly daydreaming
- ☐ Refuses to have diaper changed
- ☐ Sucks their thumb, or does so more often than before
- ☐ Reaches for a cuddly toy, or does so more often than before
- ☐ Is more babyish than they were

OTHER CHANGES YOU NOTICE

They May Seem More Babyish Now

For the first time, some parents will notice the recurrence of infantile behavior that they thought had been left behind. They have probably experienced setbacks before, but the older the baby gets, the more obvious they become. Mothers and fathers dislike seeing setbacks. It makes them feel insecure, but they really are perfectly normal. They are the promise that something new is on the verge of breaking through. Try to find out what it is. Brief setbacks may happen during every fussy phase. Be happy with them; your baby is doing well.

They May Lose Their Appetite

Many babies seem less interested in food and drink at this time. Some seem to have no appetite and may dig in their heels and refuse some meals altogether. Others will only eat what they put into their mouths themselves. Others still are picky, spill things, and spit things out. Because of this, mealtimes may take longer than they used to.

If you have a fussy eater, they may also be unmanageable during meals, not wanting to eat when they are given food and wanting it as soon as it has been taken away. Or they may demand a lot of food one day and refuse to eat the next. Every variety of behavior is possible.

"My son refused my breast for three days. It was terrible. I felt like I was going to explode. Then, just when I decided it might be time to start cutting down on breastfeeding because it was getting to be that T-shirt time of year again, he decided he wanted to nurse all day long. So then I was afraid I might not have enough because he wasn't eating anything else anymore. But it seems to be working out okay. So far, I haven't heard him complain."

Matt's mom, 34th week

How This Leap May Affect You

Like the leaps that preceded it, the changes that your baby is going through will inevitably affect you. Here are some emotions you may encounter.

You May Feel Insecure

A fussy baby usually makes parents worry. They want to understand what is making their baby behave this way, and when they believe they have found a good explanation, it puts their minds at ease. At this age, most parents decide it must be teething pain, but this may not be the case.

"My daughter's top teeth are bothering her. She keeps wanting me to do things with her, such as go for walks or play with her."

Eve's mom, 34th week (She did not cut her next tooth until the 42nd week.)

You May Be Exhausted

If you have a demanding little terror who needs little sleep, you may feel extremely tired, especially toward the end of the fussy phase. Most parents of demanding babies get very exhausted. They may think they can't go on much longer. Some also complain of headaches, backaches, and nausea.

"It makes me feel so discouraged at times when my little one stays up until midnight, even if she keeps playing happily. When she's finally asleep, I completely collapse. I feel drained and unable to think straight. My husband gives me no support whatsoever. He's even angry that I pay so much attention to her. His philosophy is Just let her cry."

Nina's mom, 37th week

"The days seem to linger on forever when my son's cranky, cries, and sulks a lot."

Bob's mom, 35th week

You May Become Aggravated

Almost all parents become increasingly irritated by their baby's behavior during fussy periods. They become more and more annoyed by bad tempers, impatience, crying, whining, and constant demands for physical contact or attention. They are aggravated by the constant clinging, the trouble they have to go through to change or dress their babies, and finicky eating habits.

"When my baby was having another one of her moods, not wanting anything and being terribly restless, I put her to bed. I am dog tired of it and terribly annoyed."

Jenny's mom, 37th week

"While I was getting my daughter dressed, her whining really got to me, and I put her down very roughly. I just couldn't stand her whining and wriggling anymore. She'd been whimpering all day."

Juliette's mom, 35th week

"When my son became so unmanageable during changing, I put him on the floor in his room and left him there. That made him stop immediately. A few moments later, he came to get me, with a howl. Then he was willing to be a bit more cooperative."

Kevin's mom, 37th week

"This week, I got angry with my baby once. He'd been screaming so relentlessly that I suddenly shouted out angrily, 'Now shut up!' That frightened him out of his wits. First he looked at me with big, round eyes, then his head drooped, as if he was genuinely ashamed of his behavior. It was such a touching sight. After that, he became a lot calmer."

Paul's mom, 37th week

"I've decided to let my son breastfeed only twice a day. I'm fed up with his fickleness. One day, he wants it all, the next he wants nothing. At home, I don't lull him to sleep at my breast anymore either. That seems to be working out fine. But when we're at someone else's house, I still do it."

Matt's mom, 37th week

You May Quarrel

Toward the end of every fussy period, most breastfeeding mothers consider stopping. The baby's fickle behavior, sometimes wanting to nurse, sometimes not, irritates them. And the demanding fashion in which a little one continuously tries to get their way is another reason mothers think seriously about giving up breastfeeding.

"My son wants my breast whenever it suits him. And he wants it immediately. If it happens to be in some way inconvenient for me, he'll throw a raging temper tantrum. I'm afraid those tantrums are starting to turn into a habit and that pretty soon he'll try getting his way every single time by kicking and screaming. So I'm stopping right now, I think."

Steven's mom, 36th week

Quarrels can also develop when parents and babies fail to negotiate the amount of physical contact and attention the little person wants and their mommy and daddy is willing to give.

> "I keep getting more and more annoyed by my baby's clinging and whining. When we go to visit friends, he'll hardly let go of me. It makes me feel like just pushing him away from me, and sometimes I do. But that only makes him angrier at me."
>
> **Kevin's mom, 37th week**

It's just part of life. Having feelings of anger and frustration at times is not abnormal or dangerous, but acting on them is. It's critical that you get help long before you lose control.

How Your Baby's New Skills Emerge

When your baby is approximately 37 weeks, you will notice them calming down. If you watch closely, you may see them trying or doing new things. For example, you may see them handling their toys in a different way, enjoying new things, or behaving in a more concentrated and inquisitive manner. Congratulations! Your baby is making another leap. They are beginning to explore the world of categories.

> "I noticed a big change. My son's toys are lying somewhere in a corner. They have been for some weeks now. I think that I need to supply him with more stimulating toys that will challenge him. But outside, he's very lively because there's plenty to see."
>
> **Bob's mom, 36th week**

The Magical Leap Forward

After the last leap, your baby started to understand relationships between different things they came across, both in the outside world and in relation to their own body. They became more familiar with every aspect of their world. They discovered that they are the same kind of being as their mommy and daddy are, and that they could move in exactly the same way they do. They learned that other things can move as well, but that they move in very different ways than human beings, and that other things can't move on their own at all.

Once your baby acquires the ability to perceive and experiment with categories, they begin to understand that they can classify their world into groups. It will dawn on them that certain things are very much alike, that they look similar, or they make similar sounds, or they taste, smell, or feel the same. In short, they discover that different things can share the same traits. For instance, they can now discover the meaning of the word "horse." They can learn that every horse falls into this category, whether it is brown, white, or spotted; whether the horse is out in a field, in a stable, in a photograph, in a painting, or in a picture book; whether it is a clay horse or a live horse. It's still a horse.

Naturally, this new understanding will not happen overnight. They must first get to know people, animals, and objects well. They have to realize that things must possess certain similarities in order to belong to a specific category. Therefore, they have to be able to spot these similarities, and this takes practice and time. When your baby acquires the ability to perceive categories, they will start experimenting with them. They will start to study people, animals, and objects in a particular way. They will observe, compare, and arrange them according to similarities, and then place them in specific categories. Your baby's comprehension of a category is the result of a lot of research that they conduct much as a real researcher would.

More Like One of Us

The use of different categories in our speech is indicative of our way of thinking. Now your baby will be able to start understanding and using this way of thinking as well. This will make it easier for you and your baby to understand one another from now on.

They observe, listen to, feel, taste, and experiment with both similarities and differences. Your baby works hard at their investigations. Later on, when your child starts talking, you will see that they have already discovered many of the categories we use and sometimes will have made up their own names for them. For instance: they may call a garage a "car house," an apartment building a "block house," or a fern a "feather plant." The names they use refer directly to whatever trait they found most characteristic.

As soon as your baby acquires the ability to divide their world into categories, they can start doing just that. They not only examine what makes something a *horse, dog,* or *bear*, but also what makes something *big, small, heavy, light, round, soft,* or *sticky,* as well as what makes something *sad, happy, sweet,* or *naughty*.

Games played during research with babies clearly show that from this age on, babies' reactions take on a different quality. Some researchers believe that intelligence makes its first appearance at this age. At first look, it might seem that way, but it does not mean that babies didn't have any thoughts prior to this age. In fact, they have had their own way of thinking that perfectly suited each stage of their development. Unfortunately, these ways are lost to adults, and we can only imagine what they might be like. When the baby begins to classify the world in groups as we do, though, their way of thinking becomes more like an adult's does. Because they start to think in the same way we do, we are able to understand them better than before.

This ability to perceive and experiment with categories affects everything a baby does. Their way of experiencing things has changed, and it is now time to make sense of it.

Your Baby's Choices: A Key to Their Personality

A new world, full of possibilities, is open to your baby in the world of categories. Between the ages of 37 and 42 weeks, your baby will make their own selection from the wide array of things available for them to experiment with. They will choose whatever suits them best at this stage in their development and matches their interests. You may find them building on certain strong inclinations they have previously displayed, or they may launch out into new territory at this point. There's a very big world out there for them to explore, and it's important not to compare your baby too closely to other babies. Every baby is unique.

Watch your baby closely as you check off the skills they select from the list "How My Baby Explores The New World Of Categories" on page 214. You will learn where their interests lie and what makes them unique. Respect their choices, and help them explore the things that interest them. Babies love anything new and it's important that you respond when you notice any new skills or interests. They will enjoy it if you share these new discoveries, and their learning will progress quickly.

Brain Changes

Your baby's brain waves will show dramatic changes again at approximately eight months. In addition, the baby's head circumference increases, and the glucose metabolism in the brain changes at this age.

My Diary

How My Baby Explores the New World of Categories

Don't be alarmed if many of these activities don't appear until much later. What your baby is really learning in this world is the concept of categories, and once they have got a grasp of this through learning one skill, it will sooner or later be carried forward into other skills. The golden rule is "help, don't push."

RECOGNIZING ANIMALS AND OBJECTS

☐ Shows that they can recognize a category, such as animals, in pictures, toys, and real life

☐ Shows that they distinguish shapes

☐ Shows that they think something is dirty, for instance by wrinkling their nose

☐ Shows that they think something is fun or good by making a characteristic sound or movement

☐ Understands names of animals or objects, such as toothbrush, sock, bread stick, cat, lamb, or duck. When you ask, "Where's...?" they will look for it. When you say, "Get your..." they will sometimes get it

☐ Repeats words after you now and then

☐ Compares things seen directly and through a screen, for instance through a sieve, the mesh of a screen door, or glass

RECOGNIZING PEOPLE AS PEOPLE

☐ Relates more to other people with sounds and gestures than before

☐ Imitates other people more often than they did before; mimics what they do

☐ Clearly wants to play games with other people more often than before

☐ Calls family members. Each has their own sound

RECOGNIZING PEOPLE IN DIFFERENT CIRCUMSTANCES

☐ Recognizes people, even in unrelated situations

☐ Makes silly faces at their mirror image and laughs

☐ Looks at a thing or person in the room and then tries to find the same thing or person in the mirror

RECOGNIZING EMOTIONS

☐ Becomes jealous for the first time when another child is receiving mother or father's attention

☐ Comforts a cuddly toy when dropped or thrown

☐ Acts extra sweet when they want something

☐ Exaggerates their mood to let everyone know how they are feeling

☐ Starts to cry when another child is crying

SWITCHING ROLES

☐ Can initiate a game by themselves

☐ Plays peek-a-boo with a younger baby

☐ Uses the bottle to feed their mother or father

☐ Asks their mother or father to sing a song, then starts clapping their hands

☐ Asks to play hide-and-seek by crawling behind something

☐ Asks you to build blocks by handing you their blocks

OTHER CHANGES YOU NOTICE

What You Can Do to Help

Your baby needs time and help to enable them to understand why something does or does not fall into a certain category. You can help them with this by giving them the opportunity and the time to experiment and play in such a way that they will learn why something belongs to a certain category. You can encourage and console them when necessary and present them with new ideas.

Give your baby the opportunity to expand their understanding of categories. It makes no difference which categories they explore first. Once they get the idea about one or two categories, it will become easier for them to apply this understanding to other categories later on. Some little ones will prefer to start out with recognizing objects, while others will begin with recognizing people. Let your baby be your guide. After all, it is impossible for them to learn everything at once.

Help Your Baby Explore the New World through Examination

When your baby starts experimenting with categories, you will notice that they are actually busy examining an entire range of characteristics and comparing them. They are using relationships to work out what categories are about. By doing this, they will learn the most important characteristics of whatever they are examining. They will find out whether or not something bounces back, whether it's heavy or light, how it feels to the touch, and so on. They will examine something from all sides, hold it upside down or hold their head sideways, move it around quickly and slowly. This is the only way for them to find out: "This is a ball, that isn't" or "This block is round, the other one isn't."

Some babies are particularly interested in different shapes, such as *round, square,* and *notched* shapes. They look at the shape and trace its perimeter with one little finger. Then they do the same with a different shape. They are comparing shapes, so to speak. With blocks, they usually pick out round

ones first, which shows they are able to recognize them. If your baby seems fascinated by shapes, give them a set of blocks with all sorts of different shapes.

You may also see that your baby will find plenty of things in the house that have shapes that interest them. Have you ever noticed how your baby looks at things that are at a distance and attract their attention? They usually do this while moving their head from left to right. They do this to learn that even when they move around, things stay the same size and shape. Find out what your baby likes to explore and how they want to do it. Offer them the opportunities they need.

"My son tries to catch the running water in the tub when the tap is on. Apparently he thinks it's something he can grab. He'll close his hand around the water, and then when he opens it there's nothing in it. He finds this most peculiar. But he can keep it up for some time."
Paul's mom, 43rd week

Many babies like to examine the different components of things. By exploring an object this way, they will eventually find out how that object is assembled and to which category it belongs. If your baby is such a scientist, they may suck successively on different sides of an object, for instance, or press on the top, in the middle, and on the bottom of something. Their explorations can have surprising side-effects.

Some babies love touching things with their hands to find out how they feel. This way they test for categories such as *firmness, stickiness, roughness, warmth, slipperiness*, and so on. Allow your baby to explore.

The Advantages of Demolishing

If your baby is examining the different components of things, they often ends up by taking something apart bit by bit. If your baby starts to demolish things, give them playthings they can explore in this way. Stack some blocks for them so that they can remove them one by one. Show them how to do it. You can do the same with doughnut rings of different sizes that stack on a rod. Also try giving them a pile of magazines, which they can move one by one. See what other games your baby invents by themselves and support them if it is not dangerous or too costly. You may also show how you take things apart yourself. This experience is very important, because after the next leap they can use this knowledge to their advantage when they start to assemble instead of demolish.

Sometimes, a baby loves rubbing other parts of their body against objects, or they will pick something up and run it past their body. This way, the baby will become even more familiar with whatever they are examining, so give them this opportunity.

In the world of categories some babies like to experiment with handling people, animals, and objects *roughly* and *carefully*. If you see yours doing this, let them know that certain things hurt and objects can break. If they experiment like this, they soon know perfectly well what they are doing.

> "When we were in the bath, my son started to examine my nipple very carefully, with one little finger, only to continue pushing, pulling, and poking it around. His own penis was next. He was a bit more careful with that!"
>
> **Matt's mom, 41st week**

> "First, my baby examines my eyes, ears, and nose with her little index finger. Then she tickles them. Then, as she gets more and more excited, she gets rougher, pushing and poking at my eyes, pulling at my ears and nose, and sticking a finger up my nostril."
>
> **Nina's mom, 39th week**

Some babies compare the weights of playthings and other objects. If yours is discovering the categories *heavy* and *light*, give them the opportunity to experiment.

> "My baby lifts everything she walks past up for a moment."
>
> **Jenny's mom, 41st week**

Usually, your baby studies the concepts *high* and *low, little* and *large* through crawling, climbing, standing, or walking. They will climb onto, over, and under everything. They will do this sedately, in a controlled manner, almost as if they are planning how to do things.

> "My son tries to crawl under and through everything. He looks for a while, then off he goes. Yesterday, he got stuck under the bottom step of the stairs. We all panicked!"
>
> **John's mom, 40th week**

Give an Active Baby Room to Investigate

From this age on, it usually becomes more and more important to give a mobile baby enough room in order to provide them ample opportunity to investigate all sorts of categories. An already physically active baby may now become increasingly dexterous and stable while sitting, standing, crawling, and walking. As a result, they will be able to do much more with their body than they could do before. They can choose to squat, crawl, or climb up onto furniture or stand on their toes when they want to reach something. Allow them to crawl through your home, climb onto things, and hoist themselves up on the most impossible ledges. Secure the safety gates by the stairs on the second or third step, and allow them to practice going up and down stairs. Place a mattress at the bottom of the stairs, so that they can't hurt themselves.

"My son clambers up everything. He even tried to scale the smooth surface of a wall."

John's mom, 42nd week

"My little girl was sitting in her high chair at the table, and before I knew it, she had climbed onto the table. I guess I need eyes in the back of my head now."

Emily's mom, 42nd week

Your little crawler can learn a lot outside as well. Give them room there, too. For instance, walk with them in the woods, at the beach, at a lake, in the park. Just as long as you do not lose sight of them.

Baby Care

Make Their Surroundings Baby-Proof

Make sure the space your baby is exploring is safe. But nevertheless, do not take your eyes off them for a single second. They will always manage to find something that can be dangerous that you might not have thought of.

Top Games for This Wonder Week

Here are games and activities that most babies like best now and that will help them practice their newly developing skills.

EXPLORING

Some things will seem absolutely fascinating to your baby, but venturing out on their own voyage of discovery may be dangerous or impossible. So help them. You can help them handle breakable picture frames or heavy figurines, for instance, so that they won't break them or hurt themselves but will satisfy their curiosity.

BELLS AND SWITCHES

Allow your baby to ring a doorbell. They will be able to hear right away what they are doing. You could let them press a button on the elevator as well. This way, they will feel they're doing something grown-up. Allow them to turn on the light when it is very dark, so that they can see what the effect is. Let them push the button in the bus sometimes, or at a pedestrian crossing, and explain to them what is happening so they know what to look for. This will teach them something about the relationship between what they are doing and what happens next.

OUTDOOR EXPLORATION

At this age, most babies can't get enough of being outdoors. Taking your baby outdoors will teach them a lot as well. They will see new things. Whether you're bike riding, walking, stroller jogging, or backpacking, be sure to stop now and then to allow your baby to look closer at, listen to, and touch things.

DRESSING

Many babies seem to have no time for dressing and grooming. They are far too busy with other things. But they love to look at themselves and are even more interested when something is being done to them.

Use this to its advantage. Towel off your baby, dress, and undress them in front of a mirror so they can play a sort of peek-a-boo game with themselves at the same time.

WORDS

Your baby often understands a lot more than you think, and they love being able to demonstrate this. They will now start to enjoy expanding the range of words and phrases they understand.

NAMING

Name the things your baby looks at or listens to. When your baby uses gestures to express what they want, translate their question for them by putting it into words. This will teach them that they can use words to express themselves. Let your baby choose a book and hand it to them. Take them on your lap or seat them close beside you. This way they can turn the pages by themselves. Point to the picture they are looking at and name the object. You can also make the appropriate sounds for the particular animal or object you are pointing to. Encourage your baby to make that word or sound as well. Don't try to continue if your baby loses interest. Some babies need a momentary cuddle or tickle after each page to keep their attention focused.

TASKS

Ask your baby if they will give you whatever they are holding by saying, for instance, "Give it to Mommy, please." Ask them to give it to Daddy as well sometime. You can also ask them to get something for you – for instance, "Pass me the toothbrush, please" and "Please get me the ball." Also try calling them when you are out of sight: "Where are you?" and get them to answer. Or ask them to come to you, "Could you please come over here." Praise them if they participate, and continue for as long as your baby enjoys it.

COPYCAT

Many babies study other people with great interest and love imitating what they see other people do. If your baby does this as well, mimic them and encourage them to mimic you.

DO THIS

First, challenge your baby to imitate whatever you are doing, then imitate them again. Often, they will be able to go on forever, taking turns doing the same thing over and over. Try alternating your gestures as well. Make the gestures a little faster or slower. Try making them with the other hand, or with two hands. Try making them with sound or without, and so on. Try doing this game in front of a mirror as well. Some babies love repeating gestures in front of a mirror while watching themselves to see how everything is done.

TALKING TO THE MIRROR

If your baby is interested in the positions of the mouth, try practicing them in front of a mirror. Turn it into a game. Sit down in front of the mirror together and play with vowels, consonants or words, whatever your baby likes best. Give them time to watch and copy. Many babies love watching themselves imitating gestures as well, such as movements of the hands and head. Try this too. If your baby can see themselves while they are imitating you, they will immediately be able to see whether they are doing it in the same way you are.

PAT–A–CAKE

Sing Pat-a-cake, pat-a-cake, baker's man, and let your baby feel every movement that goes with the song. In order to do this, take their hands in yours and make the movements together. Sometimes babies will imitate the clapping of their own accord, or they will raise their hands. They are still unable to imitate all the movements in sequence at this age, but they are able to enjoy them.

ROLE SWITCHING

Encourage your baby to take up a role they have seen you or an older child perform. Then try switching roles.

CHASE

You can consider this the first game of tag. It can be played crawling or walking. Try turning the game around sometimes as well – crawl or walk away, and clearly indicate that you expect them to come after you. Try to escape if your baby makes attempts at catching you. If your baby does catch you, or you have caught them, cuddle them or raise them up high in the air.

HIDE-AND-SEEK

Hide yourself in such a way that your baby sees you disappear, then let them look for you. Also try pretending sometime that you have lost them and are looking for them. Sometimes babies are quick to hide and will stay behind their beds or hide in corners very quietly. Usually, they will pick the spot you were just hiding in or one that was a smash hit the day before. React with enthusiasm when you have found each other.

Top Toys for This Wonder Week

Here are toys and things that most babies like best as they explore the world of categories.

- Anything that opens and closes like doors and drawers
- Pans with lids
- Doorbells, bus bells, elevator buttons, traffic light buttons
- Alarm clocks
- Magazines and newspapers to tear
- Plastic plates and cups with plastic cutlery
- Things that are larger than they are , such as boxes or buckets
- Cushions and duvets to crawl over and under
- Containers, especially round ones, pots, and bottles
- Anything that they are able to move, such as handles or knobs
- Anything that moves by itself, such as shadows or branches
- Balls of all sizes, from ping-pong balls to large beach balls
- Dolls with realistic faces
- Blocks in all shapes and sizes, the larger the better
- Baby pools
- Sand, water, pebbles, and plastic tools
- Swings
- Picture books with one or two large, distinct pictures per page
- Posters with several distinct pictures
- Toy cars

But beware of other things they are attracted to like electrical plugs and switches, washing machines, dishwashers, vacuum cleaners, hair dryers, other appliances and stairs.

Help Your Baby Explore the New World through Play-acting

If your baby is very socially aware, from this point on they will be able to pretend they are sad, sweet, or distressed. Such emotional states are categories, too. This means that they can start manipulating or taking advantage of you. Usually, mothers and fathers fall for this at first. Some simply refuse to believe that their children, still only babies, could be capable of doing anything like this deliberately. Others are secretly a little proud. If you see your little one is putting on an act, allow them to have a taste of success, if possible. But at the same time, let them know that you know what they are doing. This will teach them that using emotions is important, but that they can't use them to manipulate you.

"During the day, my girl is very troublesome, really pesky, but when it's time for her to go to bed in the evening, she plays like a little angel. It's as if she thinks, 'As long as I behave myself, I don't have to go to bed!' It's useless, anyway, trying to put her to bed when she isn't tired yet, because she'll refuse to stay lying down. Last Friday, she went to bed at 11:30 P.M."

Jenny's mom, 37th week

"If I'm talking with someone, my son will suddenly need instant help, or he'll pretend that he injured himself on something."

Matt's mom, 39th week

Sometimes a baby will take up a role they have seen their parents or an older child perform. This is possible now because they know that they are a person, the same way other people are. In other words, both they and other people belong to the same category. As a result they are able to do the same things that other people can do. They can hide, just as their mother and father used to, and make their parents the seeker. They can go and get their own toys when they feel like playing with them. Always respond to this behavior, even if only for a short while. This will teach them that they are making themselves understood and that they are important.

"This week, another child a little older than my son visited our home. My son and the other little girl each had a bottle. At a certain point, the little girl stuck her bottle in my baby's mouth and started feeding him. She kept holding the bottle herself. The next day, I had him on my lap and was giving him a bottle. Suddenly, he took the bottle and stuck it in my mouth, then started laughing, drank some himself, then stuck it back in my mouth. I was amazed. He'd never done anything like that before."

Paul's mom, 41st week

The Importance of Consistency

Parents are always proud of their babies' progress and accomplishments, and they automatically react with excitement and surprise. But some of those accomplishments can be mischievous. At first, a mischievous accomplishment may be amusing and your baby may take your delight or surprise as approval. They think they are being funny and will repeat the behavior time after time, even when mother or father tells them "No."

You will now need to be more consistent with your baby. When you disallow something once, it is better not to condone it the next time. Your baby loves putting you to the test.

"My baby's getting funnier and funnier because she's starting to become mischievous. She says *brrr* when she's got a mouth full of porridge, covering me with the stuff. She opens cupboards she's not allowed to touch and throws the cat's water all over the kitchen."

Laura's mom, 38th week

"My daughter won't listen to me. When I tell her 'No,' she laughs, even if I'm really angry with her. But when her babysitter says 'No,' she cries. I wonder if this is because I work. Perhaps I give in too much when I'm home, out of guilt."

Laura's mom, 39th week

Some little ones love to play the role of giver. It doesn't matter what they are giving, just as long as they can keep giving and receiving – preferably the latter. If your baby gives you anything at all, it goes without saying that they expect to get it back immediately. They will often understand the words "Can I have... ," as well as "Please." So you can combine the giving-and receiving game with speech, which will greatly improve their understanding of things.

Show Understanding for Irrational Fears

When your baby is learning a new skill, they may also discover a new danger and develop fear. One of these is the fear of the category heights. Another, is the fear of being confined. When your baby suddenly acts scared, sympathize with them, try to find out what is bothering them, and help them. Babies tend to be wary of new things until they are sure they are harmless.

... oe!

LEAP 6

After the Leap

Between 40 and 45 weeks, another relatively easy period sets in. For the following one to three weeks, many babies are admired for their progress, independence, and cheerfulness. They find a wide range of things interesting now, from people on horseback to flowers, leaves, ants, and mosquitoes. Many children want to spend more time outdoors now. Other people suddenly start to play an increasingly important part in their lives, as well. They make contact with them much more often and are more willing to play games with them than they were before. In short, baby's horizon is broader than ever.

"At the moment, my boy's a doll. He laughs all day long. Sometimes, he'll play by himself sweetly for an hour. He seems like a completely different child this past week. He doesn't look as bloated anymore, and he feels very lithe. He was always a little unwieldy, but now he seems to have loosened up a lot more. He's now much livelier, more energetic, and adventurous."

Frankie's mom, 42nd week

"My son understands much more, so he's getting to a new place, somewhere with more possibilities. I have to make it easier to talk to him. He needs to be where he can communicate with everyone, at the table for instance. It's important now. He's focusing on other people much more outside of the house as well. He makes contact with them right away by blowing bubbles, making certain calling sounds, or by tilting his head questioningly."

Bob's mom, 40th week

Wonder Week 46

The World of Sequences

... oe!

**DOING TWO THINGS
CONSECUTIVELY**

Babies are natural mess-makers and during the past leap in your baby's mental development, this talent probably seemed at its peak. You may have marveled at your baby's knack for destruction as they disassembled, tossed around, and squished everything in their path. If you are alert for newly developing skills in your baby, at around 46 weeks you may suddenly notice them doing things that are quite the opposite. They will begin, for the first time, to try to put things together.

Your baby is now ready to discover the world of sequences. From this age on, they have the ability to realize that to reach many of their goals, they have to do things in a certain order to be successful. You may now see your baby first looking to see which things go together and how they go together before trying to put them in each other, pile them on top of each other, or piece them together. For instance, they may focus on taking their best possible aim before attempting to pile one block on top of another. They might push a peg through a hole in a peg board but only after they have compared the shape of the peg to the hole.

This world offers whole new areas of exploration for your baby. You will notice that for the first time, they really seem able to put two and two together. They are sometimes able to follow one action with another quite spontaneously. It may become apparent that the baby is more conscious of their actions than ever before – that they are aware of what they are doing now. The onset of this new leap in their mental development begins at around 42 weeks, or between 40 and 44 weeks. While they grow into their new skills and learn to be comfortable in this new world, your baby

Note: *The first phase (fussy period) of this leap into the perceptual world of "sequences" is age-linked and predictable, emerging between 40 and 44 weeks. Most babies start the second phase (see box "Quality Time: An Unnatural Whim" on page 17) of this leap 46 weeks after full-term birth. The initial perception of the world of sequences sets in motion the development of a whole range of skills and activities. However, the age at which these skills and activities appear for the first time varies greatly and depends on your baby's preferences, experimentation and physical development. For example, the ability to perceive sequences is a necessary precondition for "pulling a string to attach a ring toy to it," but this skill normally appears anywhere from approximately 46 weeks to many weeks or even months later. The skills and activities in this chapter are stated at the earliest possible age they could appear so you can watch for and recognize them. (They may be rudimentary at first.) This way you can respond to and facilitate your baby's development.*

will tend to be fussy and demanding once again. After all, it's a lot harder to figure out how things go together than to take them apart. The sudden alteration in their thinking can understandably be upsetting. This fussy period will often last for five weeks, but it may last anywhere from three to seven weeks. If your baby is cranky, watch them closely to see if they are attempting to master new skills.

This Week's Fussy Signs

Your baby may cry more than they did during the past weeks. Most babies do. They may be fussy, cranky, whiny, weepy, grumpy, bad-tempered, unmanageable, and restless. They will do whatever they can to be able to be with their mothers and fathers. Some are preoccupied by this all day long. Some little clingers get more frantic at the prospect of separation than others. They will use every possible means they can think of to be able to stay with their parents.

> "Whenever my baby's brother comes anywhere near him and touches him, he'll start to cry immediately because he knows it will get a reaction out of me."
>
> **Kevin's mom, 41st week**

Your baby may cry less when they are near you. Most fussy babies cry less when they are with their mothers and fathers. And they complain even less when they have their undivided attention.

> "Because I want to keep my baby's sniveling down to an absolute minimum, we do everything together. I do my housekeeping carrying her on my hip or my arm because otherwise I can't move an inch with her clinging to my leg. I explain to her what I'm doing, for example, how I'm making tea or folding towels. We also usually go to the bathroom together. When I do go on my own, I leave the door open. I do this firstly so that I can see if she's doing anything dangerous, but also because then she can see me and follow me to her heart's content. And she always does. This way of going about things is the only way either of us will get any peace of mind."
>
> **Emily's mom, 43rd week**

LEAP 7

How You Know it's Time to Grow

Here are some of the signals that your baby may give you to let you know they're approaching this leap into the world of sequences.

They May Cling to Your Clothes

Your baby may go to great lengths to stay as close to you as possible. They may literally wrap themselves around you, even when there are no strangers present. Some babies don't necessarily cling to their parents but do want to stay extremely close to them so that they can keep an eye on them at all times. And there are those who keep coming back to their parents, as if they need a "mommy and daddy refill," as reassurance before they leave them again.

"My son wants to sit on my lap, ride on my arm, crawl all over me, sit on top of me, or cling to my legs all day long, like a parasite clings to a fish. When I put him down, he bursts into tears."

Bob's mom, 41st week

"My daughter will sit on my shoe and wrap her little arms round my leg. Once she's hanging on, she won't let go if she can help it. I really need to think of some kind of diversion to get her to let go."

Emily's mom, 43rd week

"At the moment, my daughter tends to stay near, but she still does her own thing. It's almost as if she's circling around me like a satellite orbits the earth. If I'm in the living room, she'll be doing something next to me, and when I go to the kitchen, she'll be emptying a cupboard next to me there."

Jenny's mom, 47th week

They May Be Shyer with Strangers

When there are strangers near them, looking at them, talking to them, or, worse still, reaching a hand out towards them, your little one may become even clingier with you than they already are. Many babies are shy now.

LEAP 7

They May Want Closer Physical Contact with You Now

Some little worriers hold on to their mothers and fathers as tightly as they can once they have a hold on them or when they are sitting on their parents' laps, as if they don't want to give their parents the chance to let go. Other babies react furiously when they are set down or when their parents walk across the room.

They May Want to Be Kept Busy

Most babies start asking for more attention now. Your baby may do the same. Even an easy little one will usually prefer doing things with you. A demanding little person would, if they could have their way, keep you busy occupying them night and day. They are often not satisfied until they have their mother or father's undivided attention. They may only have eyes for their mother or father and be focused only on them.

They May Be Jealous

Your little one can be extra cranky, naughty, or sweet when you pay attention to someone or something else. This change in behavior usually makes a parent wonder if their baby might be jealous. This discovery usually comes as a surprise.

"I babysit a 4-month-old baby. My son always finds it very interesting when I give her a bottle. But this week, he was impossible. He kept doing things he normally never does. He was really causing trouble, being obnoxious. I think he was a bit jealous."

John's mom, 44th week

They May Be Moody

Your baby might be cheerful one day and the total opposite the next. Their mood can also change suddenly. One moment, they may be busy and happy doing something, the next they could start whining and complaining. The mood swings come out of the blue for no apparent reason as far as their parents can tell. At times this can make a mother and father feel insecure.

"My baby would cling and cry her eyes out one moment and seem to be having the greatest fun the next — as if she could turn it on and off at the flick of a switch. I just don't know what to do. I wonder if something could suddenly be hurting her."

Nina's mom, 43rd week

They May Sleep Poorly

Your baby may sleep less well than before. Most babies do now. They either refuse to go to bed, have more difficulty falling asleep, or wake up earlier than usual. Some are particularly troublesome sleepers during the day. Others are worse at night, and still others are reluctant to go to bed at any time.

They May Have "Nightmares"

Your baby may turn into a restless sleeper. They could even toss and turn so much that you suspect that they are having a nightmare.

They May Be Listless

Your baby may temporarily be a little apathetic, some babies are. They are less active or babble a little less than before. They may even stop all activity for a while and simply lie down and stare. Parents don't like seeing this happen. They think it's abnormal, and they may try to get the little ones moving again.

> "My daughter is not as active anymore. Often she just sits there, wideeyed, looking around."
>
> **Hannah's mom, 45th week**

> "Occasionally, my son will just sit there, gazing into thin air. This is a change because he always used to be doing something."
>
> **Matt's mom, 43rd week**

> "My son is more passive, quieter. Sometimes, he'll sit there, staring off into the distance for a few moments. I don't like it one bit. It's as if he's not normal."
>
> **Bob's mom, 41st week**

They May Refuse to Have Their Diaper Changed

Your little one may become more impatient and unmanageable now when they are being dressed, undressed, or changed. They may whine, scream, and writhe as soon as you touch them. Sometimes parents become aggravated with or concerned about a troublesome squirmer.

> "My son won't stay still for a minute. Sometimes, getting his diaper off is like being in a wrestling match. I love the fact that he's become more active, but I don't see why he can't lie still for a few seconds."
>
> **Frankie's mom, 43rd week**

> "Dressing, undressing, and changing are a nightmare. This happened a while ago as well. Back then, I thought the lower part of her back might be troubling her. I started to worry more and more. So I took her to the pediatrician, but he said that her back was perfectly fine. He had no idea what could be causing it, either. But then, it cleared up by itself."
>
> **Juliette's mom, 46th week**

LEAP 7

They May Lose Their Appetite

Many babies seem less interested in food and drink at this time. Your baby may lose their appetite, or they may be very choosy, eating something only if, and when, they feel like it. Mothers and fathers are often worried and aggravated by poor appetites and fussy eating.

"My son is not eating well. But all of a sudden, he does want to breastfeed in the middle of the day, and he'll start whining and pulling at my blouse to get what he wants. He wakes up a lot during the night as well, wanting to breastfeed. I wonder whether he's getting good nutrition this way."

Matt's mom, 43rd week

They May Behave More Babyish Again

Sometimes a babyish behavior that you thought was long gone suddenly reappears. Mothers and fathers don't appreciate such revivals. They see them as backward steps and would put a stop to them if they could. Yet it's perfectly normal to have relapses during fussy periods. It simply means that another huge leap forward is about to happen.

"My daughter relapsed into crawling this week. I just hope it's nothing to do with her hips or because she started walking so early."

Jenny's mom, 44th week

"My son doesn't want to hold his bottle himself anymore but prefers to lie back in my arms and be fed like a tiny baby. A while ago, however, he insisted on holding the bottle himself. His relapse is actually bothering me quite a bit. I kept thinking, 'Cut it out, son, I know you can do it yourself.' A few times I put his hands on the bottle, but he wouldn't budge."

Bob's mom, 41st week

"Very often, I have to rock my son again before he will go to sleep."

Steven's mom, 41st week

They May Act Unusually Sweet

A fussy baby can now also find nicer ways of asking for more physical contact or attention. This happens more and more often and in increasingly sophisticated ways. They may bring their parents books or toys "asking" that they play with them. They may charm you into playing games with them with a variety of ploys, such as laying their little hand on your lap, snuggling up to you, or resting their head against you. Often, they may alternate between being troublesome and sweet, using whichever works best at the time, to get the desired touch or attention.

Parents of independent babies who don't usually seek much physical contact are overjoyed at the prospect of finally being able to give them a cuddle again.

"My daughter would come up to me now and again for a cuddle. She was extremely charming this week."

Ashley's mom, 46th week

"My son was very cuddly and kept clinging to me this week."

Matt's mom, 42nd week

"When my son is in the bicycle seat or stroller, he keeps looking back to check if I'm still there, and then he'll give me his tiny hand."

Paul's mom, 44th week

"My daughter wants to sit on my lap with a book more often. When she does, she'll stay there, snuggling up wonderfully close to me."

Jenny's mom, 47th week

LEAP 7

My Diary

Signs My Baby Is Growing Again

Between 40 and 44 weeks, your baby may show signs that they are ready to make the next leap into the world of sequences.

☐ Cries more often than usual and is bad-tempered or cranky

☐ Is cheerful one moment and cries the next

☐ Wants to be kept busy, or does so more often than before

☐ Clings to your clothes, or wants to be closer to you than they did before

☐ Acts unusually sweet

☐ Is mischievous

☐ Throws temper tantrums, or throws them more often than before

☐ Is jealous

☐ Is shyer with strangers than before

☐ Wants physical contact to be tighter or closer than was the case

☐ Sleeps poorly

☐ Seems to have nightmares, or has them more often than before

☐ Loses appetite

☐ Babbles less than usual

☐ Sometimes just sits there, quietly daydreaming

☐ Refuses to have their diaper changed

☐ Sucks their thumb, or does so more often than before

☐ Wants to cuddle toys, or does so more often than before

OTHER CHANGES YOU NOTICE

> "My daughter keeps crawling after me. When she rounds the corner by the door, she'll give me a big smile and quickly crawl back in the other direction again. We love this little game."
>
> **Ashley's mom, 43rd week**

They May Be Mischievous

Some parents notice that their babies are naughtier than they used to be. It may seem your baby does everything they are not allowed to. Or they may be especially mischievous at times when you are rushing to finish something and can least spare the time to deal with them.

> "We're not allowed to attend to our own business. If we do, then everything we told our daughter not to touch suddenly becomes extremely interesting, such as the telephone and the knobs on the stereo. We have to watch her every second of the day."
>
> **Jenny's mom, 47th week**

> "My daughter keeps crawling after me. I think that's adorable. But if she doesn't do that, she makes a mess of things. She'll pull the books off their shelves and scoop the dirt out of the flower pots."
>
> **Ashley's mom, 43rd week**

> "Whenever my baby sees I'm busy, she crawls over to things she's not allowed to touch."
>
> **Nina's mom, 43rd week**

> "My son clings to me all day long, and when he doesn't, I have to keep disciplining him and taking things away from him."
>
> **Kevin's mom, 43rd week**

LEAP 7

How This Leap May Affect You

As your baby's new world expands to include sequences, their fussiness and changes that follow will affect you, too. Here are some feelings you may encounter.

You May Feel Insecure

Mothers and fathers often worry when their baby is upset. They try to find a cause for their baby's now more frequent crying. As soon as they have found one, it puts their mind at ease. Because of baby's age, they are often inclined to decide it's cutting teeth.

"I think that my son's mouth was troubling him. He wasn't his normal, easygoing self."

John's mom, 43rd week

"My son cried a lot. I don't think he had enough sleep."

Frankie's mom, 43rd week

"My daughter is whiny and fussy whenever I'm busy doing something. Perhaps she's having more difficulty dealing with her sisters at the moment."

Juliette's mom, 42nd week

You May (Yet Again) Be Exhausted

Parents of babies who demand a lot of attention and need little sleep feel thoroughly exhausted toward the end of a fussy period. Some complain of headaches, backaches, nausea, and lack of concentration, as well.

"I feel that I've broken down completely because I'm not getting any support or recognition. I'd really love to have one evening of rest. At night, I keep running upstairs to the nursery and back down again. Often, this goes on into the middle of the night. To me, this is the most difficult age so far. I even kept putting off writing this diary. I just couldn't concentrate on it."

Emily's mom, 46th week

You May Become Annoyed

Toward the end of this fussy period, mothers and fathers become increasingly irritated by their fretful little clingers. They are annoyed that they are constantly preoccupied with baby's demands and they don't seem to have a life of their own any more.

"It's tedious, literally not being able to move an inch. My son constantly demands attention, or else he throws a temper tantrum, and it's slowly but surely becoming very irritating. Sometimes, I feel like he's pulling my strings, and that makes me feel rebellious. Then I get fed up. I keep contemplating if I should take him back to the daycare, after all. I've kept him at home for a few weeks now. In the beginning it felt better, but now, once in a while, I can feel myself getting slightly aggressive again."

Bob's mom, 46th week

"I'm very busy, and I can't have my daughter clinging to my legs or sitting in front of the sink anymore when I'm working. Now, when I've had enough, it's off to bed with her. Perhaps I'm starting to lose my patience."

Juliette's mom, 45th week

"Even though I have the easiest baby anyone could ever wish for, when he starts crying hysterically, I notice I do get a bit impatient with him and whisk him off to bed."

John's mom, 43rd week

Sometimes mothers and fathers get annoyed because deep down they know that their baby is capable of more than they are showing and they suspect that their little one's behavior is just too babyish for their age. They think it's time for them to start behaving more independently by now.

"When I set my son down for a clean diaper, he always starts to yell. It's the same with clean clothes, as well. This is starting to annoy me more and more. I think he's too old for that kind of behavior. In fact, it's about time he started cooperating a little."

Bob's mom, 47th week

LEAP 7

You May Start to Quarrel

Toward the end of every fussy period, many breastfeeding mothers think about whether it might be time to stop. One of the reasons is that the baby wants to nurse all day long. This is annoying and exhausting, and mothers begin to refuse babies sometimes. The little one, however, finds this unacceptable and before you know it, they quarrel with their mother.

"I keep getting more and more annoyed because I have to lull my son to sleep at my breast. I had to start doing it again when he was having so much trouble falling asleep. Now it's starting to become a habit again. Besides, he wants to nurse an awful lot and starts screaming when he doesn't get his way. I just don't feel like doing it anymore."

Matt's mom, 47th week

The good news for mothers who do persist with breastfeeding is that the normal feeding pattern will restore itself as soon as the fussy period is over. Once everything has settled down again, mothers seem to forget their irritations.

Another battleground is the familiar territory of negotiating deals between the parent and child about the amount of physical contact and attention.

"I'm aggravated by my son's continuous crying just so he can sit on my lap. I get terribly angry when he bites me, if I don't respond to him fast enough. It hurts so much that I automatically give him a shove. Once, he fell and hit his head really hard. That wasn't my intention, but I was so furious it just happened."

Kevin's mom, 44th week

It's critical to remember that having feelings of anger and frustration at times is not abnormal or dangerous, but acting on them is. Try to get help long before you lose control.

How Your Baby's New Skills Emerge

At about 46 weeks, you will see your baby calming down and attempting to do things that are brand new to them. You will see them handling their toys in different ways and enjoying new activities. Their actions will be more precise than ever before and they will pay even greater attention to detail now.

Your baby can now understand that sometimes one thing must follow another to make a sequence. They will realize that they can find and construct sequences in all of the senses, and as usual, your baby is unable to explore them all at once. Their inclinations, preferences, and temperament will help them to select the aspects of the world that they find most interesting and the skills that they will develop. Help them to do what they are ready to do, rather than trying to push them.

The Magical Leap Forward

LEAP 7

During the last leap forward, your baby realized that certain things have so much in common that they belong to one group or category. In order to categorize things, they would often examine them by breaking them down and taking them apart. For instance, they might have taken a tower of blocks apart one by one, removed a key from a lock, or loosened a handle on a chest of drawers. This paved the way for the current leap where the very opposite takes place, they begin to experiment with putting things back together. Every baby needs to learn how to take a tower apart before they can build one. Even the seemingly simple activity of choosing the next block and then deliberately placing it in position requires a mental leap that, until this point, your baby was not ready to take.

(continued on page 253)

My Diary

How My Baby Explores the New World of Sequences

Check off the boxes below as you notice your baby changing. Stop filling this out once the next stormy period begins, heralding the coming of the next leap.

This world is just as multifaceted as all the others that your baby has entered in their short life. Each baby has their own ideas about what is interesting. Your baby can't experiment with everything at once. If they have always been a listening and looking baby, this may continue at the expense of more physical activities. It is perfectly normal if most of these skills don't become evident until several months later.

POINTING AND TALKING

- ☐ Follows and points to a person, animal, or object that you have just named, whether in real life or a picture
- ☐ Points out one or two items for you to name, such as people, animals, or objects
- ☐ Points out and names one or two items in turn
- ☐ Deliberately looks through a book, making different sounds to go with one or two pictures
- ☐ Points to their nose when you ask, "Where's your nose?"
- ☐ Points to a body part, for instance, their nose or your nose, wanting you to name it
- ☐ Imitates the sound when you name an animal, for instance, when you ask, "What does the cat say?" they say, "Meow"
- ☐ Raises their arms when you ask, "How tall are you going to be?"

- ☐ Says "Yum" when they want the next bite
- ☐ Says "No, no" when they don't want to do something
- ☐ Uses a word in an extended way, for instance, says "Yuck" for something dirty but also when they have to be careful of something, because to them, "Yuck" has come to mean "Don't touch"

WHAT GOES TOGETHER AND WHAT COMES NEXT

- ☐ Knows that they can push a round peg through a round hole; for example, they will choose the round peg from a pile of pegs and try to push it through the round hole of a peg board
- ☐ Tries to put together three pieces of a simple puzzle
- ☐ Tries pushing coins through a slot
- ☐ Tries fitting two different sizes of containers inside each other
- ☐ Takes a key from somewhere else and tries to insert it into a keyhole
- ☐ Looks at the lamp and reaches for it when you flick the light switch
- ☐ Tries to talk into a telephone receiver
- ☐ Puts objects in a container, covers the container, removes the cover, removes the objects, and repeats the cycle again
- ☐ Tries to put a "doughnut" ring over an upright rod
- ☐ Pushes toy cars around, making a vrrrm sound
- ☐ Scoops up sand with a spade and then empties it into a bucket
- ☐ Fills bath toys with water and empties them again
- ☐ Examines two Primo blocks and then tries fitting them together
- ☐ Tries scrawling on a piece of paper with a pencil or crayon

MAKING AND USING TOOLS

☐ Helps themselves learn to walk by finding an object to push

☐ Finds something to use as a step to reach a desired place or object

☐ Points with their finger in the direction they want to go when being carried

LOCOMOTION

☐ Clambers down the stairs or off a chair or sofa backward. In the beginning, they sometimes even start crawling backwards toward the stairs before starting their descent

☐ Puts their head down in position to initiate a somersault, with help

☐ Bends their knees, then stretches their legs powerfully, so that they jump off the ground with both feet

☐ Tries to aim before throwing or kicking a ball

☐ Looks first to see whether they can reach another supporting object within the number of steps they can take by themselves

PLAYING WITH OTHERS

☐ Plays with you. Clearly expresses which games they want to play by starting them and then looking at you expectantly

☐ Repeats a game

☐ Entices you to play with them, perhaps by pretending they are unable to do something that you have seen them doing before on their own

HIDE AND SEEK

- ☐ Looks for something that you have hidden by completely concealing it with something else – either as a game, or because you do not want them to get hold of it
- ☐ Hides something that belongs to someone else, waits and watches, then laughs when the other person finds it

COPYING A SEQUENCE OF GESTURES

- ☐ Imitates two or more gestures in sequence
- ☐ Studies the way the same sequence of gestures looks in reality and in the mirror
- ☐ Copies one or two movements while you are singing a song with them

HELPING OUT WITH THE HOUSEKEEPING

- ☐ Hands you things one by one that you want to put away
- ☐ Goes and gets simple objects, if you ask them to
- ☐ Picks up the clothes that you have just taken off them and puts them in the laundry basket
- ☐ Gets their own bucket with dolls' laundry, and puts it in the washing machine
- ☐ Gets out a broom and sweeps the floor with it
- ☐ Gets a cloth out and dusts things off
- ☐ Imitates you cooking; for example, they bang a fork in a bowl or stir with a spoon

DRESSING AND GROOMING

☐ Tries to undress themselves; for instance, they try to take a sock off by pulling at their toes

☐ Tries putting on their shoe or sock by themselves; for instance, they hold on to their shoe or sock and their foot and put them together

☐ Helps when you dress them. Leans toward you when you pull a sweater on or off or sticks their foot out when the sock or shoe is coming

☐ Brushes their hair

☐ Uses a toothbrush

☐ Sometimes uses a potty

EATING AND FEEDING

☐ Offers others a bite or sip while eating and drinking

☐ Blows steam off food themselves before taking a bite

☐ Sticks a piece of bread on a baby fork and eats it

☐ Can scoop up food with a spoon and put it in their mouth

OTHER CHANGES YOU NOTICE

As their new skills begin to take wing, for the first time your little one concerns themselves with constructing, putting things together, and linking things. For instance, they may now take a key off a table and try putting it in a lock. They can learn to dig up sand with a spade and then put it in a bucket. They can learn to aim a ball first and then throw it. While singing a song, such as Pat-a-cake, pat-a-cake, baker's man, they can begin to make different gestures successively, without you having to set the example. They can learn to scoop up food with a spoon and then put it in their mouth. They may learn to pick up their clothes from the floor and then put them in the laundry basket. At this age, babies are just beginning to be aware of sequences, and it's quite a feat if they manage to string two actions together. Although they know what belongs together, their attempts may not always succeed. For instance, your baby may try putting on their shoes by getting them out but then sit down and rub them against their feet trying to put them on.

You can also tell by your baby's reactions that they are now beginning to realize how certain events usually follow one another in the normal course of events. You will notice that they now know what the next step is in any particular sequence. For instance, if they see you push a doorbell, you may see your baby pause to listen for the bell.

"When a music is finished, my son now looks up at my phone, not at the speaker. He now knows that I have to do something on my phone if he is to hear more music."

Bob's mom, 48th week

Your baby can now also start pointing out and naming different people, animals, and objects. When they do this on their own, they may often still say da instead of using the proper word. When they do this together with you, they may point out things and want you to name them or have you make the appropriate sound. They might like to play the game the other way around, having you point while they tell you what they call the object. When you are carrying them around, you may also start to notice that your baby will point in the direction that they want you to go.

Babies who haven't been doing much in the way of talking may now for the first time begin to name people, animals, and objects, or parts of these. The very act of naming is a way of relating a spoken word or sound to a person, animal, or object. Pointing or looking followed by a word is a sequence as well. But some babies will still put off talking in favor of other skills, such as walking.

Your Baby's Choices: A Key to Their Personality

Babies can now perceive and play with sequences. This opens a new world of possibilities, and your baby will make their own choices according to their mental development, build, weight, and coordination. Some babies are very social and like to focus on skills that involve people; others prefer playthings. Some pick at every little detail and others are more interested in getting an overall impression of many different skills. You may find it irresistible to make comparisons with other babies, but remember that every baby is unique.

Watch your baby closely to determine where their interests lie. Between 46 and 51 weeks, they will select the skills they like best from this world. Respect their choices. You will find out what it is that makes them unique, and when you follow their interests, you will be able to help them with their playing and learning. Babies love anything new and it's important you respond when you notice any new skills or interests. They will enjoy it if you share these new discoveries, and this will accelerate their learning progress.

What you Can Do to Help

Every baby needs time and help to learn new skills. You can help your baby by giving them the opportunity and time to toy with sequences. You can encourage them when they succeed and console them when they don't. You can try to facilitate their attempts and make their failures easier to bear.

Your baby will find plenty of opportunities to come into contact with sequences themselves. Allow them to see, hear, feel, smell, and taste and indulge in whatever they like best. The more they encounter and play with sequences, the better they will learn to understand them. Pay attention, however, they might think they know it all. It doesn't matter whether they prefer learning about sequences through observing, handling toys, speech, sounds, music, or locomotion. Soon they will be able to put the expertise they have gained in one area into practice in other areas with no trouble at all.

Help Your Baby Explore the New World through Experimentation

When your baby enters the world of sequences it dawns upon them that they have to do things in a certain order, if they want to succeed. They have observed how adults perform a particular sequence, but they have to master it themselves through trial and error. Often their "solutions" are peculiar. The sequence they perform may be correct (grabbing something and putting it into something else), but they may apply the wrong objects to the wrong targets. They know that dirty cloths go into a container. So why only in the laundry basket and not in the dustbin or the toilet as well? The sequence is much the same, after all!

"My son pulls plugs from their outlets and then tries putting them into the wall. He also tries sticking other objects with two protrusions in the outlets. I have to watch him even closer now and take safety precautions."

Bob's mom, 48th week

"When my daughter wants to climb onto our bed, she opens a drawer of our nightstand, stands on it, and then climbs onto the bed. If she opens the drawer too far, the whole nightstand starts swaying back and forth. She makes me very nervous."

Jenny's mom, 49th week

The sequence itself may also be peculiar. For instance, your baby knows how their mother walks up the stairs, but the steps are too high for them, so they have to crawl. However, on every step they stand up.

"My son desperately wants to climb the stairs on his own, but he behaves dangerously. He crawls on his knees to the next step, stands up, then continues upwards on his knees, stands up again, and so it goes. I don't like it one bit. I have to keep a sharp eye on him."

Steven's mom, 45th week

Once they are of the opinion that they have mastered a particular sequence, it is "fixed". They will not accept it done in any other way and they may be quite stubborn if you try to change their mind. So always pay close attention, your young wiseacre does not yet know the meaning of danger.

Help Your Baby Explore the New World through Independence

Many babies refuse to be helped and resist any form of interference by others. These babies want to do everything they can, or think they can, by themselves. If yours is this type of baby, try to have as much consideration for their feelings as possible. This is just the age when many little ones like to start asserting their independence.

"My son always liked practicing walking together. But if I hold his hands now, he'll immediately sit down. Then when I leave he'll give it another try. At every successful attempt, no matter how slight, he'll look at me triumphantly."

Paul's mom, 46th week

"My son keeps trying to scribble something on paper with a pencil, just like his older brother does. But whenever his brother tries to guide his hand to show him how it's supposed to work, he'll pull his hand away."

Kevin's mom, 48th week

"When we push pegs through my son's peg board together, he'll start throwing them. But as soon as he's on his own in the playpen, he will try to copy it. To tell the truth, it annoys me."

Paul's mom, 53rd week

"My daughter will eat only if she can put the food in her mouth herself. When I do it, she'll take it out again."

Laura's mom, 43rd week

LEAP 7

At this age, many parents spend huge amounts of time taking things away from their children and disciplining them. It's important to consider that your baby isn't necessarily being disobedient. They just want to do things by themselves.

"My daughter is being troublesome and wants her own way with everything. She gets angry when I refuse her something. It's really tiresome."

Jenny's mom, 50th week

"My son tries to get things done by screaming and throwing temper tantrums."

Matt's mom, 46th week

"When I complain, my daughter screams and lashes out at everything and everybody around her, or pulls a plant from its pot. This annoys me to no end. She behaves much better with her babysitter."

Laura's mom, 49th week

Show Some Understanding for Frustrations

Many mothers and fathers see their baby's strive for independence as rebellious. But if you stop to think, it's not. Your baby simply wants to do things by themselves. After all, they are becoming aware of what belongs together and the order in which things need to be done. They are convinced they know it all and are capable of doing anything. They no longer want you to interfere or to tell them how things should be done. They want to make their own decisions. But, as their mother or father, you are not really used to this. You naturally help them as you always have, without giving it a second thought. You know perfectly well that your baby is still unable to properly carry out the things they want to do. And you know that they will inevitably make a mess of things if they try. Parents and babies may often have different views of things. This can lead to conflicts.

The parents see the baby as being difficult, and the baby feels their parents are causing all the trouble. Adolescents may go through the most difficult phases, but babies and toddlers run a close second.

Help Your Baby Explore the New World through Feedback

At this age, babies start testing the limits of how far they can go before someone stops them. If you make it clear to them when they are doing something wrong and just why it's bad or dangerous, they can learn a lot from it.

Similarly, you should let your baby know what they're doing right by praising them. This will teach them what is good and what is bad behavior. Most babies ask for praise themselves, anyway. When they do something right, they ask to be rewarded all the time. They look at you and laugh, full of pride, or call for attention. They can keep repeating behaviors many times as well, asking for a reward after each time.

LEAP 7

If your baby is frustrated by things they are not able or allowed to do, you can still quite easily distract them with a favorite toy or game. This is of course, different for every baby.

"My son keeps wanting to help out. He thinks that's the best thing ever and starts beaming. I do have to take my time with him, though. It takes me 10 times longer to put a pile of diapers away in the cupboard with his help. He'll hand me each diaper separately, but before he lets me have each one, he'll put it on his shoulder and rub the side of his chin against it."

Matt's mom, 48th week

Help Your Baby Explore the New World through Language

A baby who lives in the world of sequences may start pointing out and naming different people, animals, and objects. Pointing or looking, followed by a word, is a sequence. If you notice your baby doing this, listen to them and let them know you understand them and that you think they are wonderful. Do not try to improve their pronunciation. This will spoil your baby's fun and will make no difference to the way they speak.

Do make sure that you use the correct words all the time. This way, your baby will automatically learn the right pronunciation in due time. For a while they will "translate" what you say into their own baby pronunciation.

"My daughter is starting to use words and point at whatever she's talking about. At the moment, she's in love with horses. When she sees a horse, she points to it and says 'Hoss.' Yesterday at the park, a large Afghan dog ran past her. She called that a 'Hoss,' as well."

Hannah's mom, 48th week

"My son suddenly said 'Nana' to a toy cat. We have never used that word. He has a lot of toy animals. When I asked, 'Where's nana?' he kept pointing to the cat."

Paul's mom, 48th week

Understand Your Baby's Fears

When your baby is learning new skills, they may also perceive things that they don't yet fully understand. In a way, they discover new anxieties – dangers that up until now they didn't realize existed. As soon as they recognize these dangers, and until they can be sure they are harmless, their fears will stay with them. So show them a little understanding.

"My daughter keeps wanting to sit on her potty. Even if she hasn't done anything, she'll take the potty into the lavatory to empty it and flush the toilet. But while she seems fascinated by flushing, at the same time she's also scared of it. She doesn't get as frightened when she flushes the toilet herself, only when someone else does. Then she doesn't like it at all."

Jenny's mom, 50th week

"My daughter is fascinated by airplanes. She recognizes them everywhere: in the air, in pictures, and in magazines. This week, she suddenly became frightened by the sound, even though she's heard it before."

Laura's mom, 46th week

Some babies can use body language and sounds to tell you that they remember certain situations or that they have seen certain people before. If you notice your baby doing this, talk to them a lot, explain to them what you are seeing, and react to what they tell you about it later on.

LEAP 7

"We go swimming every week. Usually, we see the same people there. One day, we saw one of the mothers on the street. Immediately, my son called out 'Oh oh' and pointed to her as if he recognized her. Then, he saw girl in the swimming pool who lives near us and whom he's seen only a couple of times, and he reacted the same way."

Paul's mom, 49th week

Top Games for This Wonder Week

Here are games and activities that most babies like best now. Remember, all babies are different. See what your baby responds to best.

HELPING OUT GAMES

Your baby likes to feel needed. Let them know that you can certainly use some help from them. At this age, they will not be of any real help, but they will be able to understand the actions involved in many common activities. Plus, it is a good way of preparing them for the next leap.

DOING HOUSEWORK

Show your baby how you cook and clean. Involve them and explain what you are doing. Give them one of your dusters. This will be much more interesting than using their own cloth. When you are baking a cake, give them their own plastic mixing bowl and spoon.

DRESSING

This is the most fun in front of a mirror. Try undressing your baby, toweling them down, and dressing them while they watch themselves. Name the parts you are drying. When you notice they are starting to cooperate, ask them to help out. Ask them to raise an arm or stretch their leg when you are about to put a jumper or sock on them. Praise them when they do it.

GROOMING THEMSELVES

Allow your baby to groom themselves. This is most fun in front of a mirror, too. This way, the baby can see for themselves what they are doing, learn quickly, and have a lot of fun. Brush their hair in front of a mirror, then let them try it themselves. You can do the same with brushing their teeth. You can also see if they will wash themselves. Give them a washcloth when they are in the bath, and say something such as, "Go on, wash your face." Respond with enthusiasm at every attempt. You will see how proud this makes them.

FEEDING THEMSELVES WITH A SPOON

Allow your baby to eat by themselves with a spoon. Or give them a baby fork to eat cubes of bread or pieces of fruit. Lay a large sheet of plastic under their chair so that afterward you will easily be able to clean up the mess they make.

NAMING GAMES

Your baby often understands a lot more than you think, and they love being allowed to prove it.

THIS IS YOUR NOSE

Touching and naming parts of their anatomy will help your baby to discover their own body. You can play this game while dressing or undressing them or when you are sitting together. Also, see if they know where your nose is.

POINTING OUT AND NAMING

For many babies, pointing out and naming things, or making the appropriate sounds, is a fun game. You can play this anywhere: outside, in a store, or with a book. Enjoy your baby's misnomers as well.

SONG AND MOVEMENT GAMES

Now your baby may want to actively participate in songs. They may start to make one or two movements that go with them by themselves, as well.

PAT-A-CAKE, PAT-A-CAKE, BAKER'S MAN

Sit facing your baby and sing:

Pat-a-cake, pat-a-cake, baker's man
(Clap your hands, and let your baby follow.)
Bake me a cake as fast as you can
Prick it and pat it, and mark it with "B"
(Make pricking and patting movements,
and let your baby follow.)
And put it in the oven for baby and me.
(At the word "baby," point to them or poke them in the stomach.)

ITSY BITSY SPIDER

Sit facing your baby and sing:

The itsy bitsy spider
Climbed up the water spout
(Walk your fingers up in the air or on the baby like a spider.)
Down came the rain and washed the spider out.
(Mimic raindrops coming down and make
an action of washing water away.)
Out came the sun and dried up all the rain.
(Draw the sun in the air.)
And the itsy bitsy spider climbed up the spout again.
(Walk your fingers up in the air or on the baby like the spider
coming back again.)

ROW, ROW, ROW YOUR BOAT

Sit on the floor opposite your child. Place your baby in between your legs. Take their hands in yours and sing while gently rocking back and forth:

Row, row, row your boat
Gently down the stream
Merrily, merrily, merrily, merrily
Life is but a dream.

HIDE-AND-SEEK GAMES

Many babies like uncovering playthings that you have made disappear completely.

UNWRAPPING A PARCEL

Wrap a plaything in a piece of paper or crackly crisp bag, while your baby watches. Then give them the parcel and let them retrieve the plaything, it appears as if by magic. Encourage them with each attempt they make.

UNDER THE CUP

Put a plaything in front of your baby and place a cup over it. Then put an identical cup next to the first one and ask your baby where the plaything is. Praise them every time they look for the hidden plaything, even if they do not find it immediately. If this game is still a bit too complicated, try playing it with a cloth instead of a cup. They will be able to see the contour of the plaything through the cloth. Play this game the other way around, too – let your baby hide something that you have to find.

> "On our way to the store, we saw a large pile of stones. I said, 'Look at all those stones.' My son gazed at them intently. The next day, he began pointing at the stones from a distance, looking at me and shouting 'Eh, eh.'"
>
> **Steven's mom, 51st week**

The Virtue of Patience

It's important to keep your patience with your baby as they try to learn new skills. When you see they're not interested, stop. They have enough other things that they may find more interesting to occupy themselves with at that moment.

> "I'm very busy practicing saying 'Daddy' with my boy and playing games like 'Where's your nose?' But so far, we've had little result. He just laughs, jumps around, and would rather bite my nose or pull my hair. But I'm happy enough that he's become such a lively little fellow."
>
> **Frankie's mom, 49th week**

> "I try to sing songs with my son, but I don't feel as if they are doing much good. He doesn't seem particularly interested. He seems to be preoccupied by his surroundings."
>
> **John's mom, 47th week**

After the Leap

Between 47 and 52 weeks, another period of comparative ease sets in. For one to three weeks, you may be amazed by your baby's cheerfulness and independence. They may pay much better attention when you talk now. They may seem calmer and more controlled when they are at play, and they may play well on their own again. They may want to be put back in their playpen – they may not even want to be taken out. And finally, they may look remarkably older and wiser. They are growing into a real toddler now.

Top Toys for This Wonder Week

Here are toys and things that most babies like best now.

- Wooden trains with stations, bridges, and sidings
- Toy cars
- Dolls with toy bottles
- Drum, pots, and pans to beat on
- Books with pictures of animals
- Sandboxes with a bucket and spade
- Balls of all sizes, from ping-pong balls to large beach balls
- Giant plastic beads
- Stuffed animals, especially the ones that make music when you squeeze them
- Bicycles, cars, or tractors that they can sit on themselves and move around
- Primo blocks
- Small plastic figures of people or animals
- Mirrors

Remember to put away or take safety precautions with electrical outlets, stairs, stereo equipment, televisions, vacuum cleaners, washing machines, pets, and small objects such as knickknacks, pins, or little pieces of colored glass.

LEAP 7

"My daughter is getting lovelier by the day. She keeps getting better at entertaining herself. She can really keep herself occupied with something now. I got the playpen out again this week. But the thing I found most striking was that she doesn't at all seem to mind spending an hour or so in it anymore, whereas a few weeks ago she'd scream hysterically if I took her anywhere near it. It's as if she's discovering her toys all over again and enjoying the peace and quiet in the playpen."

Ashley's mom, 52nd week

"My daughter has become a real playmate for her older sister. She responds exactly like you'd expect her to. They do a lot more things together. They take their bath together as well. Both of them enjoy each other tremendously."

Hannah's mom, 47th week

"These were lovely weeks. My son is more of a buddy again. The day care center is working out fine. He always enjoys seeing the other children and comes home in a good mood. He sleeps better at night. He understands a lot more and seems fascinated by the toys he plays with. He crawls into another room on his own again, too, and laughs a lot. I'm enjoying every minute with him."

Bob's mom, 51st week

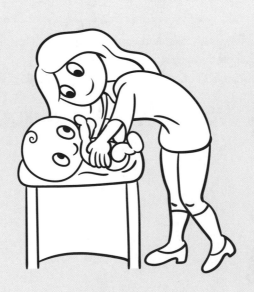

LEAP 8

Wonder Week 55

The World of Programs

**THE PARTS BELONG
TOGETHER**

Every child's first birthday is a significant occasion. For many parents, the end of the first year means the beginning of the end of babyhood. Your little cherub is about to become a toddler. In many ways, of course, they are still a baby. They still have so much to learn about their world – which has become such an interesting place to explore. They can get around so much better now and they have become adept at getting into everything that interests them.

Shortly after the first birthday, at around 55 weeks, your little one will go through another big change in their mental development and will be ready to explore the world of programs. This will make them seem even more like a little person with their own way of approaching the world. A watchful parent will begin to see the blossoming of a new understanding in the toddler's way of thinking.

The word "programs" is very abstract. Here's what it means in this context. In the past leap in development, your baby learned to deal with the notion of sequences – the fact that events follow one after another or objects fit together in a particular way. A program is a degree more complicated than a sequence since it allows the end result to be reached in any number of ways. Once your child becomes capable of perceiving programs, they can begin to understand what it means to do the laundry, set the table, eat lunch, tidy up, get dressed, build a tower, make a phone call, and the millions of other things that make up everyday life. These are all programs.

Note: *The first phase (fussy period) of this leap into the perceptual world of "programs" is age-linked and predictable, emerging between 49 and 53 weeks. Most babies start the second phase (see box "Quality Time: An Unnatural Whim" on page 17) of this leap 55 weeks after full-term birth. The first perception of the world of programs sets in motion the development of a whole range of skills and activities. However, the age at which these skills and activities appear for the first time varies greatly and depends on your baby's preferences, experimentation and physical development. For example, the ability to perceive programs is a necessary precondition for "washing dishes" or "vacuum cleaning," but these skills normally appear anywhere from 55 weeks to many months later. The skills and activities in this chapter are stated at the earliest possible age they could appear so you can watch for and recognize them. (They may be rudimentary at first.) This way you can respond to and facilitate your baby's development.*

The main characteristic of a program is that it has a goal but that the steps taken to accomplish it are flexible. This is how it differs from a sequence, which is the same every time. An example of a sequence is counting from 1 to 10. You do it the same way each and every time. Dusting is an example of a program. You don't necessarily have to dust an object in the same way each time – you can dust the legs of a table first and then the top, or the other way around. Every time that you dust, you can choose the sequence you feel is best for that day, that room, that chair, and your mood. However you choose to do it, the program you are working with remains "dusting." So, a program can be seen as a network of possible sequences that you can carry out in a variety of ways. The options may be limited with dusting, but if you think of examples such as going on vacation or changing jobs, the programs become very complex. Your child can now think of a goal, such as going shopping, and know that this may mean putting on hats, coats, and boots and getting in the car. Or they may be eager to "help" you – doing the cleaning, taking the dog for a walk, and putting away the groceries. They may insist on doing things themselves – washing their hands, feeding themselves, even undressing themselves.

As your child changes, you may feel they are more unpredictable than ever. It used to be easy to interpret their actions when they were part of simple sequences, because one thing always led to the next in a familiar pattern. Now their world is much more flexible than before and any action can form part of any program. This is confusing for you both. Until you get used to the way they are operating, some of their actions may be hard to understand because you can no longer guess what they're trying to achieve. This leap will also be apparent in their play. They will begin to be interested in some of their toys all over again, and for the first time, you may notice a budding imagination and more complex play.

Between 49 and 53 weeks, your child begins to perceive that their world is changing again. While they are sorting out this new complexity, they will need some extra comfort and support, and this makes them appear fussy and demanding for a while. This fussy period will often last for four or five weeks, but it can be as short as three weeks or as long as six. If your baby is cranky, watch them closely. There's a good chance that they're attempting to master new skills.

This Week's Fussy Signs

Your child may cry more easily than they did during the past weeks. Children are usually quicker to cry now than their parents have been used to. They want to be near their mothers and fathers, preferably all day long. Some children are much more insistent about this than others are, of course. They may also seem cranky, unmanageable, and temperamental.

"My son could be pretty bad-tempered at times. Not all the time – he would play on his own for a while, but then suddenly it was all over and he would be terribly weepy for quite some time. Then he would want me to hold him. And all of this commotion would take place in just one morning."

Bob's mom, 52nd week

"My daughter was very quick to cry. All I had to do was say 'No,' and she'd have an immediate crying fit. It was not like her at all."

Eve's mom, 52nd week

Children usually cry less when they are with their mothers or fathers or when their parents are occupied with them in some way, playing with them, or watching them.

"While my little girl is doing things, I'm supposed to stay sitting on the sofa, preferably not doing anything myself. I long for the day when I'll be able to knit something quietly while I'm sitting there."

Emily's mom, 53rd week

How you know it's Time to Grow

It's still too early for your little one to use words to tell you how they're feeling. But still, they are able to express the turmoil they feel inside.
Here's how.

They May Cling to Your Clothes

Your little one may start clinging more to you again – many children do at this age. They may want to be carried around or cling to your legs to prevent you from walking away and leaving them behind. Others don't necessarily need physical contact, but they may keep coming back to be near their mothers for only brief moments or to touch them. Every child comes back for their own brand of "mommy refill."

"My daughter stays around me more again, plays for a moment, and then comes back to me."

Hannah's mom, 54th week

"I can't do a thing as long as my son is awake. When he's out of his playpen, he is constantly underfoot, and when he's in the playpen, I have to stay near him. Otherwise, he'll throw a screaming fit."

Frankie's mom, 55th week

"When I stand up and walk into the kitchen, right away my daughter will come after me and want to be carried. She'll really make a scene. It's all terribly dramatic. You'd think something awful was happening."

Emily's mom, 53rd week

LEAP 8

They May Be Shyer with Strangers than Before

When there are strangers near, your little one may cling to you even more fanatically than they already did. Once more, many children suddenly want to have less to do with strangers now. This even includes their own family members on occasion.

"This week, my daughter would suddenly become extremely upset, and she'd want only to be with me. If I put her down or gave her to my husband, she'd panic."

Jenny's mom, 56th week

"My little girl won't accept anything to eat from strangers, not even a slice of bread or a cookie."

Nina's mom, 54th week

But there are also children who only want to be with their fathers.

"My daughter was completely crazy about her father for two days. She didn't want to have anything to do with me then, even though I hadn't done her any wrong. If he didn't pick her up right away, she'd start crying."

Juliette's mom, 53rd week

They May Want Physical Contact to Be as Close as Possible

Some children hold on as tightly as they can, even when they are being carried. They don't want to be put down – and very likely, yours doesn't either. There are also little ones who don't mind being put down, as long as their parents don't walk away. The only one who's allowed to leave is the little terror themselves.

"One evening I had to go away. When I set my son down to put on my coat, he started crying, grabbed me, and tugged at my hand, as if he didn't want me to leave."

Paul's mom, 52nd week

> "I really have to keep a close eye on my daughter. If I want to set her down to go into the kitchen for a second to get something, she'll go for the dog, pretend to pet him, while at the same time she pulls out whiskers and tufts of fur."
>
> **Emily's mom, 53rd week**

They May Want to Be Entertained

Your little one may start asking for more attention at this point. Most children do. Demanding ones do this all day long. But even easy, even-tempered children prefer doing things together with their mothers and fathers.

> "My daughter keeps coming to get me, pulls me along by my hand so we can play together, with her blocks or dolls or to look at a book together."
>
> **Jenny's mom, 53rd week**

They May Be Jealous

Some possessive children seem to put on an act when their mothers or fathers pay attention to someone or something else. They pretend to be cranky, mischievous, or determined to hurt themselves. Others act sweetly and cuddly in an exaggerated way in order to get their parents' attention.

> "My son gets jealous when I give something to the tiny baby I look after."
>
> **Matt's mom, 53rd week**

> "My friend came over with her baby. Every time I said something to her baby, mine would step in between us with this big grin on her face."
>
> **Jenny's mom, 54th week**

They May Be Moody

Your little one may be happily occupied one moment, then become sad, angry, or infuriated the next, for no apparent reason. You may not be able to pinpoint a particular cause.

> "Sometimes, my son will sit and play with his blocks like a little angel, but then suddenly he'll become furious. He shrieks and slams his blocks together or throws them across the room."
>
> **Steven's mom, 52nd week**

They May Sleep Poorly

Your child may sleep less well than usual. Most children resist going to bed, have difficulty falling asleep, and wake up sooner than you are used to. Some sleep less well during the day, others are restless at night, and still others simply refuse to go to bed quietly at any time.

> "This week, I noticed for the first time that my toddler often lies awake for a while at night. Sometimes, she'll cry a little. If I pick her up, she goes back to sleep in seconds."
>
> **Ashley's mom, 54th week**

> "We'd really like our daughter to make less of a fuss about going to sleep. Right now, it involves a lot of screaming and crying, sometimes almost hysterics, even when she's exhausted."
>
> **Jenny's mom, 52nd week**

> "My son is awake a lot during the night, terribly distressed. He really panics. Sometimes, it's hard to get him to calm down again."
>
> **Bob's mom, 52nd week**

They May "Daydream"

Occasionally, some children may just sit, staring out into nothingness, as if they are in their own little worlds. Parents don't like this dreaming one bit, and they will often try to break these reveries.

> "Sometimes, my daughter will sit, slouching and rocking back and forth, gazing into thin air. I always drop whatever I'm doing to shake her and wake her up again. I'm terrified there might be something wrong with her."
>
> **Juliette's mom, 54th week**

They May Lose Their Appetite

Many little ones are fussy eaters. Their mothers almost always find this troubling and irritating. A child who is still being breastfed usually wants the breast more often than before, not because they really want to nurse, but so they can stay close to their mother.

"My daughter is suddenly less interested in food. Previously, she would finish everything within 15 minutes. She was like a bottomless pit. Now it sometimes takes me half an hour to feed her."
Ashley's mom, 53rd week

"My son sprays his lunch around with his mouth. He dirties everything. The first few days, I thought it was quite funny. Not anymore, I should add."
Bob's mom, 53rd week

They May Be More Babyish Again

Sometimes, the babyish behavior that supposedly vanished will resurface. Parents don't like seeing this happen – they expect steady progress. Yet, during fussy phases, relapses such as these are perfectly normal. It tells you that progress, in the shape of a new world, is on its way.

"My daughter crawled again a couple of times, but she probably just did it to get attention."
Jenny's mom, 55th week

"My daughter is putting things in her mouth a little more often again, just like she used to."
Hannah's mom, 51st week

> "My son wants me to feed him again. When I don't do this, he pushes his food away."
>
> **Kevin's mom, 53rd week**

They May Act Unusually Sweet

Some little clingers suddenly come up to their mothers or fathers for a few moments just to cuddle with them, then they are off again.

> "Sometimes, my son comes crawling up to me just to be a real sweetie for a moment. He'll lay his little head very softly on my knees, for instance, very affectionately."
>
> **Bob's mom, 51st week**

> "My daughter often comes up for a quick cuddle. She says 'Kiss,' and then I get one, too."
>
> **Ashley's mom, 53rd week**

They May Reach for a Cuddly Object More Often

Your little one may cuddle a favorite object with a bit more passion than before. Many children do this, especially when they are tired or when their mothers or fathers are busy. They cuddle soft toys, rugs, cloths, slippers, or even dirty laundry. Anything soft that they can lay their little hands on will do. They kiss and pet their cuddly things as well. Parents find this endearing.

> "My son cuddles away while I'm busy. He'll hold his toy elephant's ear with one hand and stick two fingers from his other hand in his mouth. It's a sight to see."
>
> **John's mom, 51st week**

They May Be Mischievous

Your child may try to get your attention by being extra naughty, especially when you are busy and really have no time for them.

"I have to keep telling my daughter 'No' because she seems to do things just to get my attention. If I don't react, she will eventually stop. But I can't always do that because sometimes there's a chance she might break whatever it is she's taking apart."

Jenny's mom, 53rd week

"My son is being a handful at the moment. He touches everything and refuses to listen. I can't really get anything done until he's in bed."

Frankie's mom, 55th week

"Sometimes I suspect that my son doesn't listen on purpose."

Steven's mom, 51st week

They May Have More Temper Tantrums Now

If you have a hot-headed little terror, they may go berserk as soon as they fail to get their own way. You may even see a tantrum that comes out of nowhere, perhaps because they are anticipating that you may not allow them to do or have what's on their mind.

"My son wants me to put him on my lap and feed him his bottle of fruit juice again. If he even suspects it might not happen quickly enough, he'll toss his bottle across the room and start screaming, yelling, and kicking to get me to take it back to him."

Matt's mom, 52nd week

"If I don't respond immediately when my daughter wants attention, she gets furious. She'll pinch the skin right off my arm, nastily, quickly, and violently."

Emily's mom, 53rd week

"My son refuses to have anything to do with 'bed.' He gets so angry that he bangs his chin on the railings of his crib, hurting himself every time. So now I'm really afraid to put him in bed."

Matt's mom, 52nd week

My Diary

Signs My Baby Is Growing Again

Between 49 and 53 weeks, your child may show signs that they are ready to make the next leap, into the world of programs.

- ☐ Cries more often than before and is cranky or fretful
- ☐ Is cheerful one moment and cries the next
- ☐ Wants you to keep them busy, or does so more often than before
- ☐ Clings to your clothes or wants to be closer to you than ever
- ☐ Acts unusually sweet
- ☐ Is mischievous
- ☐ Throws temper tantrums, or throws them more often than before
- ☐ Is jealous
- ☐ Is more obviously shy with strangers all of a sudden
- ☐ Wants physical contact to be tighter or closer now
- ☐ Sleeps poorly
- ☐ Has "nightmares," or has them more often than before
- ☐ Loses appetite
- ☐ Sometimes just sits there, quietly daydreaming
- ☐ Sucks their thumb, or does so more often than usual
- ☐ Reaches for a cuddly toy, or does so more often than they did
- ☐ Is more babyish than they were

OTHER CHANGES YOU NOTICE

How This Leap May Affect You

No doubt you're feeling the stress of your baby's changes as well, if only vicariously. Here are some of the signs.

You May Feel Insecure

When a mother and father are confronted with a little fusspot, they may be worried at first. They want to know what is wrong with their child. But at this age, irritation soon sets in.

Also during this period, some parents wonder why their child is not walking as quickly as they expected them to. They worry there might be something physically wrong with them.

You May Become Really Frustrated

Toward the end of the fussy period, parents often become increasingly aggravated by their baby's demands on them. They become increasingly annoyed by seemingly purposeful mischief and the way their baby uses temper tantrums to get their own way.

LEAP 8

"I'm so annoyed by my daughter's crying fits whenever I leave the room. I can't stand the fact that she immediately crawls after me either, clutching my leg and crawling along with me. I can't get anything done this way. When I've had enough, it's off to bed with her, I'm afraid."

Juliette's mom, 52nd week

"My son keeps pulling at the big plant to get my attention. Distracting him doesn't work. Now I get angry and push him away, or I give him a gentle slap on his bottom."

Matt's mom, 56th week

"My daughter flies into a rage every other minute whenever she's not allowed to do something or can't manage it. She'll throw her toys and start whining like mad. I try to ignore this. But if she has several tantrums in a row, I put her to bed. When she first started doing this two weeks ago, I thought it was very amusing. Now I'm terribly aggravated by it. Her sisters just laugh at her. Sometimes, when she sees them doing that, it brightens her up and she'll start smiling back at them, shyly. It usually does the trick, but not all of the time."

Ashley's mom, 53rd week

You May Argue

During this fussy period, quarrels are usually brought on by temper tantrums.

"I feel myself getting angry when my daughter starts bawling if she isn't getting her own way. This week, she got furious when I wouldn't immediately follow her into the kitchen. So I gave her a good smack on the bottom, after which her rage turned into real tears. I know I shouldn't have done it, but I was fed up."

Jenny's mom, 54th week

It's understandable that things can get too much sometimes. But hitting or a "good smack on the bottom" does not solve anything. It hurts your baby unnecessarily and damages the trust your baby has in you. During each fussy period, breastfeeding mothers feel a desire to stop. At this age, this is because the baby keeps wanting the breast in fits and starts, or because their demands are accompanied by temper tantrums.

> "I've really given up now. My son would throw temper tantrums from just thinking about my breast. It messed up our entire relationship with him tugging at my sweater, kicking, screaming, and me getting angry. Perhaps those tantrums will start to disappear now, too. The last time he nursed was on the night of his first birthday."

Matt's mom, 53rd week

How Your Baby's New Skills Emerge

Around 55 weeks, you will notice that your little one is less fussy than before. At the same time, you should notice that they are attempting and achieving entirely new things again. They deal with people, toys, and other objects in a more mature way and they enjoy doing new things with familiar toys and household objects that have been there since they were born. At this point, they don't quite feel like your little "baby" any more but will seem to have transformed into a little toddler. This is because they are entering the world of programs where they are beginning to see that the world is full of goals and sequences of actions leading up to a specific goal. This new flexible world is theirs to discover, but, as usual, they will want to do this in their own way and at their own speed. As a parent, your help will be as vital as ever, although it may not always feel that way when another temper tantrum rolls in.

The Magical Leap Forward

In the past leap in development, your baby learned to deal with the notion of sequences – where events follow one after another or objects fit together in a particular way. A program is more complicated than a sequence because you can reach the end result in any number of ways.

An adult's world is filled with complicated programs. Fortunately, your child's world is simpler. Instead of dealing with enormous programs like "going on a vacation," your child will be working with programs such as "eating lunch." However, operating a program entails choices at each crossroad – rather like finding your way across town. During lunch, after every bite they will have to decide after every bite whether they would rather take another bite of the same food, switch to something different, have a sip of their drink, or perhaps even three sips. They can decide whether to take the next bite with their hands or use a spoon. They can decide to finish what they have or clamor for dessert. Whatever they opt for, it will still be the "eating lunch" program.

Your toddler will, as usual, experiment with this new world. Expect them to play with the different choices they can make at every juncture – they may just want to try everything out. They need to learn the possible consequences are of the decisions they make at different points – so they could decide to empty the next spoonful on the floor instead of in their mouth.

They can also decide when to put a program into operation. For example, they can get the broom out of the closet because they want to sweep the floor. They can get their coat because they want to go out and do the shopping. Unfortunately, misunderstandings are quick to occur. After all, they can't yet explain what they want yet and their mother or father can easily interpret them wrongly. This is very frustrating for such a young person, and a temperamental child might even throw a tantrum. Even if a

parent does understand their child correctly, they may simply not want to do whatever their child wants at that very moment. This, too, can frustrate a toddler quite quickly, as they can't understand the idea of "waiting" at this age.

Besides being able to learn how to carry out a program themselves, they can now perceive when someone else is doing the same thing. So they can begin to understand that if their mother is making tea, a snack will follow shortly and they can expect a cookie – or not. Now that your toddler can learn to perceive and explore this world, they also understand they have the choice of refusing a program they don't like – at least, in theory. If they don't agree with their parents' plan, they may feel frustrated and sometimes even have a temper tantrum. You might be seeing a lot of them these days.

Brain Changes

Your child's brain waves will show changes again at approximately 12 months. Also, their head circumference will increase, and the glucose metabolism in their brain will change.

Your Toddler's Choices: A Key to Their Personality

At this age, all toddlers will begin to understand and experiment with the world of programs, a world that offers a wide range of new skills to play with. Your child will choose the things that interest them, things that they have perhaps watched others do in the world around them, but also the things that most suit their own inclinations, interests, and physique. Every little individual learns about programs in their own way. Some children will be acute watchers, carefully studying the way things are done around them. Others may want to "help" all the time. And still others will want to do things themselves, and they will let you know in no uncertain terms that they don't want any interference.

(continued on page 289)

LEAP 8

My Diary

How My Baby Explores the New World of Programs

Check off the boxes below as you notice your baby changing. Some of the skills in the list below may not appear until weeks or months later. Your toddler will exercise their own choices in exploring what they can do in their new world.

STARTING A PROGRAM THEMSELVES

☐ Gets out a broom or duster and tries sweeping or dusting

☐ Goes to the bathroom and tries cleaning the toilet bowl

☐ Comes to you with things they want to be put away

☐ Gets out the cookie jar and expects a snack

☐ Comes to you with their coat, cap, a bag to go shopping

☐ Gets out their coat and shovel, ready to go to the sandbox

☐ Gets out their clothes and wants to put them on

JOINING IN WITH YOUR PROGRAM

☐ Throws the cushions from the chair in advance to help when you are cleaning

☐ Tries to hang the towel back in place when you are finished

☐ Puts an object or a food item away in the right cupboard

☐ Brings their own plate, silverware, and place mat when you are setting the table

☐ Tells you by words, sounds, or gestures that it's time for dessert when they have finished eating

☐ Puts spoons in cups and usually starts stirring

☐ Grabs an item from you and wants to carry it themselves

☐ Tries to put something on by themselves while they are being dressed or helps by pulling on their leggings or sleeves

☐ Picks out a song or movie on the TV and helps put it on. Knows which button to press for play or stop

EXECUTING A PROGRAM UNDER SUPERVISION

☐ Puts different shaped blocks through the correct holes in a box when you help by pointing out what goes where

☐ Uses the potty when you ask them to or when they need to. Then carries the potty to the bathroom by themselves or helps you carry it (if they don't walk yet) and flushes

☐ Gets out pens and paper and scribbles when you help them

INDEPENDENT PROGRAMS

☐ Tries feeding dolls or cuddly toys, copying their own eating program

☐ Tries giving a doll a bath by copying their own bathing ritual

☐ Tries putting doll on the potty, maybe after using it

☐ Eats everything on their plate without help; often they want to do this while sitting politely at the table like the grown-ups

☐ Eats raisins from a packet by themselves

☐ Builds a tower of at least three blocks

☐ Starts and continues a telephone conversation, sometimes dialing at the start or ending the conversation with "Bye"

☐ Crawls through the room following "paths" of their own choice, under chairs and tables and through narrow tunnels, and often indicates which direction they intend to go first

LEAP 8

- ☐ Crawls through the room with a toy car or train saying "Vroom vroom." Follows all sorts of different routes – under chairs and tables, or between the sofa and the wall
- ☐ Is capable of finding something you hid

WATCHING OTHERS CARRYING OUT A PROGRAM

- ☐ Watches cartoons or children's shows on television, which manages to keep their attention for about three minutes
- ☐ Listens to short stories
- ☐ Expresses an understanding of what is happening in pictures – for example, by saying "Yum" when the child or animal in the picture is eating or being offered something to eat
- ☐ Looks and listens when you play "pretend" games – feeding, bathing and dressing their dolls and cuddly toys, or making them talk and answer
- ☐ Studies how older children carry out a program with their toys – how they play with a tea set, a garage with cars, doll's bed, or train set
- ☐ Studies other family members when they are carrying out an everyday program, for instance, when they are getting dressed, eating, drawing, or telephoning

OTHER CHANGES YOU NOTICE

You are probably getting to know your toddler's personality quite well by now, and many of their choices will follow patterns that you've already noticed as they have grown. They are still capable of exploring new skills and interests as the opportunity presents itself. Watch your toddler carefully to determine where their interests lie. Use the list on pages 286-288 to mark or highlight what your child selects. Between 55 and 61 weeks, they will start to choose what they want to explore from the world of programs. Remember to respect those choices and to let your child develop at their own pace. Focus on helping them do what they are ready to do. Young children love anything new and it's important you respond when you notice any new skills or interests. They will enjoy it if you share these new discoveries, and this will accelerate their learning progress.

What you Can Do to Help

Help your toddler as they make their first tentative steps toward their encounters with programs. Talk about what they're going to achieve and how they're going to do it. If they enjoy watching you, encourage this. Talk about what you are doing as you are carrying out your program. Offer them opportunities to help you. Allow them to try carrying out their own program when you notice that they seem to have one in mind.

Help Your Baby Explore the New World through Independence

If your child is interested in dressing, undressing, and grooming themselves, then show them how you do these things. Explain to them what you are doing as well as why you are doing it. They will be able to understand more than they are able to tell you. If you have a little time, let them toy with washing and dressing themselves or, if they want to, somebody else in the family.

"My daughter tries pulling her trousers up by herself or putting her own slippers on, but she can't do it yet. Then suddenly I found her walking around in my slippers."

Jenny's mom, 55th week

"My daughter likes walking around with a cap or hat on. Whether it's mine, hers, or a doll's — it's all the same to her."

Eve's mom, 57th week

"This past week, my son kept putting all sorts of things on his head: dishcloths, towels, and, a few times, someone's pants. He'd walk around the house impervious to his surroundings while his brother and sister were on the floor laughing."

Frankie's mom, 59th week

"As soon as my daughter is dressed, she crawls over to my dressing table and tries to spray herself with perfume."

Laura's mom, 57th week

"Yesterday, when I went into my son's room to get him, he was standing up in his crib grinning like mad. He had gotten almost completely undressed by himself."

John's mom, 58th week

"My daughter feeds her dolls, bathes them, and puts them to bed. When she's used her potty, she'll put her dolls on the potty, as well."

Jenny's mom, 56th week

If your little one wants to eat on their own, let them try it as often as you can. Keep in mind that they are creative enough to want to test different methods of eating – and all of them will probably be messy. If cleaning up gets tiring, you can make cleaning easier by putting a large sheet of plastic on the floor under their chair.

"Since my son has learned how to eat his dinner by himself with a spoon, he insists on doing it completely on his own. Otherwise, he won't eat. He also insists on sitting in his chair at the table when he's eating."

Kevin's mom, 57th week

"Suddenly, my daughter discovered it was great fun to first stir something with a spoon, then stick it in her mouth."

Jenny's mom, 56th week

"My son loves eating raisins from a packet by himself."

Matt's mom, 57th week

"My daughter says 'Pie' when she's finished eating her food, so she knows there's more to come. As soon as she's finished her dessert, she has to be taken out of her chair."

Emily's mom, 60th week

Bags, purses with money inside, the television set, the radio, cleaning utensils, makeup – many little ones want to use everything the same way their parents do. Some children now leave their own toys lying somewhere in a corner. Try to work out what your little one is trying to do, even if they do not always make life easy for you.

"I saw my son pushing phone buttons for the first time today, putting the receiver to his ear, and babbling busily. A few times he said 'Dada' before hanging up."

Frankie's mom, 56th week

"My daughter picked up the phone when it rang and I was out of the room for a second and really 'talked' to her grandma."

Emily's mom, 60th week

"My little girl knows exactly which button to press to start the movie. When she comes to me with the remote control, she really prefers to press the buttons herself."

Jenny's mom, 57th week

"My son is in love with the toilet bowl. He throws all sorts of things in it, and cleans it with the brush every two minutes, drenching the bathroom floor at the same time."

Frankie's mom, 56th week

"My son brings me newspapers, empty beer bottles, and shoes. He wants me to tidy up and put them away."

Frankie's mom, 56th week

Help Your Baby Explore the New World through Toys

Many children now become interested in more complex playthings that allow them to imitate programs, such as garages with cars, trains with tracks, farmhouses with animals, dolls with diapers or clothes, tea sets with pots and pans, or play shops with packages and boxes. If your little one shows an interest in such toys, offer them opportunities to play with them. Help them once in a while. It's still a very complicated world for them.

"When I sit next to my son on the floor and encourage him, he'll sometimes build towers as high as eight blocks."

Matt's mom, 57th week

"When my daughter plays on her own and needs help, she'll call out 'Mama.' Then she'll show me what she wants me to do."

Hannah's mom, 55th week

Most children are interested in seeing the "real thing," too. For example, if your baby is interested in garages, take them to see cars being repaired. If they are interested in horses, tour a riding school. And if their tractor, crane, or boat is their favorite toy, they will certainly want to see a real one working.

Help Your Baby Explore the New World through Language and Music

When they leap into the world of programs, your child becomes fascinated by stories. You can enable them hear and see them. You could let them watch stories on television, you could let them listen to a story, or best of all, you could tell them a story yourself, with or without a picture book. Just make sure that the stories correspond with whatever your child is experiencing themselves or with their interests. For some children, this will be cars, for others it will be a special flower, animals, the swimming pool, or their cuddly toys. Keep in mind that each story must contain a short and simple program. Most little ones of this age can only concentrate on a story for about three minutes.

LEAP 8

Also offer a budding little talker the opportunity to tell their own story when you are looking at a picture book together.

> "My daughter can understand a picture in a book. She'll tell me what she sees. For instance, if she sees a kid in a picture giving a treat to another kid, she'll say, 'Yum'."
>
> **Hannah's mom, 57th week**

Many little children are eager chatterboxes. They will tell you entire "stories" complete with questions, exclamations, and pauses. And they expect a response. If your toddler is a storyteller, try to take their stories seriously, even if you are still unable to understand what they are saying. If you listen closely, you may sometimes be able to make out a real word.

> "My son talks until your ears feel like they're about to drop off. He really holds a conversation. Sometimes he'll do it in the questioning mode. It sounds really cute. I would love to know what he's trying to tell me."
>
> **Frankie's mom, 58th week**

> "My son chatters away like crazy. Sometimes he'll stop and look at me until I say something back, and then he'll continue his story. This past week, it sounded like he was saying 'Kiss,' and then he actually gave me a kiss. Now I pay 10 times more attention."
>
> **Frankie's mom, 59th week**

Many little ones love listening to children's songs as long as they are simple and short. Such songs are programs as well. If your toddler likes music, they may now want to learn how to make all the appropriate gestures too.

Some children also have a lot of fun playing their own piece of music. Drums, pianos, keyboards, and flutes seem to be their particular favorites. Naturally, most budding musicians prefer grown-up instruments, but they will be able to do less harm with a toy instrument.

Be Happy with Their Help

When you notice your child is trying to lend you a hand, then accept it. They are beginning to understand what you are doing and are learning to do their own share.

"My daughter wants to help with everything. She wants to carry the groceries, hang the dishcloth back in place when I'm done, carry the place mats and silverware to the table when I'm setting the table, and so on."

Emily's mom, 62nd week

"My daughter knows that apple juice and milk belong in the fridge and runs to the door to open it. For cookies, she goes straight to the cupboard and gets out the tin."

Jenny's mom, 57th week

Teach Them to Respect You

Many children are now beginning to understand that you can also be in the middle of a program, such as when you are busy cleaning. When you notice your baby is starting to comprehend these things, you can also start asking them to have consideration for you so that you can finish what you are doing. At this age, however, you can't expect them to wait too long.

Help Your Baby Explore the New World through Experimentation

If your toddler is a little researcher, you could see them performing the following program or experiment: How do these toys land, roll over, and bounce? Your little Einstein can go on examining these things for what seems like forever. For instance, they might pick up different toy people and drop them on the table 25 times and then repeat this up to 60 times with all sorts of building blocks. If you see your child doing this, then just let them carry on. This is their way of experimenting with the objects' characteristics in a very systematic way. They will be able to put this information to good use later on when they have to decide in the middle of a program whether to do something this way or that. Toddlers are not simply playing – they are working hard, often putting in long hours, to discover how the world works.

"When my son is doing something, for instance building, he suddenly shakes his head, says 'No,' and starts to do it in a different way."
Kevin's mom, 55th week

"My daughter gets out her little locomotive to stand on when she wants to get her things from the closet. She used to always use her chair."
Jenny's mom, 56th week

Do Remember

Breaking old habits and setting new rules are also part of developing each new skill. You can only demand of your baby that they follow the new rules they understand – no more, but also no less.

Good to Know

LEAP 8

Some children are exceptionally creative when it comes to inventing and trying out different ways to attain the same final goal. Gifted children can be particularly exhausting for their parents. They continually try to see if things can be done some other way. Whenever they fail or are forbidden to do something, they always look for another way around the problem or prohibition. It seems like a challenge to them never to do something the same way twice. They find simply repeating things boring.

Top Games for This Wonder Week

Here are games and activities that most toddlers like best now. Remember, all children are different. See what your little one responds to best.

DOING A JOB BY THEMSELVES

Many toddlers love being allowed to do something very mature all by themselves. Making a mess with water is the most popular job. Most children calm down when they play with water.

GIVING THE DOLL A BATH

Fill a baby bath or a washing-up bowl with lukewarm water. Give your child a washcloth and a bar of soap, and let them lather up their doll or cuddly toy. Washing hair is usually a very popular part of this game.

DOING DISHES

Tie an apron on your child, and put them on a chair in front of the sink. Fill the bowl with lukewarm water, and give them your dish sponge and an assortment of baby-friendly items to be washed, such as plastic plates, cups, wooden spoons, and all sorts of strainers and funnels. A nice topping of bubbles will make them even more eager to get to work. Make sure the chair they are standing on does not become slippery when wet, causing the busy one to lose their footing in their enthusiasm. Then stand back and let the fun begin.

HELPING OUT

Your toddler may prefer to do things with you. They can help prepare dinner, set the table, and shop for groceries. They will have their own ideas about the job, but they will learn a lot by doing it with you. This helps them feel grown-up and content.

UNPACKING AND PUTTING AWAY GROCERIES

Put fragile and dangerous things away first, then let your little assistant help you unpack. You can have them hand you or bring you the groceries one by one, as they choose. Or you can ask them "Could you give me the . . . please, and now the . . ."

You can also ask them where they would put things. And finally, they can close the cupboard doors when you are finished. Encourage and thank them.

HIDE-AND-SEEK GAMES

Now you can make these games more complicated than before. When your child is in the right mood, they will usually enjoy displaying their talents. Adjust the pace to your child. Make the game neither impossibly difficult nor too easy for them.

DOUBLE HIDING GAME

Place two cups in front of them and put a plaything under one of them. Then switch the cups around by sliding them across the table. This way, cup A will be where cup B was, and vice versa. The object of the exercise here is not to fool your toddler but quite the reverse. Make sure that your child is watching closely when you move the cups and encourage them to find the toy. Give them plenty of praise for each attempt. This is really very complicated for them.

SOUND GAME

Many toddlers love looking for sounds. Take your child on your lap and let them see and hear an object that can make a sound – for instance, a musical box. Then close their eyes and have someone else hide the object while it is playing. Make sure that your little one cannot see where it is being hidden. When it has vanished from sight, encourage them to look for it.

> "When I ask my daughter, 'Do you need to use your potty?' she'll use it if she really does need to. She pees, carries it to the bathroom herself, and flushes. But sometimes she'll be sitting on it, then she'll get up and pee next to her potty."
>
> **Jenny's mom, 54th week**

Show Understanding for Irrational Fears

When your little one is busy exploring their new world, they will run into things that they don't fully understand. Along the way, they discover new dangers, ones that they never imagined existed. They are still unable to talk about them, so show them a little understanding. Their fear will only disappear only when they start to understand everything better.

> "All of a sudden, my son was frightened of our ship's lamp when it was on, probably because it shines so brightly."
>
> **Paul's mom, 57th week**

> "My daughter is a little scared of the dark. Not once she is in the dark, but to walk from a lit room into a dark room."
>
> **Jenny's mom, 58th week**

> "My son gets frightened when I inflate a balloon. He doesn't get it."
>
> **Matt's mom, 58th week**

> "My daughter was frightened by a ball that was deflating."
>
> **Eve's mom, 59th week**

> "My son gets terribly frightened by loud noises, like jet airplanes, telephones, and the doorbell ringing."
>
> **Bob's mom, 55th week**

> "My daughter is scared of everything that draws near quickly. Like the parakeet, fluttering around her head, her brother chasing her, and a remote-control car belonging to her brother's friend. It was just too fast for her."
>
> **Emily's mom, 56th week**

Top Toys for This Wonder Week

Here are toys and things that most babies like best now:

- Dolls, doll strollers, and doll beds
- Farmhouses, farm animals, and fences
- Garages and cars
- Wooden trains with tracks, platforms, bridges, and tunnels
- Unbreakable tea sets
- Pots, pans, and wooden spoons
- Telephones
- Primo blocks
- Bicycles, cars, toy horses or engines that they can sit on themselves
- Push-along wagons that they can use to transport all sorts of things
- Rocking horses or rocking chairs
- Boxes with differently shaped blocks and holes
- Stackable containers and rods with stackable rings
- Mops, hand brooms, dustpans, and brushes
- Colored sponges to scrub with or play with in the bath
- Large sheets of paper and markers
- Books with animals and their young, or cars and tractors
- Musical instruments, such as drums, toy pianos, and xylophones
- Baby TV or Youtube movies with short stories

Remember at this time to put away or take precautions with closets and drawers that might contain harmful or poisonous things, knobs on audio and video equipment, electrical appliances, ovens, and lights and power outlets.

LEAP 8

After the Leap

Around 59 weeks, most toddlers become a little less troublesome than they were. Some are particularly admired for their friendly talkativeness and others for their cute eagerness to help out with the housekeeping. Most are now beginning to rely less on temper tantrums to get their own way. In short, their independence and cheerfulness assert themselves once again. With their new liveliness and mobility, however, many parents may still consider their little ones to be a bit of a handful. That's because their child thinks they know it all, but you know they still have so much to learn.

"My daughter is painstakingly precise. Everything has its own little place. If I make changes, she'll notice and put things back. She also doesn't hold onto anything anymore when she's walking. She will happily walk right across the room. To think I've been so worried over this."

Emily's mom, 60th week

"My son is perfectly happy in the playpen again. Sometimes he doesn't want to be taken out. I don't have to play along with him anymore, either. He keeps himself occupied, especially with his toy cars and puzzles. He's much more cheerful now."

Paul's mom, 60th week

"My daughter doesn't play with toys anymore; she won't even look at them. Watching, imitating, and joining in with us is much more fascinating to her now. She's enterprising as well. She gets her coat and her bag when she wants to go out and the broom when something needs cleaning. She's very mature."

Nina's mom, 58th week

"Now that my son runs like the wind and wanders through the entire apartment, he also does a lot of things he shouldn't. He keeps putting away cups, beer bottles, and shoes, and he can be extremely imaginative. If I take my eye off him for a moment, those things end up in the trash can or the toilet. Then when I scold him, he gets very sad."

Frankie's mom, 59th week

"My daughter is such a lovely little girl, the way she plays, chit-chatting away. She's often so full of joy. Those temper tantrums seem like a thing of the past. But perhaps I'd better knock on wood."

Ashley's mom, 59th week

LEAP 9

Wonder Week 64

The World of Principles

**THE CONSCIENCE
EMERGES...**

After the previous leap, your little one began to understand what a "program" is. Your daily programs of eating, shopping, taking a stroll, playing, and washing the dishes seem normal to them at this stage. Sometimes they appear to be following your lead and other times they grab the opportunity to show you what they can do. You might also have noticed that your little helper has a slightly different approach to household chores than you have. They use a piece of string to 'vacuum'. They use a rag to 'mop', wetting it in their mouth. And, they 'clear up' by using their magical powers to banish anything and everything in their way to that one special out-of-the-way spot: the bathroom, the trash or over the balcony. No more mess. Your little helper is still bound by certain strict routines, which tend to be a tad mechanical in nature. They are therefore, just a beginner in the complex world of programs. They are not yet able to adapt the program they are carrying out to different circumstances. It will require several years of experience before they become proficient in such matters.

As adults, we have the benefit of experience. You are able to adapt to change. You vary the order in which you do things. While grocery shopping, you opt for the short line at the butcher instead of joining a long line at the deli counter. Whether you are in a hurry or you want special ingredients for a recipe, you adapt. We also adapt our programs to those around us. If anyone asks your opinion, you measure your response in kind, given their status and age. You also adapt your mood or the direction you want your moods to go. You prepare a meal in different ways depending on whether you have time to relax and enjoy it or whether you have to rush off to an important meeting. You anticipate everything happening around you that concerns you. You know what you want and how best to get it. You make sure that you achieve your goals. It's because of this that your programs appear to be so flexible and natural.

Note: *The first phase (fussy period) of this leap into the perceptual world of "principles" is age-linked and predictable, and starts between 59 and 63 weeks. Most babies start the second phase (see box "Quality Time: An Unnatural Whim" on page 17) of this leap 64 weeks after full-term birth. The first perception of the world of principles sets in motion the development of a whole range of skills and activities. However, the age at which these skills and activities appear for the first time varies greatly and depends on your baby's preferences, experimentation and physical development. For example, the ability to perceive principles is a necessary precondition for "pretending to cook for their dolls," but this activity normally appears at anywhere from 64 weeks to many months later. The skills and activities in this chapter are stated at the earliest possible age they could appear so you can watch for and recognize them. (They may be rudimentary at first.) This way you can respond to and facilitate your baby's development.*

Your little angel will start to pick up on how they can better deal with certain situations as soon as they take their next leap. They will land in the world of "principles." Around 64 weeks – approaching 15 months – you will notice them stepping up to try new things. It is a leap that previously revealed itself to your little angel. Around 61 weeks – 14 months – your little one starts noticing that "things are changing." A maze of new impressions is turning their reality on its head. Initially, it's quite a task for them to deal with the changes. First, they will have to create some order in this new-found chaos. They return to familiar surroundings. They become clingy. They need a "mommy or daddy refill."

Do Remember

If your little one becomes clingy, watch for new skills or for them attempting new things

This Week's Fussy Signs

Is your baby quick to cry? Many parents complain that they rarely hear their baby laugh any more. They label their toddler now as "earnest more often" or "sad more often." The moments of sadness are unexpected, and are usually short lived with no clear cause.

"This week he cried a lot. Why? I don't know. All of a sudden he burst out in tears."
Gregory's mom, 64th week, or 14½ months

Your little one could also be irritable, impatient, frustrated or angry; for instance, if they even think that mommy or daddy is not standing by at their beck and call, or if mommy or daddy does not understand what they want

LEAP 9

or say, or if mommy or daddy corrects them or tells them "NO!" This could even happen if their latest building project was to topple or if a chair refuses to move or if they run into a table.

"If she does not receive my direct attention, she sprawls out on the ground bawling."

Josie's mom, 62nd week, or 14 months

"She is more quickly irritated, angry and impatient than she was. If she wants to tell me something and I don't fully understand what she wants, she starts to scream and fuss even louder."

Eve's mom, 64th week, or 14½ months

"He was very whiny this week. His crying became louder and more insistent if he didn't get his way or if he was made to wait. The same was the case if my hands were full and I was unable to pick him up."

Kevin's mom, 65th week, or approaching 15 months

"He is really struggling. If he is unable to do something right the first time, he throws a tantrum."

Gregory's mom, 66th week, or 15 months

How You Know it's Time to Grow

Here are some of the signals that your baby may give you to let you know they're approaching this leap into the world of principles.

They May Cling to Your Clothes

Most toddlers do whatever is necessary to be around mommy and daddy. But little kids become bigger. Occasionally, some toddlers are content if they can tempt mommy and daddy into a game of briefly making eye contact and then looking away. This is a considerable step towards independence. However, more often than not, the toddler is more like a small baby. They are only happy if sitting on a lap or being carried around. Sometimes when they are especially clingy, mother may decide that the best form of transport is the baby carrier – and the little clinger happily submits.

"He followed me constantly, dragging his toy. If I stood still or sat down, he would play at my feet or even under them. It began to wear on me."

Kevin's mom, 62nd week, or 14 months

"She constantly wanted to climb on my lap, but that was inconvenient because I was ironing. I put her in the center of the room a few times with her toys, but no, she only had eyes for my lap. The next time she went for my lap, she caught the cord of the iron bringing it down on my foot. Because she was tangled in the cord, I was unable to get the iron off my foot right away, which made me shout in pain. She then clamped on to my leg and let out a cry. By the time I had finally freed myself, she was so upset that I had to carry her with me to the bathroom so that I could put my foot under some cold running water. Lesson one: no ironing with her around!"

Julia's mom, 63rd week, or 14 months and a week

"He loves to get my attention from a short distance, just glancing at each other. He glows from our mutual relationship."

Luke's mom 63rd week, or 14 months and a week

LEAP 9

"This week he clung to me, literally. He climbed up my back, hung in my hair, crawled up against me. He sat between my legs and clamped on so that I was unable to take a step. All the while, making a game of it, and making it difficult to become impatient. And, in the meantime, he had it his way."

Matt's mom, 65th week, or approaching 15 months

"He crawls onto my lap more often now, but doesn't stay there. Even if he is walking around he likes to be picked up for a bit."

Frankie's mom, 66th week, or 15 months

They May be Shyer with Strangers Than Before

Most children don't stray from their mother or father's side when in the company of strangers. Some seem to try to climb back into mommy. They certainly don't want to be picked up by another person. Their mother is the only one who may touch them, sometimes the only one who can talk to them, even father may be too much. Mostly, they seem frightened. You think sometimes that they are becoming shy.

"When we are visiting or we have guests, he stays right around me for a while before slowly venturing further. But as soon as it even looks like someone else wants to pick him up, he hurries to me to cling for a while."

Gregory's mom, 64th week, or 14½ months

"He is shy with strangers. If there is a group, he crawls and puts his head between my legs and stays there for a bit."

Kevin's mom, 63rd week, or 14 months and a week

"He cries if I leave him in a room with other people. If I go to the kitchen, so does he. Especially today, he never left my side, and this while his grandmother was in the room. He knows his grandmother well and sees her every day."

Frankie's mom, 63rd week, or 14 months and a week

> "Even if her father wants her attention, she turns her head away. And when he puts her in her bath, she starts to scream. She only wants to be with me."
>
> **Josie's mom, 64th week, or 14½ months**

They May Want Physical Contact to Be as Close as Possible

Often a small child does not want the distance between them and their mother or father to increase. If anyone is going to go anywhere, then the toddler wants to be the one. Mommy or daddy must remain exactly where they are and not move one bit.

> "She hates when I leave. She doesn't even want me getting up for a shower. If when I get out of bed in the morning she is left with her father, she starts shrieking. I have to take her if I want to get out of bed. She never did that before."
>
> **Laura's mom, 62nd week, or 14 months**

> "When I take her to daycare and try to leave, she cries her eyes out. She only did that in the beginning though."
>
> **Ashley's mom, 65th week, or approaching 15 months**

> "He gets angry when I drop him at daycare and he lets me know when I pick him up. He ignores me for a while, as if I don't exist. However, when he is done with ignoring me, he is really sweet and snuggles up by putting his head on my shoulder!"
>
> **Mark's mom, 66th week, or 15 months**

They May Want to Be Entertained

Most toddlers don't like to play alone. They want mommy or daddy to play along. They don't want to feel alone and will follow mommy or daddy if they

walk away. With this behavior, what they are really saying is: "If you don't feel like playing with me, then I'll just tag along with you." And because mommy's tasks are usually domestic, household tasks are very popular, although not for every child. Now and then some clever little one thinks up a new strategy with a playful trick or antic to lure mother to play. Such an enterprise is difficult to resist. Even though mother may be held up with her work, they are willing to overlook it. Her toddler is already getting big.

"When it is least convenient, he wants us to listen to a Children's Song. I have to snuggle up to him, grin and bear it. Even peeking in a magazine is out of the question."
Robin's mom, 63rd week, or 14 months and a week

"She hardly plays anymore, she follows me around constantly. Just wants to see what I'm doing around the house and put her nose in the middle of it."
Jenny's mom, 64th week, or 14½ months

"He almost never wanted to play by himself. The whole day long it was horse riding and mommy was the horse. He kept me occupied with cute little ploys, all the while thinking that I wasn't on to his little game."
Matt's mom, 65th week, or approaching 15 months

They May Be Jealous

Sometimes toddlers want extra attention from their mother or father when they are in the company of others – especially if the others are children, otherwise, they become insecure. They want mommy or daddy for themselves, they must be the center of their mother or father's attention.

> "He particularly wants my attention when I'm around others, especially if the others are children. Then he gets jealous. He does listen though if I tell him that it's time to go and play by himself, but he stays around me."
>
> **Thomas' mom, 61st week, or 14 months**

> "Sometimes he gets jealous if another child is on my lap. I never saw him do this before."
>
> **Taylor's mom, 62nd week, or 14 months**

They May Be Moody

Some parents notice that their little one's mood can completely change very quickly. One moment the little chameleon is grumpy, the next they are all smiles. One minute they are very cuddly, the next so angry that they sweep their cup clean off the table, then they can become sad with gushing tears, and so on. You could say that your toddler is practicing for puberty. Little ones at this age are capable of many forms of behavior to express their feelings. And a child that is at odds with themselves tries them all.

> "She went back and forth from sulky to cheerful, clingy to independent, earnest to silly, unruly to compliant. And all these different moods took turns as if everything was completely normal. It was quite a chore."
>
> **Juliette's mom, 62nd week, or 14 months**

> "One moment he is into mischief, the next he's an example of obedience. One moment he is hitting me, the next he is kissing me. One moment he insists on doing everything himself and the next he's pitiful and needs my help."
>
> **Mark's mom, 65th week, or approaching 15 months**

LEAP 9

They May Sleep Poorly

Many little ones sleep less well at this stage. They don't want to go to bed and cry when it's time, even during the day. Some parents say their child's entire sleeping pattern seems to have changed. They suspect that their child is on the verge of moving from two naps a day to one. Although the children do fall asleep, many mothers and fathers are not at peace. The poor sleepers cry in their sleep, or they regularly wake up seeming helpless. They are clearly afraid of something. Sometimes they fall back asleep if comforted. But some little ones only want to continue sleeping if mom stays with them or if they can occupy the precious spot between mom and dad in the big bed.

"Because she doesn't want to take daytime naps anymore, I put her with me in my bed during the day, thinking perhaps that would help. Nope. We ended up getting out of bed again. Result: She and I were dead tired! I think she is bordering on moving from two naps to one."

Josie's mom, 62nd week, or 14 months

"If she wakes up during the night, she clamps herself onto me. As if she were afraid."

Jenny's mom, 62nd week, or 14 months

"Sleeping was hopeless. He slept a lot, but he was tossing and turning. I kept hearing his cries. It didn't seem like he was getting his rest."

Mark's mom, 63rd week, or 14 months and a week

"She gets very busy, bothersome and tries to bite when bedtime comes. It seems like she doesn't want to sleep by herself. It takes some doing. After crying a while, she does finally fall asleep, but after that I'm mentally drained. Last night, she slept in between us. She spreads out with an arm and a leg on daddy and an arm and a leg on mommy."

Emily's mom, 64th week, or 14½ months

"It seems like he requires less sleep now. He goes to bed later. He's also awake for half an hour every night. Then he wants to play."

Gregory's mom, 65th week, or approaching 15 months

They May Have "Nightmares"

Many toddlers have nightmares more often than before. Sometimes they wake up looking helpless, sometimes afraid or in a panic. And other times very frustrated, angry or hot-tempered.

"Twice this week he woke up screeching, covered in sweat and completely in a panic. It took him half an hour to stop crying. He was practically inconsolable. This has never happened before. I also noticed that it took him a while before being at ease again."

Gregory's mom, 62nd week, or 14 months

"At night he was often awake. He seemed helpless or really in a panic. One night he slept with me because he couldn't shake his anxiety. Lying next to me relaxes him."

Thomas' mom, 62nd week, or 14 months

"I saw that she was sound asleep, went downstairs and all of a sudden I hear a thump and loud screaming. I ran back upstairs and when I picked her up to console her, she was in the middle of a fit. She rolled on the ground, kicking and screaming. I tried to hold her close to me, but she resisted with everything she had. She simply had to get rid of her rage, which took a very long time."

Julia's mom, 64th week, or 14½ months

They May "Daydream"

Sometimes little ones sit staring off in the distance. It's a time of self-reflection.

"I noticed that he was rather quiet. He sat there staring. He'd never done that before."

Thomas's mom, 63rd week, or 14 months and a week

LEAP 9

They May Lose Their Appetite

Not all toddlers have the best eating habits. Sometimes they simply skip a meal. Mothers find it difficult if their child does not eat well, and this gives the little one the attention they need. Breastfeeding toddlers, however, do seem to want to feed more often. But as soon as they have sucked a little, they let go of the nipple and look around, or they just hold the nipple in their mouth. After all, they are where they want to be: with their mom.

They May Be More Babyish Again

It could seem like your toddler is a baby again. That's not really the case. Regression during a clingy period means that progress is coming. And because children at this age are capable of so much more, a regression is more evident.

"He's crawling more often again."

Luke's mom, 63rd week, or 14 months and a week

"She is ready for her playpen again, full of baby toys!"

Hannah's mom, 63rd week, or 14 months and a week

"If we timed it right and asked if she needed to pee, she would generally go to her potty, but now she is back to solely using diapers. As if she has completely forgotten how."

Jenny's mom, 62nd week, or 14 months

"I am back to giving her bottles like when she was a baby. She won't even hold it herself."

Emily's mom, 62nd week, or 14 months

They May Act Unusually Sweet

Some parents succumb to a generous hug, kiss or barrage of petting from their children. The little ones have certainly noticed that it's more difficult for mother or father to resist these displays of affection than the whining, clinging and being a nuisance. And this way they can "fill-up on mommy and daddy" if need be.

"Now he climbs up behind me in the chair and proceeds on to my neck to give me a massive hug."

Matt's mom, 63rd week, or 14 months and a week

"Sometimes she is really affectionate. She comes and hugs with one arm around my neck, pressing her cheek into mine, strokes my face and kisses me. Even strokes and kisses the fur collar on my coat. She was never this affectionate before."

Nina's mom, 65th week, or approaching 15 months

They May Reach for a Cuddly Object More Often

Sometimes toddlers use blankets, stuffed animals and all things soft to snuggle. They especially do this if their mother or father is busy.

They May Be Mischievous

Many toddlers are naughty on purpose. Being naughty is the perfect way to get attention. If something breaks, is dirty or dangerous, or if the house gets turned upside down, mommy and daddy will have to address this misbehavior. This is a covert way of getting a "mommy or daddy refill."

"She is not allowed to touch the stereo, TV or other such devices. She knows they're off limits! She gets one warning and then a swat on her fingers."
Vera's mom, 62nd week, or 14 months

"I was really angry when he deliberately threw some things over our balcony. There's no getting the things back because they landed in the water below. After that, if he did it again, I snatched him up and put him in his playpen explaining that such things are not allowed."
Luke's mom, 62nd week, or 14 months

"She purposefully misbehaves. She lays her hands precisely where she knows that they are not allowed. She shakes the gate for the stairs (it is destroyed by now), pulled out the knitting needles from my knitting, just for starters. It's really getting on my nerves."
Vera's mom, 65th week, or approaching 15 months

"He repeatedly has periods where he only does what is not allowed. I am left doing nothing but saying 'No' and keeping an eye on him."
Gregory's mom, 66th week, or 15 months

They May Have More Temper Tantrums Than Before

Many toddlers get more irritable, angry and out of sorts quicker than parents are used to from them. These little ones roll kicking and screaming on the ground if they don't get their way, if they can't manage something first time, if they are not understood directly, or even without any clear reason at all.

"She had her first temper tantrum. It's the newest thing. At first we thought that it was teething pain. She dropped to her knees and began screeching. It turned out to be a temper tantrum. No walk in the park!"
Josie's mom, 63rd week, or 14 months and a week

"When his father put him back in bed at 5:30 A.M., he really threw a fit. He obviously had other plans than we did."
Frankie's mom, 62nd week, or 14 months

"She wanted to eat without any help and we didn't get it at first. She screamed, started kicking and practically broke her chair. I had no idea that she could be such a pain. Quite a trial!"
Nina's mom, 62nd week, or 14 months

"When we're around other people, I can't move away an inch or he'll fall to the ground and throw a fit."
Frankie's mom, 63rd week, or 14 months and a week

"If she doesn't get her way, she throws herself to the ground screeching and refuses to sit or stand up. Then I pick her up and draw her attention to something else."
Julia's mom, 62nd week, or 14 months

LEAP 9

My Diary

Signs My Baby Is Growing Again

Between 59 and 63 weeks, your child may show signs that they are ready to make the next leap, into the world of principles.

- ☐ Cries more often and is cranky or fretful more often than before
- ☐ Is cheerful one moment and cries the next
- ☐ Wants to be entertained, or does so more often than usual
- ☐ Clings to your clothes or wants to be closer to you now
- ☐ Acts unusually sweet
- ☐ Is mischievous
- ☐ Throws temper tantrums, or throws them more often than before
- ☐ Is jealous
- ☐ Is more obviously shy with strangers than you are used to seeing
- ☐ Wants physical contact to be tighter or closer than before
- ☐ Sleeps poorly
- ☐ Has nightmares, or has them more often than before
- ☐ Loses appetite
- ☐ Sometimes just sits there, quietly daydreaming
- ☐ Reaches for a cuddly toy, or does so more often than usual
- ☐ Is more babyish than they were
- ☐ Resists getting dressed

OTHER CHANGES YOU NOTICE

How This Leap May Affect You

You May Become Really Frustrated

Parents clearly have less patience with clinging, whining and provocation from a child of this age. When they were still a little baby, such behavior made them worry. Now it annoys them.

"She never had problems sleeping before. Now she does. For the last couple of nights it's been nothing but crying. I am completely annoyed by it. The evenings are my time and now she is dominating them too. Hope this doesn't become a habit."

Maria's mom, 69th week, or approaching 16 months

The moment parents get annoyed, they will show it. At this age, a persistent toddler will hear when their parents disapproves of their behavior. Using words the baby understands, mothers explain what they don't like. Language starts to play a greater role in this. And a whining nuisance is quicker to land in their playpen or in their bed than when they were younger. Mother's and father's patience is shorter. Parents think that their child is big enough to behave better. Additionally, they think that their toddlers should learn to be more considerate of them.

"I have arranged that she stay with a nanny. It really annoys me that she clamps on to me when we go somewhere. All the other children are running around and playing with toys. She rarely does that. Only after she's stood aside and observed long enough does she begin to let go of my dress. I only hope that she can get over the clinging when she goes to the babysitter."

Julia's mom, 64th week, or 14½ months

"When I am cooking, he comes and sits right at my feet. If it becomes too much and he doesn't want to move out of the way when I ask, I put him in his playpen. Then my patience has run out."

Frankie's mom, 64th week, or 14½ months

"He constantly wants to climb on my lap and, even better, go on the nipple-preferably from sun up till sun down. It really bothers me. First, I try to get him off me a bit by playfully distracting him. But if he continues coming and pulling on me, he has a good chance of winding up in bed. It just gets to be too much."

Robin's mom, 65th week, or approaching 15 months

"Sometimes he wants to be picked up at the very moment I am busy with something and that bothers me. I try to explain in simple terms why I can't pick him up. And explaining helps!"

Gregory's mom, 65th week, or approaching 15 months

"I can get rather perturbed when he pretends not to hear what I say. I grab him and turn him to face me, so that he has to look at me and listen when I say something."

Taylor's mom, 65th week, or approaching 15 months

"If he persists in being naughty, doesn't know what he wants, cries for any little thing and doesn't listen to what I say, I assume that he is very tired and that it's time to go to bed. I need to let off a bit of steam, because then my patience is at its end."

Taylor's mom, 67th week, or 15 months and a week

You May Argue

Your toddler is getting bigger. More and more often they and their mother and father do not see eye-to-eye. If they are not allowed to interrupt, to cling or to be unruly, they rebel fiercely, and this results in real quarrels. Such an eruption is most likely at the end of the difficult period. That's when both the parents and child are most short tempered.

"We just had a real fight! He kept grabbing the kittens and pushing them around the floor like toy cars. I had to stop him."

Mark's mom, 63rd week, or 14 months and a week

Luke's mom, 63rd week, or 14 months and a week

"She's driving us nuts. She cries a lot and requires constant attention from 7 in the morning until 10:30 at night. Sometimes, a good smack on the bottom is really necessary. Trying to talk to her is like talking to a brick wall; she won't listen. Her naps are only an hour and a half. We don't have time for ourselves or each other any more because she practically runs our lives. Maybe we should pay less attention to her. I'd like to know if other children are this difficult at this age. We never hear other parents complaining. We're out of ideas. At the moment, we're finding parenthood a rather thankless task."

Jenny's mom, 65th week, or approaching 15 months

If your baby seeks attention in such a willful way, it can make you desperate. That is quite normal. However, you should not react in desperation. Hurting your baby or child is never a good way to teach them the rules.

"If he doesn't get his way, he gets furious and hits me. That has been bothering me for some time and now my patience had reached its end. I gave him a rap so that he could just feel it. Then I explained to him at length that the hitting must stop."

Mark's mom, 65th week, or approaching 15 months

Your child does what you do. If they are not allowed to hit you, then you shouldn't hit them. If you hit your child, then there's not much sense in saying that they shouldn't strike out. Your words must match your actions. Hitting solves nothing and it's not good for your little one.

LEAP 9

"She refuses to listen and that can really get tedious or dangerous. Sometimes she needs a rap. But a rap doesn't always work. This week as things were already heated, I said, 'Mommy doesn't like you now, go away,' and her reaction got to me. She started crying uncontrollably. She really was mortified, worse than a rap. I hope that I never say that again in desperation. I didn't mean for it to be taken so literally."

Jenny's mom, 66th week, or 15 months

How Your Baby's New Skills Emerge

Around 64 weeks – almost 15 months – you will notice that much of the clinginess starts to disappear. Your toddler is a bit more enterprising again. Perhaps you already see that they are different, and act differently. They are getting much more willful. They think differently. They handle their toys differently. Their sense of humor has changed. You see these changes because, at this age, your toddler's ability to observe and implement "principles" is breaking through. Getting this ability is comparable with discovering a whole new world. Your toddler, with their talents, preferences and temperament, chooses where they want to begin. Find out where they are going and help them with it. This new ability they have acquired sometimes "gives them a headache," to use a figure of speech.

"He doesn't want to sit on my lap as much, he's active again."

Thomas' mom, 67th week, or 15 months and a week

"All listlessness and bad moods have passed. She even was happy to go to daycare. The difficult period has passed."

Josie's mom, 66th week, or 15 months

"Sometimes I worry. I have the feeling that he is busy inside. In a way he keeps more to himself. But at the same time, he does like to be near me. Not to do anything together, but just to be near me."

Luke's mom, 67th week, or 15 months and a week

Compared to before, they play longer by themselves and are calmer, more focused, more solemn, enterprising, testing, observant, and independent in the sense that they do things by themselves. They are less interested in toys now. Their interests are more towards the domestic. Furthermore, they really like being outside just wandering and exploring. They do need you to be around, though.

The Magical Leap Forward

Now that your toddler takes their first steps into the world of "principles," you will notice they complete various "programs" more smoothly and naturally than before. You can now understand what they are doing and what they want. Principles will influence their thought process. They start to get on top of things, just like a teacher has to be on top of things in order to be able to explain them. Your child is no longer "caught up" in a program, but rather they can "create" or change and judge for themselves what's what. They start to think about programs. And just as when executing programs, they deliberate each move and decide if they will do it this way or that. In the world of principles your little one starts thinking about thinking. They are busier in their heads. And they feel that.

"He's feeling his way with his head. Literally. Several things he touches with his forehead: the ground, the table leg, a book, his plate and so forth. He calls to show me. I can't follow him. Certain times I think he wants to say that you can bump into these things. Other times it seems to be the start of a new way of thinking, as if he feels that he can mentally comprehend the world."

Luke's mom, 67th week, or 15 months and a week

In the world of principles your little one will think ahead, contemplate, consider the consequences of their actions, make plans and evaluate them. They will come up with strategies: "Should I ask Dad or Grandma to get the candy?" "How can I create a subtle delay?" Naturally, your toddler is not very adept at devising plans, nor are they as complex as ours. As adults, it has taken us years to master this. Through practice, every one of us has learned principles by executing programs and confronting several thousand different situations. Your little rookie can't fully comprehend the meaning of so many new things. As an "Alice in Wonderland," they wander the complicated world of principles. It begins to sink in that from morning till night they will have to make choices. They notice that it's unavoidable: they must choose, choose and choose again. Perhaps you have noticed your little one endlessly hesitating over what they should do. Thinking is a full-time job.

"He now realizes that he has to make all kinds of choices the whole day through. He chooses very consciously and takes his time. He hesitates endlessly if he should turn on the TV, or perhaps not. If he should throw something off the balcony, or better not. If he will sleep in the big bed or the little one, and if he will sit with his father or with me. And so on."

Luke's mom, 67th week, or 15 months and a week

In the world of principles your child not only has to choose what they will do, but while they are doing it, they must continually make choices: "Should I wreck my tower, just leave it or build it higher?" And if they choose the latter, they must choose how to do it: "Should I put a block on my tower next or a doll or this time?" With everything they do, they will have to choose: "Should I go about it carefully, sloppily, recklessly, quickly, wildly, dangerously or carefully?" If mother or father thinks that it is bedtime, they will have to choose whether to go along quietly or whether to try to delay it. Again, they must choose: "Which is the best strategy for keeping me out of bed the longest? Just scampering away as fast as I can? Pull a plant out of its pot? Or pull some other stunt?" And if they know full well that something is not allowed, they must choose whether or not to just go for it or whether to wait until the coast is clear. They contemplate, choose, test and make mom and dad desperate.

With all these choices, it dawns on your toddler that they too can manage things, just like mom, dad and everyone else. They become possessive as well. They don't readily share their toys, especially not with other children. They now count as a person. They are kings and queens of their own world. Their own will is on overtime. One moment they decide to place a full cup on the table carefully and the next they let the cup fall down and spill the contents. One moment they try to get a cookie off their mother or father with kisses and caresses. The next moment they opt for a less subtle approach, and mother or father has no idea that their toddler is after a cookie! Your toddler is full of surprises. By using their whole arsenal and by studying your and others' reactions, your little terror discovers that the various strategies they employ give different results. So, your toddler discovers when they can best be friendly, helpful, aggressive, assertive, careful or polite. And that's not all. Your child thinks up some of the strategies by themselves, others they imitate: "Oh, that kid hit their mother, should I try that?" Your toddler wanders around in the world of principles and really needs mom and others in their learning process.

We adults already have years of experience in the world of principles. We have become skilled in this world through trial and error. We know, for example, what justice, kindness, humanity, helpfulness, ingenuity, moderation, thriftiness, trust, frugality, caution, cooperation, care, empowerment, assertiveness, patience and caring mean to us. We know what it means to be considerate of others, to be efficient, to cooperate, to be loving, respectful and we know how to put others at ease. Yet we don't all interpret these principles in the same way. We know, for instance, that it is polite to shake hands when we introduce ourselves – that is, in the Dutch culture. In England, however, people do not expect a handshake; there, a nod and a greeting are sufficient. And in Tanzania, people expect both hands; one hand is just a half-offering. We fulfill our principles according to our personality, family and the culture in which we have grown up.

In general, you could say that when pursuing a certain goal, a principle is a common strategy that we use without having to go through all the specific steps one by one. The previous examples are mainly moral principles, which deal with standards and values. But there are other types of principles that

concern the way we do things. For example, there are the strategies you use when playing a board game. Another example is that when planning a weekend trip, you plan for enough time to sleep. Yet another example is the principle that when writing an article, you must take your intended audience into account. Or the principle of keeping dual accounting, or developing a musical "theme." Then there are the laws of nature that dictate how things move, chemical equations describing how complex matter is built up by simple elements, or the geology that describes the movements of the earth's crust. All these belong to what we call the world of principles.

Your toddler is naturally nowhere near being ready for such adult applications of principles, such as strategy in chess, laws of nature or grown-up standards or norms. Those are all very big words that we don't usually associate with toddlers. But in their own rudimentary way, your one gets started in the world of principles. They have already devised strategies to get to stay up longer! And some toddlers spend all day playing with toy cars, watching them descend an incline.

There can be stark differences with the way in which an adult handles a principle in practice. We constantly ready ourselves for the changing conditions that present themselves. Thus, we are not always patient, careful or thrifty, and as caring, careful and respectful towards everyone in the same way. That wouldn't be prudent. Sometimes for instance we find it less important to be open with someone, at other times we find it more important to consider another's situation or age. Suppose your spouse and your toddler both give you a drawing of an ape and look at you full of expectation. You will most likely be more honest with your spouse. You might even tell them that they should stick to their day job. But you praise the little scribbler for their effort. Even if you can't tell what it is, you say that this is the most charming ape you've ever seen. And as a show of appreciation, you put the ape up on the fridge. Without even thinking about

it, you took the maker's age into account. It wouldn't have been beneficial if you had been forthcoming with your toddler. You might have permanently destroyed their will to draw.

At this age your toddler can't yet prepare themselves for all the various conditions. They have yet to acquire the subtleness. They are still attached to the strategies that they first learned. This is because they have just gotten their first whiff of principles and they are only able to apply them in set ways. It's only after they have made their next leap that will you notice your child beginning to become more adaptable to their surroundings. They will adapt their strategy. Just like your child was able to grasp the programs after making their leap into the world of principles, your toddler will, after the next leap, grasp that they can choose what they want to be: honest, friendly, helpful, careful, patient, resourceful, efficient, just, caring or frugal. And that they can choose to be none or all of those things. They begin to understand that they can pay attention to grandpa, or that they don't have to, that they can comfort a friend, or choose not to. Or, that they can treat the dog gently, or they can be rough, that they can be polite to the neighbor and cooperate with mother and father, or not...

"Nora snuck off! Grandma was cooking and she was playing sweetly with her doll and things. Slowly she expanded the bounds of her territory to the hall. But she was not planning on stopping there. She must have closed the hall door very quietly and with the same skill, opened the front door. Grandma found it all too quiet in the hall. She looked around and the closed door made her fear the worst. She ran outside before knowing what to do. Two streets down she saw her. She was running like a rabbit behind her buggy with her baby doll into the wide world, far away from Grandma's house. When she saw Grandma, she was very startled and began a loud protest: 'Nora doesn't like this! Nora doesn't like this!' She wanted to continue on wandering on her own. She couldn't stand getting caught. From now on Grandma's front door will be locked."

Nora's mom, 87th week, or 20 months

"She has been wanting to give the bathroom a good going over, but had yet to succeed. All of a sudden, she found a solution to her cleaning urge. Suddenly, we heard the door to bathroom lock and this enormous cleaning sound emerged from the smallest room. There was scrubbing, flushing and waist bins rattling. A flush, and another and another. The splashing of water brought the whole family knocking and calling at the door. But however much Grandpa, Grandma and I begged, the door remained locked with the continuing sound of cleaning from inside. Slowly some water seeped under the door. But the door stayed shut. Some twenty minutes later the door opened and out came the little cleaning lady. Soaking wet, proud and satisfied: 'All done,' she said and walked away. Everything was wet—the walls, the commode, the floor. The rolls of toilet paper lay in the toilet and sheets of toilet paper were stuck on the wall. And on the floor lay a pan, a brush and a towel. She had prepared well for the job."

Angela's mom, 92nd week, or 21 months

Brain Changes

From U.S. research on 408 identical twins it was concluded that around 14 months of age there was clear hereditary influence upon mental development. The development concerned both non-verbal skills as well as speech comprehension.

Your Toddler's Choices: A Key to Their Personality

All toddlers have been given the ability to perceive and uphold principles. They need years in order to completely familiarize themselves with the wide range of new skills they have to play with, but as toddlers they take their first tender steps in the world of principles. At this age, for example, your toddler chooses how they will go about things: carefully or recklessly. They choose whether or not to pay heed to mother and father or to try to get their own way with a fit of obstinacy. In short, they choose which strategy they will use to reach the goal they set for themselves. And like every other toddler, first they choose that which best suits their talents, mobility, preferences and their particular circumstances. The very first choices become apparent when they are 64 weeks or almost 15 months old. Don't compare your child with other toddlers. Each child is unique and will choose differently.

Take a good look at your toddler. Establish what their interests are. Use the list in "My Diary" on pages 332-333 to mark or highlight what your child selects. You could also look to see if there are any principles you think your child could use or learn. Stop marking when your child begins with the next leap. That is usually when they are 71 weeks old, or 16½ months.

Toddlers Are Like This

Your toddler will like anything that's new to them best of all. Therefore, always react to new skills and interests your toddler shows. In that way they learn more pleasantly, easier, quicker and more.

What you Can Do to Help

In the world of principles your toddler will discover that there are several ways to accomplish a goal. All the strategies they can utilize: "Should I do it carefully, recklessly, pushy or sweetly? Or should I try a prank?" Your little one is becoming more resourceful. They owe this to the fact that they are

(continued on page 334)

My Diary

How My Baby Explores the New World of Principles

EXERCISING THEIR OWN WILL

☐ Chooses consciously

☐ Takes initiatives

☐ Wants a say if others do something

☐ Feels more need to belong now, to be accepted

☐ Possessive with toys

☐ Other things that I have noticed:

COPYING AND IMITATING

☐ Observes grownups

☐ Observes other children

☐ Imitates sweet behavior

☐ Imitates aggressive behavior

☐ Imitates overt physical actions, like somersaults, climbing

☐ Imitates subtle motor skills, like holding a pencil

☐ Imitates "oddities," like limping, walking like a hunchback

☐ Imitates what they see on TV or in a book

☐ Other things that I have noticed:

PRACTICING STRATEGIES, EXPLORING LIMITS AND BECOMING RESOURCEFUL

☐ Experiments with motor skills

☐ Experiments with stashing and recovering objects

☐ Experiments with crawling in or behind something and getting out again

☐ Experiments with manipulating things with caution and care

☐ Experiments with making choices: What shall I choose?

☐ Experiments with the meaning of "Yes" and "No"

- ☐ Experiments with fooling mother or father; acts disobediently to get a reaction
- ☐ Experiments with ramps and rises; feels with their finger and studies them or runs their cars up and down them
- ☐ Other things that I have noticed:

IMPLEMENTING STRATEGIES AND TACTICS

- ☐ Is or tries to be helpful (more often than unhelpful)
- ☐ Is or does their best to be obedient (more often than naughty)
- ☐ Is or tries to be careful (more often than not careful) and caring
- ☐ Accepts (more often than not) that they are still small, require help and therefore must obey. Grasps, for instance, that streets are dangerous and therefore they must walk hand and hand
- ☐ Plays around to get something or to get others to do something
- ☐ Is extra sweet (more often than not) to get their way
- ☐ Tries to get their way by being pushy (more often than before)
- ☐ Shows their feelings in fits of obstinacy (more often than before)
- ☐ Does what they feel like, goes their own way (more often than before)
- ☐ Makes use of others to get something done they were otherwise unable to do and that mom disapproved of; for instance, "Perhaps Dad will give me a cookie?"
- ☐ Other things that I have noticed:

OTHER CHANGES YOU NOTICE

LEAP 9

quickly growing sharper in all areas. They begin walking more adeptly and are able to get around quickly. They understand you better now and can sometimes answer back. They practice playing with their emotions, and not always around you. They can think ahead and know that they count as a person, too. They are better at eating and drinking, with cleaning up, building towers, putting things together, pushing and kicking other kids than ever before. Their throwing aim has improved, as have other things. Everything will come more naturally to them in the coming weeks. And, they will continue to use new strategies to get to their objectives. Of course, not every strategy your child thinks up achieves the desired effect, that requires time and practice. By trying things out, your toddler realizes that various strategies bring different results. Some are a smashing success, others the opposite and most are just so-so. Give your child the opportunity to experiment with all sorts of strategies, to test them out and reflect on them. The only way they will learn how to behave in certain situations is being resourceful, by gauging your reaction and through lots of practice.

Skillfulness

Physical Antics

When your toddler is trying to make their way in the world of principles, they will also want to know what their little body is capable of – in other words, how to use their body when they want to be quick, slow, careful, funny or clever. Your little one will be experimenting with their body. They will test its capabilities. Which stunts can my body do? Can I fit between there? How do I climb the stairs? How do I go down? How do I go down the slide? Is that a good spot to lay down, between the toys and furniture? How strong am I? In short, your little one is becoming resourceful with their body. They sometimes appear reckless, which frightens mother and father.

"She goes up and down a step upright. She practices that the whole day through. Now I keep my eyes open for other objects of different heights so she can develop this skill."

Hannah's mom, 67th week, or 15 months and a week

"We put a mattress on the ground so that she can jump around on it. She loves galloping over it; she dives on the mattress and tries a somersault. She keeps testing how far she can go on the soft surface."

Josie's mom, 66th week, or 15 months

"Thomas likes to stay on the couch the whole day. He climbs up the back rest using the wall to get up."

Thomas' mom, 66th week, or 15 months

"Every day he discovers new games. He has found a small tunnel behind his bed and chest of drawers and loves going back and forth behind them. He slides under the couch and sees how far he can go before he gets stuck. And he gets a kick sliding around the room on his knees instead of using his feet."

Matt's mom, 70th week, or 16 months

"She practices different ways of walking. Walking backwards, turning circles, walking fast, walking slowly. She is very studious about all these tricks."

Eve's mom, 64th week, or 14½ months

"She lies in and on everything: in the doll's bath, in the doll's bed and on the cushions spread on the floor."

Ashley's mom, 64th week, or 14½ months

"He laughs as he rolls himself in the curtains."
Matt's mom, 69th week, or approaching 16 months

"All of the sudden he is picking up chairs and benches."
Kevin's mom, 70th week, or 16 months

Getting Acquainted with the Outdoors

Many toddlers enjoy browsing around outside. They look like they're just fumbling about, but in fact they are surveying the area. This is not to say that they don't need their parents: they do! Many question everything endlessly: What is this and what is that called? And all children absorb what you say and what they see with the utmost concentration.

"She was startled when she walked through a puddle and got wet. She walked back to look at and investigate the puddle."
Ashley's mom, 64th week, or 14½ months

"He finds it interesting to splash through the puddles. It really pleases him."
Matt's mom, 71st week, or 16 months and a week

"She stood eye-to-eye with a real live cow and was really at a loss. This was at the children's zoo. She wasn't ready to pet the animal yet. Even when she was in her daddy's arms. On the way home, she was quiet as she mulled it over. That was the impression left on her by the living version of the cow from the book."
Victoria's mom, 61st week, or 14 months

Getting Skillful with Things

Your child will become ever more resourceful with games and objects in the world of principles. They will only eat properly if they can feed themselves. Helping them when it's not wanted could result in everything ending up on the floor. They manage quite well building things or playing with their game of rings and puzzles. But beware!

They try to open the faucet, bottles and jars with twist-off lids on a regular basis. Your toddler is, above all, interested in testing which of the strategies works best when they need it. They contemplate and experiment. What will happen if I drop the key chain behind the cabinet? What if I put it under the bed? And what will happen to the key chain if I let it slide down between the couch and the wall? And how will I make it reappear? And if I am unable to reach it, can I get to it with a pole? In short, they are learning how to hide something, put something away and recover it. Later, if they are skillful enough or think themselves to be, they will, perhaps, use their tricks to amuse you with a prank. They could also hide a game if, for instance, they don't want one of their friends to play with it. Do watch what your terror is up to. Put dangerous items out of reach and keep an eye on your little explorer.

"We do puzzles together. Now he likes it and participates gladly. Not that it always goes well, but it's a start."
Kevin's mom, 65th week, or approaching 15 months

"Now his ring game is popular. He clearly sees if he puts the wrong ring onto the pole and says: 'No.' If he gets it right, then he is very proud, looks at me and expects applause."
Harry's mom, 64th week, or 14½ months

"He stashes the ball and the balloon way behind something. The consequence is that he can no longer reach them."
Luke's mom, 66th week, or 15 months

"She throws things on the floor when you are least expecting it. She studies the effect her throwing has on the object."
Josie's mom, 64th week, or 14½ months

"He likes playing with his cars. This week he tried to see how well they stack up on top of each other."
Robin's mom, 72nd week, or 16½ months

LEAP 9

"When she is vacuuming with her battery powered vacuum, she prefers to go for the most impossible spots. She does those spots as if her life depended on it: under the cabinet, between the chairs and table legs, in open cupboards. She skips the easy large open spaces."

Victoria's mom, 61st week, or 14 months

"Again and again she pulled open my desk drawer, so I locked it. She then tried several ways to get it open, squatted and pulled, sat and pulled, the standing pull. It completely frustrated her."

Laura's mom, 65th week, or approaching 15 months

"She wanted candies that were on the fireplace mantel. I wouldn't give them to her. She then went into pushy mode. When she wouldn't stop, I put her in the hall to cool off. I had hoped that she would forget about the candy, but I was wrong. The minute she returned to the room, she dragged a chair from the dining room to the den. It took her 15 minutes. When the chair reached the fireplace, she asked her brother to lift up the chair. He realized that was a no go, so he laughed at her. She then gave up. Grandpa was visiting that evening and he was playing with her. He has a real sweet tooth and when he saw the candy, he just had to help himself. She got one too. Later when I came back into the room, she walked victoriously towards me and showed me her spoils. She prevailed in the end."

Victoria's mom, 61st week, or 14 months

"She was unable to get something out of the basket of magazines. When she finally managed after trying pulling and yanking five or six times, she laughed contentedly to herself. She'd never done that before."

Emily's mom, 68th week, or 15½ months

Becoming Skillful with Language

In the world of principles your toddler is continuously getting a better grasp of what the big people around them are saying to each other and to them. They are also getting better at understanding brief instructions and often carry them out with great enthusiasm. They feel like they count for something. They also have fun pointing to parts of the body when you name them. The same goes for various things in the home, whether they are on the floor, the walls or ceiling. Many parents think that their little one should be talking more, given that they already know so much. But that is not the case. It is only after the next leap that your toddler's speech really takes off. Your child is 21 months by then. In the world of principles most children are content with pronouncing single words, imitating animal sounds and reproducing all sorts of other noises.

Get your child to play a game of pointing and naming with you. You name something and let your child point to it, whether it's a toy, a body part or whatever. And try to see what your child thinks of a game of calling to each other. It's best if your child starts by calling you. Call their name to get them to call your name. Call out their name again. For many children, it gives them a sense of pride and importance that their egos count.

"He understands more and more. Unbelievable how quickly a child picks up new words. Yet he picks out only a few to use in his speech. He prefers words that begin with 'b' like his favorite things: ball and boy. He pronounces the words well and completely. It seems like he knows how to pronounce the words but he doesn't have the coordination."

Harry's mom, 69th week, or approaching 16 months

"She points perkily to her foot, toe, eye, ear, nose, stomach, hand and hair. She also knows that you wash your hair with shampoo as well what bottle it's in."

Juliette's mom, 69th week, or approaching 16 months

"She cried 'Daddy' when her father was busy in the kitchen. The calling out automatically evolved into a language game. Taking turns, the two called out each other's name: 'Anna....,' 'Daddy....,' 'Anna....,' 'Daddy.' Endlessly. Now it happens all the time if one of them goes out of the other's sight."

Anna's mom, 70th week, or 16 months

LEAP 9

Imitating Others

In the world of principles your toddler will observe how adults or other children do things and what effect their actions have. "How do they do that so skillfully?" "That kid gets immediate attention from everyone if they bite Grandma." "Mom and Dad regularly sit on the toilet. That must be a part of being 'big.'" "They keep kicking the leg of the lady from next door; she laughs so kicking must be funny." These are just for starters. They copy, imitate and try out what they see. The people around them are their role models. Also, the behavior they see in books and on TV gives them an inexhaustible source of ideas. React to your little one's behavior. Let them know what you think of their behavior. This is the only way you will your toddler learn what's right and wrong, and if they can do things better, quicker, more efficiently or nicer than they are doing.

"Imitating is now his main occupation. He imitates every behavior he sees: someone stamps her feet, he stamps his feet; someone hits, he hits; someone falls, he falls; someone throws, he throws; someone bites, he bites."

Thomas' mom, 63rd week, or 14 months and a week

"Everything that I do, he wants to do too. Also, he directly absorbs what other kids do. Even if he sees something only once, he picks it straight up. He copies pleasant and not-so-pleasant behavior."

Paul's mom, 64th week, or 14½ months

"She spends more time on and is ever more attentive to books and TV. One child on TV stuck his tongue out at another and she copied him straight away."

Josie's mom, 64th week, or 14½ months

"She wants to brush her teeth by herself. She brushes up and down once and knocks the toothbrush on the edge of the sink-knock, knock, knock-slides the toothbrush up and down in her mouth again and knocks again-knock, knock, knock. And on she brushes. The funny thing is that she is imitating me. I knock the toothbrush on the edge of the sink, but only after I am completely finished and have rinsed my brush. I do it to shake the water off my brush."

Victoria's mom, 61st week, or 14 months

"Initially she would turn her vacuum on with her fingers. Then she saw that I use my foot to turn mine on. Since now she uses her foot to start hers, too."

Victoria's mom, 61st week, or 14 months

Replaying

In the world of principles your child replays the daily domestic duties done indoors and out. They "cook," "shop," "take walks," "say goodbye," and "take care of their doll children." Naturally, they do all of this in their toddler way. Yet you getting better at recognizing what they are up to. Above all you see whether or not they do their best to be careful or helpful or if they are just being bossy, or if they're sweetly sucking up. They may do these things simply because they think it's part of their role or because they are imitating the people around them. Give your child the opportunity to settle into their role. Play with them once and a while. Your child then feels like they count and that what they do is important. Many toddlers at this age are very keen for signs of appreciation. They really want to be understood.

"She 'cooks' for her doll. I lay out some actual food, because that's what she wants. She puts everything in a small bowl, feeds her doll and then removes the food."

Emily's mom, 68th week, or 15½ months

"He bakes mud pies: scoops and scoops buckets full to dump them out again. He finds it all very interesting."

Thomas' mom, 66th week, or 15 months

"For the past few days he has been pouring water from one bucket into the other. It's keeping him busy. Now and again I get a request to fill up a bucket. Otherwise, he seems to have forgotten me and is consumed with his special brew."

Steven's mom, 63rd week, or 14 months and a week

"She strolled proudly on to the premises of the petting zoo behind her doll carriage. A goat blocked her way and she began an extensive discussion with the inattentive animal. Unfortunately, it was incomprehensible. It sounded as if she was calling him to order."

Hannah's mom, 64th week, or 14½ months

"He often plays 'saying goodbye.' He picks up a bag, walks to the door and says, 'Bye, Bye.' He waves while doing so."

Frankie's mom, 64th week, or 14½ months

"He often snuggles, kisses, comforts and caresses his dolls and bears. He also puts them to bed. Really loving."

Luke's mom, 66th week, or 15 months

Sometimes a child imitates being a father or mother. They study how it is to be daddy or mommy. When a little girl wants to be mom, her real mom is actually in the way. They then seem to be competing. Naturally, the same happens if father is home and they want to walk in dad's shoes. And if a little boy is playing dad, he wants to know how mom reacts to this new dad.

Try and understand what your child is doing. Give them the opportunity to play their role and play along. Your little one learns a lot from this. They feel the need to express themselves in this way and to experience how it is to be mom or dad.

"He goes and spreads out on his father's bed and looks around as if it is his. Also, just like his father, he goes and sits in his chair to read the paper. It is important to him to do as his dad does. He wants my reaction to it all as well."

Jim's mom, 66th week, or 15 months

"As soon as I take off my shoes, she's in them. And then she follows up by taking a walk around in my shoes. She also regularly wants to sit in my chair. I have to vacate it for her. She starts pulling and yanking me and if I don't concede, she throws a tantrum."

Nina's mom, 69th week, or approaching 16 months

Practicing with Emotions

In the world of the principles many toddlers experiment with their emotions. How does it feel if I am happy, sad, shy, angry, funny or emotional? And when I greet someone, what does my face do then? What does my body do? And how can I use those emotions if I want others to know how I feel? And how should I act if I badly want to have or do something?

"He walks around laughing very artificially like he is experimenting with how it feels to laugh. He does the same with crying."

Bob's mom, 63rd week, or 14 months and a week

"This time she greeted Grandpa very differently than she used to. Normally, she threw herself onto him putting her head on his neck and shoulder. When she had been still for a bit, the greeting had run its course and she began to play with him. But this time she stood up straight looking at him, only to launch herself onto him again. She repeated this a number of times. Then she gave him a cautious kiss and looked at him again. This, too, repeated itself a number of times. Never before had she greeted Grandpa in such a studious way. She was clearly experimenting with a greeting."

Victoria's mom, 61st week, or 14 months

"She wanted to read a certain book again for the eighth time and noticed that I had had enough of it. She sat there a bit with her head facing downward. Very quietly, she practiced a pout. When she thought she had the right expression, she looked at me with a perfectly pouting lip and passed the book back to me."

Josie's mom, 65th week, or approaching 15 months

"Suddenly he's become shy. If I brag about him for instance, he shies away almost in shame. I've never seen that before. Yet he's quick to notice if I talk about him."

Luke's mom, 68th week, or 15½ months

Thinking ahead has Begun

In the world of principles your toddler can think ahead, contemplate and make plans. They now understand that their mother and father can and do that too. You soon notice this by the reactions from your little one. They realize what the consequences are for something that mother or father does or wants them to do. And all of a sudden, they express their opinion of something that they used to find quite normal or even liked. Remember though that they are not unruly. Their development has just made a leap. It is progress!

"Now she has a hard time when I leave for work. Up until recently, she ran to the front door to give me a send-off. Now she protests and holds me back. I think this is because she now understands the effects. Sending someone off can be fun, but when mom leaves, she is gone for at least a few hours. And that's not so nice."

Eve's mom, 67th week, or 15 months and a week

"Thinking ahead has started! I brush her teeth after she has had a go. That always leads to terrible shouting matches. Up until recently when she heard 'Time to brush our teeth,' she came running. Now she throws the toothbrush in the corner when I hand it to her, because she knows what follows after the fun of doing it herself."

Laura's mom, 67th week, or 15 months and a week

"Sometimes she walks away having forgotten her pacifier. She then says: 'Oh, no,' and turns around to go get it."

Ashley's mom, 69th week, or approaching 16 months

"Now he remembers where he has hidden or left his things, even from yesterday."

Luke's mom, 63rd week, or 14 months and a week

"When he realized that he would have to get on the bike for the second time today in the freezing weather, he got really cross. He clearly recalled how cold it was and repeating the outing in such severe weather conditions didn't sit well with him."

James' mom, 67th week, or 15 months and a week

"This was the first time that I was able to see that she had a clear expectation. We had finger-painted and she had decorated the mirror. While she was bathing, I snuck off to clean the mirror. I shouldn't have done that. When she got out of the bath, she walked right to the mirror looking for her decoration. Very sad."

Josie's mom, 65th week, or approaching 15 months

Nagging and Getting One's Way

The Drama Class

Does your little one try getting their own way by screeching, rolling, stamping and throwing things? Do they lose their temper for the slightest reason? For example, if they don't get attention directly, if they're not allowed to do something, if their play is interrupted for dinner, if their building topples over, or just out of the blue without you detecting that anything is wrong? Why does a toddler put on such an act? It's because mom and dad and the toys aren't reacting the way the toddler thinks they should be. They are frustrated and need to express it. They do this using the most obvious strategies: getting as angry and making the biggest fuss possible. They have yet to discover and practice more successful, quicker, sweeter strategies in order to persuade you to do what they want, or to build a better building. Your nagging toddler is only able to make their wishes known by acting like they do. Understand your toddler's frustration. Let them blow off some steam if they need to. And help them discover that there are other and better strategies they can use when they want to get something done, ways that are more receptive and more successful.

"She only wants to eat if she can feed herself. A saga when we didn't get it! Everything flew through the air."
Juliette's mom, 65th week, or approaching 15 months

"At the slightest little thing or if things don't go as she has in mind, she throws herself on the floor. She lands on the back of her head with a thud, then lies on the ground stamping her feet and screaming."
Julia's mom, 65th week, or 14½ months

"He has an inordinate number of tantrums. He screams and throws things if he is corrected or if he 'bites off more than he can chew' or if his playtime is interrupted. If I distract him quickly, though, he doesn't shed any tears. But if it takes too long then his temper turns into a sad bout of tears."
Matt's mom, 68th week, or 15½ months

"He's thrown a number of temper tantrums this week. One was so bad that he went completely limp. If he doesn't get his way, he gets really angry and then it's a real battle. He is really in his own world! At the moment, he doesn't listen well at all."
James' mom, 67th week, 15 months and a week

"She throws an increasing number of temper tantrums. Yesterday, I got her out of bed and for no reason she threw a temper tantrum. This one lasted quite a long time, complete with rolling on the floor, banging her head, kicking and pushing me away, and screeching the whole time. Nothing I tried helped, not cuddling, not distracting her or stern words. After a while, I went and sat perplexed on the couch, leaned back and watched while she rolled around on the floor. Then I went into the kitchen to carve an apple. She slowly calmed down, came to the kitchen and stood next to me."

Julia's mom, 65th week, or approaching 15 months

The Gender Gap

Boys express their sense of impotence and displeasure more often than girls do. This is often because parents accept this type of manifestations more readily from boys than they do from girls, so girls learn to suppress these feelings of impotence and displeasure. Consequently, they may also become more easily depressed than boys.

They Want Their Say

In the world of principles your little one discovers that they count, too, just like all the big people. They begin to speak up for themselves. But sometimes it goes too far: their will is law and they will not be swayed. This happens because it is becoming ever clearer to them that they can impose their will. They count, too! They realize that just like mom or dad, they can decide if, when or where they want do something, how they will do it and when they will finish. On top of that, they want to put in their "two cents worth" if mom or dad wants to do something. They want to help decide

LEAP 9

how it is done. And if they don't get their way or if it doesn't go according to plan, they become angry, disappointed or sad. Show them understanding. They still have to learn that they can't always do what they want to do right away, and that they also have to learn to consider the wishes of others, even though they want to stand up for and assert themselves.

"She emphatically wants to choose which breast she takes. She hesitates a bit, looking which breast to take, points to the winner and says 'Tha.' Sometimes it looks as if she is deciding between two different flavors."

Juliette's mom, 65th week, or approaching 15 months

"If he gets something into his head, it's impossible to change his mind. It's like talking to a brick wall. He just goes on to the next room and gets up to no good. The toys in his brother's and sister's drawers were this week's target. He really had designs on the modeling clay. He knows full well what he is allowed, but he is less concerned with what I think of it all."

Frankie's mom, 65th week, or approaching 15 months

"If he doesn't want to listen, he shakes his head 'No.' These days, he walks around the whole day shaking his head, meanwhile just going about his business. Recently, when he was fishing through the garbage can, I got angry at him. A bit later, I saw him sulking in the corner crying."

John's mom, 70th week, or 16 months

"All of a sudden she's developed her own will! We picked out a book in the children's book store. It was really fun. When I decided that it was time to go, she had other ideas. First, she screamed her head off in the store and then kept on screaming when we went outside. On the bike, she kept standing up in her seat. I had to keep pushing her down in her chair. We almost got into a real fight. She didn't want to leave the bookstore, and I had no say in the matter. I'm still amazed."

Josie's mom, 68th week, or 15½ months

"Three weeks ago we went shopping for Thomas. He needed a 'big boy's suit' for a party. When we had chosen a suit, he came tip-toeing back with a pair of shoes – dainty, shiny, black patent leather. He tried to convince Dad that he needed these shoes. Dad didn't think that that was such a good idea and put the shoes back in the rack.

A week later, Thomas and I went back to the shoe store. He was getting his first pair of shoes. I went straight for the macho gear. It seemed a shoo-in that my big boy would want the same, but he had other ideas. He found a pair of shiny lace-up boots with feathers on the girls' rack. He loved them and had to have them. With his prize in hand, he came wobbling up to me. I was astounded. There was my boyish Thomas with a pair of dainty patent leather boots in his slightly less dainty hands, beaming. They were exactly the princess boots that I loved so much as a child, it was bewildering that my little guy would fall for the same thing. I quickly recommended a series of boyish styles while sneaking the shiny boots back were they belonged. Thomas looked at the boy's rack and quickly found something much to his liking. 'Vroom, vroom,' he cheered and grabbed a pair of thick-soled shoes with trucks sticking out the sides of the shoes. This made them shoes on wheels. As a true car-lover, they caught his eye. He wanted them and was very content; as was I. But when I was paying for the shoes on wheels, he nudged me. There he was trying to put something onto the sales counter. It were the boots."

Thomas' mom, 69th week, or approaching 16 months

"She is increasingly insistent. When she won't cooperate, we get into a fight. It happens while getting dressed, eating or if I'm in a hurry. Yesterday, it happened again. I lost my cool and ended up screaming and cursing at her."

Julia's mom, 66th week, or 15 months

Aggression

Many parents say that their sweet toddler sometimes turns into an aggressive tiger and this makes them uneasy. Yet it is an understandable change. In the world of principles your child tries all types of behavior. Being aggressive is one of those. Your toddler studies how mom, other adults and children react if they hit, bite, push or kick, or if they deliberately break something. Show your child what you think of their behavior. This is the only way that they will learn that being aggressive isn't sweet, interesting or funny. This way they learn that it's hurtful and that adults are not amused by aggressive or destructive behavior.

Mine and Yours

In the world of principles your little one discovers that some toys in the house are theirs and only theirs. Just like big people, they are suddenly the proud owner of their own stuff. This is quite a discovery for a toddler. They also need time to grasp what "mine and yours" means. Things aren't easy for them while they are figuring this out. Some children find it disturbing if another child grabs something out of their hands for no reason without recognizing them as owner. Such lack of understanding starts them crying. Others become very wary and protect their territory as best they can. They come up with all sorts of strategies to prevent others from getting close to their things. They especially don't trust children. Your toddler still has to learn to lend, share and play with others.

"She is developing a certain urge to own. When we have guests, she comes and proudly shows her possessions. If we go over to play at a friend's house, she grabs her things and gives them to me for safe keeping. She hopes by doing so to prevent her friend from playing with them."

Eve's mom, 64th week, or 14½ months

Tips on Aggression

Research has shown that shortly after the first birthday parents report the first physical aggression. At 17 months, 90 percent of parents report that their child is sometimes aggressive. Physical aggression peaks just before the second birthday. Thereafter, this type of behavior recedes. By the time children have reached school age, under normal circumstances, it will have mostly disappeared.

Of course, some children are more prone to aggressive behavior than others. Yet, a child's surroundings are also very important. They help determine how long a child remains aggressive. If children live with adults and children who are aggressive, then they will assume that "being aggressive" is normal social behavior. However, children also live in environments where aggression is not tolerated and where sweet and friendly behavior is rewarded. The result is that the child will not start hitting and kicking when they are frustrated, want something or are corrected. They will use more acceptable ways of expressing themselves.

LEAP 9

"Suddenly, he is very possessive of my breasts. If his father comes close, he tries to protect his territory. He clamps his mouth on to a nipple and covers the other with his hand so that his dad can't get to it."

Thomas' mom, 65th week, or approaching 15 months

"Every time his little friend snatches one of his toys, he bursts out in tears."

Robin's mom, 68th week, or 15½ months

"He doesn't let anyone take anything from him. You can't even tempt him with a 'good trade' either. If he's got a hold of it, he's keeping it. He's keen, though, to snatch things from others. In that, he has no scruples at all."

Kevin's mom, 65th week, or approaching 15 months

Being Nice and Placating

The Joke Strategy

In the world of principles, tricks and antics play an ever-increasing role in your little one's day to day life. Your toddler may start making their first jokes and they themselves will get the biggest kick out of these jokes. You might notice that they appreciate others' jokes also, many toddlers do. They enjoy gags, and when people or animals do something out of the ordinary, whether in real life or on TV, it makes them laugh. They find it exciting. Some children pull pranks to try getting around the rules.

You may notice that "being funny" is being used as a strategy to get away with doing something that would otherwise be frowned upon. Something pleasant and unexpected becomes increasingly more successful for getting on mom's or dad's good side than a temper tantrum is. Give your child the opportunity to be creative while making fun and pulling pranks. Be very clear when they overstep the bounds. It is only with your help that they will learn the difference between what is and isn't acceptable.

"He is constantly kidding around and has a great time doing it. He and his friends have a barrel of laughs acting silly. He really cracks up if he sees an animal do something silly or unexpected."

Robin's mom, 68th week, or 15½ months

"He loves just being silly. He giggles and if his sister joins in, he really bursts out laughing."

James' mom, 69th week, or approaching 16 months

"Cartoons really make him laugh, especially if something sudden or unexpected happens. He even loves the monsters in 'Sesame Street.' He really starts giggling when they talk and move around."

Robin's mom, 70th week, or 16 months

"He loves me to chase after him saying, 'I'm gonna get you.' However, when I want to put on his jacket, he runs away squawking and making a game of it."

James' mom, 70th week, or 16 months

"She cracks up when she ignores me, is disobedient or is making fun of me, or when she hides something from me and it is hard for me to get at. She thinks she is very clever."

Laura's mom, 66th week, or 15 months

"She loves playing pranks. When we get to the front door, she doesn't wait for me to put the key in the lock, she just continues walking to the next door. She really thinks she's funny."

Ashley's mom, 70th week, or 16 months

Negotiating and Bargaining

It used to be that mom and dad laid down the law and children had to obey. Adults didn't take kindly to backtalk. But everything changes. Nowadays it is generally assumed that children who have learned to negotiate grow up better able to think for themselves. When your toddler lands in the world of principles, you could see a budding negotiator.

Does your toddler experiment with the words "Yes" and "No?" They sometimes do so when nodding or shaking their heads, occasionally pronouncing "Yes" or "No" out loud. They also try nodding while saying no and shaking their head while saying yes, which is very funny to them. Their stuffed animals have mandatory "yes" and "no" lessons. Other times they practice on their own while building something or wandering through the house just looking for something to get into, but mostly they practice their yes and no routine with their parents. They are also good for trying out their jokes on.

Give your child the opportunity to be inventive with the concepts of yes and no. This type of practice allows them to learn to use a yes or a no to their advantage. How does mom and dad do it? They can find the best yes and no strategy for various situations. They discover which strategy is best suited to meet their needs.

"He is able to answer all sorts of questions with just a yes or no. He sometimes makes a mistake. He says 'Yes' when he means 'No' and if I act upon his answer, he smiles and quickly changes to a 'No,' in a tone of 'not really.'"
Luke's mom, 65th week, or approaching 15 months

"She says 'Yes' and 'No' with increasing authority, but she likes to try to trick me using yes and no."
Juliette's mom, 66th week, or 15 months

Asking for Help

Your toddler can be inventive in trying to put someone on the spot. They can use clever, sneaky or sweet ways. They still require some practice in learning the tricks of the trade. Just watch your little one go to work on you or someone else when they need to get something done. Tell them what you think of it. Your child is still researching in the world of principles. They learn from your feedback.

LEAP 9

"He points at things more and more. He also points to the things he wants you to get for him. This week he lured his grandmother to the kitchen, walked to the cabinet where the cookies are and pointed to the top shelf."

Frankie's mom, 63rd week, or 14 months and a week

"With a sly look on her face, she pointed to an egg and then a plate. She meant, 'put that egg on my plate.' She was so cute that no one could refuse."

Hannah's mom, 62nd week, or 14 months

"These past weeks he has been commanding like a general. He cries out loudly and forcefully: 'Mom! Mom!' when he wants something. When I look at him, he sits there with his arm outstretched, pointing at the toy of his choosing. He wants them brought to him and when he gets his request, he pulls his arm back and carries on playing. Giving orders has become second nature to him. This week was the first time I really noticed it."

Matt's mom, 68th week, or 15½ months

"Today she showed me what she wanted when we were visiting someone. She took my hand and walked to the door, behind which were our coats, opened the door, went to our coats and pointed while looking at me with a questioning look on her face. I didn't know what hit me."

Emily's mom, 67th week, or 15 months and a week

Cooperation

In the world of principles your child has choices: "Am I going with the flow or against it?" "Do I care what Mom or Dad says or not?" In addition to that, your toddler is growing ever more outspoken and more capable. Small assignments are getting easier for them, like: "Get your shoes please" "Go get your bottle please" "Throw that in the trash please" "Give it to Daddy please" "Put it in the hall please" or "Put it in the hamper please." You might have already noticed that sometimes you don't have to say what to do. Your little toddler already grasps what you want and is working along. It is increasingly easier to lay down certain ground rules.

Try involving your child in day-to-day business and getting involved in their day-to-day, too. It makes them feel understood, appreciated and important. Their ego is growing. Praise them too, if they are thinking ahead for you. They are demonstrating that they know what needs to be done.

"Every time before we go somewhere, she gets her own jacket."
Josie's mom, 65th week, or approaching 15 months

"He now understands that he needs to stay with me when we're on the sidewalk."
Luke's mom, 66th week, or 15 months

"She puts two and two together. When I say: 'Go find your bottle,' she returns after her expedition and makes a gesture of 'gone.'"
Eve's mom, 72nd week, or 16½ months

"When she needs changing, she walks with me to her dresser. She lays still and practically helps me."
Laura's mom, 63rd week, or 14 months and a week

"She knows that she is not allowed to take the nuts from the bowl on the table. So she thought of a trick so she could eat the nuts and still conform to the rules. She got her own plate and a spoon and scooped some nuts onto her plate. She then ate her winnings with her spoon. This way she could have some nuts and eat them, too, without breaking the rules in her eyes."
Ashley's mom, 68th week, or 15½ months

LEAP 9

Being Helpful

When toddlers land in the world of principles most of them are particularly interested in all the goings-on about the house, although there is a big chance that your little one is no longer content just watching mom and dad do their things. They want to help. They want to lighten your load. Let your child do their part. They really want to believe that they are a big help and that, without them, things would be a huge mess or that dinner wouldn't be any good. Be sure they receive a well-deserved compliment.

"She helps me set and clear the table as well as do the vacuuming. She just started one day and it disappoints her if she doesn't get the necessary time and space to be creative."

Josie's mom, 62nd week, or 14 months

"She gladly helps making drinks. Sometimes, I let her make her own drink. She uses all kinds of ingredients. When she drinks it, she goes around murmuring, 'Yum, yum, yum.'"

Juliette's mom, 68th week, or 15½ months

"As soon as I grab the vacuum cleaner, she grabs her battery-powered one. She wants to help oh so badly. So what happens is that she wants to use my vacuum because it's better. Therefore, I begin with hers and when she takes it back, I can peacefully go on with the real one."

Victoria's mom, 61st week, or 14 months

"She used to like to watch me doing my thing. Now she wants to help. When she sees me slice a lemon, she runs to the counter to be picked up so that she can put the lemon in the citrus press. If she sees dirty dishes, she hurries over to the counter to do the washing up."

Nina's mom, 64th week, or 14½ months

Being Careful

Does your toddler experiment with being "rash" or "careful?" "Should I fling my cup on the ground or should I place it carefully on the table?" Reckless behavior seems to be very popular. Running, climbing, wild horseplay and treating objects recklessly seem to be the favorite pastime. But do realize that by experimenting and getting your reaction to such behavior, your little one learns what it means to be reckless or to be careful.

LEAP 9

"He practices his balance. Outside, he reaches for the sky, inside he reaches for the ceiling. He climbs onto chairs and tables so that he can reach higher and does seem to understand that space is out of reach. While reaching he all of a sudden lets himself fall down."

Luke's mom, 64th week, or 14½ months

"When you're least expecting it, she throws her bottle away, for instance when we are cycling, and then she studies our reaction to her behavior out of the corner of her eye."

Hannah's mom, 64th week, or 14½ months

"He climbs like a monkey. He climbs on everything. He climbs on chairs a lot. I also constantly find him on the dining room table, claiming that he can't get down! He is careful. He is aware of the danger, but sometimes he falls pretty hard."

Frankie's mom, 66th week, or 15 months

"Wrestling with his brother is now the top draw. Sometimes they get really rough."

Kevin's mom, 69th week, or approaching 16 months

"She spilled a few drops of her drink on the floor. I grabbed an old sock that was lying around and mopped up. She looked at me shocked and amazed, went purposefully to the baby wipes, took one out of the box and mopped all over again. When she had finished, she looked at me as if she wanted to say, 'That's how it should be done.' I was taken aback at the level of cleanliness, and I praised her for it."

Victoria's mom, 61st week, or 14 months

> *"She is very capable in expressing that something is dirty. She repeatedly says 'Poo' to the slightest smudge in bed. I hope that this is temporary and she doesn't stay such a 'neat freak.'"*

Josie's mom, 64th week, or 14½ months

> *"When her brother was looking through her dolls in search of a special robot, he swept all her dolls onto the floor. Even Elisabeth's baby doll. She immediately ran to her fallen child and picked her up, hurried to me and thrust the doll to my breast. She then gave her brother a dirty look."*

Elisabeth's mom, 63rd week, or 14 months and a week

Show Understanding for Irrational Fears

When your toddler is busy exploring their new world and working through their newfound ability, they will encounter things and situations that are new and foreign to them. They are actually discovering new dangers, dangers that until now did not exist for them. They aren't able to talk about them yet. Their fears will only disappear once they are able to understand things better. Show sympathy.

> *"He was mad for batteries. All batteries had to come out and be put back in, out, in, out, in; it was endless."*

Steven's mom, 61st week, or 14 months

"He is scared of his sister's ducky. He walks way around it if it's in the way. When he grabs it, he drops it immediately."

James' mom, 66th week, or 15 months

"It looks as if she is afraid to sit in the bathtub by herself, yelling and screeching. We don't know the reason. She wants to get in provided one of us joins her. She's not afraid of the swimming pool. She likes getting in there."

Josie's mom, 67th week, or 15 months and a week

"She is not afraid of new things, but you do notice that she is not completely convinced."

Josie's mom, 68th week, or 15½ months

Learning the Rules

Whining and whimpering to get one's way, childish behavior like constantly needing to be entertained and always wanting a pacifier, being messy without any cause, not being careful and intentionally hurting others, going out of their way to be naughty – you probably wonder if you're the only one that is having such trouble with your little one's behavior. No, certainly not. Your toddler is no longer a baby. Time has come to lay down some ground rules. Your toddler is ready for you to start asking and expecting more from them. What's more: they are searching for these boundaries. Now that they have entered the world of principles, they yearn for rules. They are looking for chances to familiarize themselves with them. Just as they must satisfy their appetite by eating, so too they must satisfy this yearning for rules. The only way they will discover most of the rules is if you present them to them. Social rules are particularly important. You must show them what is acceptable and what is not acceptable socially. There is no harm in laying down the law. On the contrary, you owe it to them, and who better to do it than someone who loves them?

"I think that he should be able to put things on the table neatly. It really annoys me if he throws his sandwich and bottle when he's finished with them. He has to stop that. He's capable of putting things down properly."

Thomas' mom, 67th week, or 15 months and a week

"She still whines and whimpers to get her way, making it difficult to be consistent. It seems that this is the point where she needs guidance. It's much easier to give her what she wants, because she stops whining then. If I don't give her what she wants, then all hell breaks loose. Then there's a power struggle, which she easily wins. I've never been quite so aware of power as I am now."

Josie's mom, 68th week, or 15½ months

"Sometimes he purposely does something he's not supposed to do. He throws rocks, puts batteries in his mouth or smears his food on the floor. I scold him, while taking everything he has in his hands and putting it out of reach. This sometimes ends in an argument."

Paul's mom, 69th week, or approaching 16 months

"Is my child the only one that rolls around on the ground kicking and screaming when she doesn't get her way? I don't hear the other parents complaining much. Do I let her get away with too much? Do I cater too much to her needs? Is it because she goes to daycare more often? What am I to do? Right, lay down clear ground rules, that's what I will do."

Vera's mom, 70th week, or 16 months

"I teach him that he is not allowed to just take things away from other children."

Thomas' mom, 70th week, or 16 months

Top Games for This Wonder Week

Here are games and activities that most 15-16 month-old toddlers like best now and that help develop their new abilities. Remember, all children are different. See what your little one responds to best.

SKILLFULNESS

In the world of principles toddlers have surpassed programs and thoroughly enjoy endlessly practicing variations and experimenting with these programs. By doing so, they become skillful and discover how and when they can best get things done. They are also keen observers.

PHYSICAL ANTICS

Your toddler will like running, climbing, chasing other kids, jumping on the bed, doing somersaults, rolling on the ground, wrestling with other kids, playing "I'll get you," walking on the stairs without holding on, walking on walls, jumping from walls, the list is endless. Take the time to give them the opportunity to do it.

EXPLORING THE GREAT OUTDOORS

Roaming around outside, doing nothing in particular while scouting about is often a favorite pastime: at the petting zoo, on the playground, or in the zoo. Even just being carried on mom or dad's back at a festival, is doable for several hours.

POINTING GAMES

Challenge your little one to play a pointing game. You say a word and have your child point to where the object, toy, or body part is.

GAMES USING HANDS AND FEET WITH SINGING AND RHYMING

Use rhymes or songs which involve using hands and feet. For instance, they love: "The Wheels on the Bus Go 'Round and 'Round" or "If You're Happy and You Know It, Clap Your Hands" or "Itsy Bitsy Spider" or "Head, Shoulder, Knees and Toes."

CALLING GAMES

See how your child likes playing a "calling game." It's best to start with your child calling you. Then call their name out and get them to call back to you. Call their name out again. Most children feel proud upon hearing their own name called out. It makes them feel like they belong.

KIDDING AROUND

In the world of principles, kidding and joking will start to play a more important role in daily life. By now, your toddler has figured out how things work to some degree. So when things get out of whack, they really get a kick out of it, whether it's someone acting funny or bending the rules.

JUST BEING SILLY

Your toddler loves acting silly: funny faces, funny walks or odd sounds. And more so if it is unexpected. It's a real mess when the little ones get together. It cracks them up when their brother and sister join the antics. They and their little friends also have the greatest time acting silly.

A JOKE AS A STRATEGY

Your toddler uses silliness to get something or get something done by someone. Pleasant surprises are far more effective in getting something out of mom or dad than temper tantrums. Some toddlers employ various antics in order to bend or get around the rules. Not listening, being unruly or teasing mom or dad are all cause for laughter. Give your kid the opportunity to play the clown. But be clear and correct them if and when they overstep the bounds. They won't always know when they have gone too far.

CARTOONS, MONSTERS AND ANIMALS

Animals that do something silly or unexpected are favorites with toddlers. For instance, the monsters in "Sesame Street" are really funny. Cartoons really make them laugh, especially if something happens that catches them by surprise.

HOUSEHOLD GAMES

In the world of principles your child re-enacts the daily business in and around the house. Give them the opportunity to do this and play with them sometimes. It makes your toddler feel they are part of the club. It's great if they can actually help out. Here below are a few examples, but you are bound to come up with more.

COOKING PRACTICE

Give them some small bowls, some real food and a bowl of water, so they can cook to feed their doll.

VACUUMING

There are toy vacuum cleaners that are exact replicas of the real thing. Vacuuming together can be fun!

DOING THE DISHES

The water goes everywhere, but that's what mops are for.

DOING EXACTLY AS MOM OR DAD DOES

Leave your shoes lying around, so that they can put them on.

GAMES WITH EMOTIONS

Your toddler will be experimenting with emotions, such as varying their expressions when they greet people or when they want something. Pay special attention and play along with the drama. For instance, you can imitate them and play at being pitiful. It will probably make them laugh.

HIDE AND SEEK

PEEK-A-BOO

Peek-a-Boo is a classic that always works.

HIDE AND SEEK

With each leap playing "hide and seek" becomes slightly more advanced. By this age, your toddler is already good at staying hidden in one place.

Top Toys for This Wonder Week

Here are toys and things that most 15-16-month-old toddlers like best now and that help develop the new ability:

- Jungle gyms, slides
- Balls
- Books
- Sandboxes
- Tea sets with water or cold juice in cups or mugs
- Puzzles
- Plastic bottles
- Cleaning utensils
- Toy vacuums
- Toys on strings
- Sesame Street
- Cartoons

Be careful with the following:

- Garbage cans
- Toilets
- Baseball bats, hockey sticks in the hallway

After the Leap

Around 68 weeks, or approaching 16 months, most toddlers become a little less troublesome than they were. They are bigger and have grown wiser and are living right along with the rest of us. You sometimes forget that they are still very little.

"He looks slimmer, less stocky, his face thinner, he is growing up. I sometimes see him sitting calmly, focused on his food. He seems rather mature then."

Luke's mom, 66th week, or 15 months

"Everything comes easier to her now, from feeding herself to cleaning up. She is really just like the rest of us. I keep forgetting that she is still a very small child."

Eve's mom, 67th week, or 15 months and a week

"All of a sudden, she seems wiser and more mature. It seems that she has taken a giant leap forward. She has entered the wide world, full of confidence and fearing nothing and nobody. She is doing extremely well, is easy-going and sweet, and at night she falls asleep much easier."

Josie's mom, 70th week, or 16 months

LEAP 9

LEAP 10

Wonder Week 75

The World of Systems

" EVERYTHING IS
CONNECTED!

Since the previous leap, your toddler has started to understand what "principles" are. They have risen above the previous confines of "programs," and they have shed their mechanical character. For the first time they were able to evaluate existing programs and even to change them. You could see them constantly changing programs, then studying the effects. You could also see them performing physical antics, exploring the great outdoors, getting skillful with objects and language, imitating others, replaying the day-to-day, trying out emotions, beginning to plan, staging their own drama classes, insisting on taking part, using aggression, learning what's theirs and what's not, using pranks as a strategy to an end, experimenting with yes and no, being resourceful by putting people on the spot, learning to cooperate, wanting to help out around the house, and experimenting with being reckless and being careful.

Just as the toddler's programs were mechanical before they rose to new heights, their principles were also lacking a certain flexibility. They were only able to apply them in set ways, always the same, regardless of the situation.

We adults are capable of adjusting our principles to fit different circumstances. We are able to see a bigger picture. We see how certain principles are linked and form an entire system. The concept "system" encompasses our idea of an organized unit. We use the term "system" if the parts it comprises are interdependent and function as a whole. There are tangible examples, like a grandfather clock that needs winding, an electrical network or the human muscle system. These systems form a coherent

---

Note: *The first phase (fussy period) of this leap into the perceptual world of "systems" is age-linked and predictable, and starts from 71 weeks onwards. Most babies start the second phase (see box "Quality Time: An Unnatural Whim" on page 17) of this leap 75 weeks after full-term birth. The first perception of the world of systems sets in motion the development of a whole range of skills and activities. However, the age at which these skills and activities appear for the first time varies greatly and depends on your baby's preferences, experimentation and physical development. For example, the ability to perceive systems is a necessary precondition for "being able to point the way to the supermarket or park," but this skill normally appears at anywhere from 75 weeks to many months later. The skills and activities in this chapter are stated at the earliest possible age they could appear so you can watch for and recognize them. (They may be rudimentary at first.) This way you can respond to and facilitate your baby's development.*

set of principles of gear ratios, electric amps and volts, and balanced muscle tensions, respectively. There are also less tangible examples. Take human organizations, they are arranged on the basis of principles that you cannot always put your finger on. There are rules (or agreements) for duties assigned to certain positions, rules for social behavior like being on time, and rules for learning the goals imposed by your boss. To name just a few examples of human organizations, take the scouts, families, drama clubs, police stations, the church, our society, our culture, and the law.

Do Remember

If your toddler is clingy, watch them closely. There's a good chance that they're attempting to master new skills.

When your toddler makes their next leap, they will land in the world of systems. For the first time in their life they will perceive "systems." Of course, it's all new to them. They will need a number of years before they fully understand what our society, our culture or the law really entail. They start with the basics and stay close to home. They develop the idea of themselves as a system, and that together with mom and dad they form a family. And their family is not the same as their little friend's, nor is their house the same as their neighbor's house.

Just as your toddler learned to be more flexible with programs after they made the leap into the world of principles, after leaping into the world of systems they start being more flexible in how they apply principles. Now they begin to understand they can choose what they want to be: honest, helpful, careful, patient, and so forth. To be or not to be: that is the question. They apply principles less rigidly and start to learn how they can refine their approach to all sorts of different circumstances. Around 75 weeks, or 17 months and a week, you usually notice that your little one starts trying new things. However, they already felt the leap into the world of systems coming at an earlier age. From week 71, or just over 16 months onwards, your toddler notices their world is changing. A maze of new impressions turns reality on its head. They cannot process the novelty all at once. First, they will have to create order out of the chaos. They return to a familiar and safe base. They get clingy. They need a "mommy or daddy refill."

This Week's Fussy Signs

In this last chapter, we are not going to describe in detail the clues that your baby is about to make a developmental leap. These will be familiar to you by now. For this reason, we are only including the "My Diary" section on the next page. A useful memory aid for what to expect is the three C's: CRYING, CLINGINESS and CRANKINESS. Remember that your toddler is only after two things – being near you and having your undivided attention. They are also bigger and smarter now and more capable of finding new ways to these same goals than ever before.

How You Know it's Time to Grow

Which of these signs did you notice as your baby started this leap?

My Diary

Signs My Baby Is Growing Again

- ☐ Cries more often and is more often cranky or fretful than before
- ☐ Is cheerful one moment and cries the next
- ☐ Wants to be entertained, or does so more often than they did
- ☐ Clings to your clothes or wants to be closer to you more than before
- ☐ Acts unusually sweet
- ☐ Is mischievous
- ☐ Throws temper tantrums, or throws them more often than they did
- ☐ Is jealous
- ☐ Is more obviously shy with strangers now
- ☐ Wants physical contact to be tighter or closer than before
- ☐ Sleeps poorly
- ☐ Has nightmares, or has them more often than before
- ☐ Loses appetite
- ☐ Sometimes just sits there, quietly daydreaming
- ☐ Reaches for a cuddly toy, or does so more often than usual
- ☐ Is more babyish again

OTHER CHANGES YOU NOTICE

LEAP 10

How This Leap May Affect You

Initially, when your baby became clingy, cranky and cried more often than usual, your sole concern was that something was wrong with them. By the time they were 6 months old, you began to become increasingly annoyed when it became clear that nothing was wrong, but generally, you let it pass. After all, they were so tiny then. After their first birthday, you started to take action if you were annoyed and that sometimes resulted in arguments. You were able to enjoy the true pleasures of parenthood! All parents report that they quarrel with their "teenaging" toddler. Teens have been known to have the ability to make life rotten for their parents. Toddlers can do it, too. It gives you a preview of what is to come ten years down the line. It's part of the bargain.

You May Become Really Frustrated

"If she asks me with a whiny voice if I want to do something, I say very in a very friendly way: 'Yes, Mommy do you want...' Then she repeats very sweetly: 'Mommy, do you want...'"

Anna's mom, 71st week, or just over 16 months

"I was really annoyed this week. He didn't want to take his nap. If he doesn't want to, then he doesn't have to. It's easier and it saves me a lot of trouble. Nor does he want to wear a diaper, so I often let him go without."

Taylor's mom, 73rd week, or approaching 17 months

"It was difficult for me when she completely dominated my time. She was driving me nuts. I thought, 'What am I doing wrong?' I try to relax and not to make plans and take things as they come, but it's not easy."

Ashley's mom, 73rd week, or approaching 17 months

"Once in a while this week I put him in his playpen, although he was whining and what-not. He was constantly being pushy and impatient. He wanted to get his way all the time."

Frankie's mom, 74th week, or 17 months

You May Argue

How Your Baby's New Skills Emerge

Around 75 weeks, or 17 months and a week, you will notice that most of the clinginess disappears. The temper tantrums and quarreling with your "teenaging" toddler subside. They're back to their enterprising selves. You may notice that they've changed, that their behavior is different, that they are becoming very aware of themselves as a person, that they think differently, and that they have a better sense of time than ever before. They play with their toys differently and their use of fantasy takes off. Their humor has changed. This change is evident because at this age your toddler's

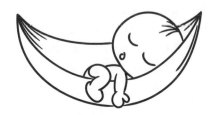

ability to perceive systems and to apply the concept of system is emerging. This new ability is the equivalent to a new world opening up. Your toddler, with their talents, preferences and temperament, chooses where they will start exploring. Try to see what they are doing and help them. But watch out! They want to do it all by themselves.

"His father claims that he has more patience."
Gregory's mom, 74th week, or 17 months

"Things went much easier with her, although she is very pig-headed and needs a lot of attention."
Juliette's mom, 75th week, or 17 months and a week

The Magical Leap Forward

When your toddler enters the world of systems, they are now able to see clearly beyond the world of principles. They no longer apply principles as rigidly as before. They are able to adjust their principles to changing circumstances. For instance, they are now able to choose to apply a moral principle, or not. From this age you can see they develop the earliest beginnings of a conscience, by systematically upholding their norms and values.

"She jumps when we catch her doing something she's not allowed. Then she blurts out 'No.'"
Jenny's mom, 73rd week, or approaching 17 months

The system your toddler lives with day in and day out is the one they themselves know best. They are their own person. When the world of systems opens up to them, they start to develop their notion of self. This has several consequences. Your toddler now discovers that they own and control their own body. They also discover that they can orchestrate things, that they can do things by themselves, that they can control things around them, and that they can make decisions, all things that stem from their growing concept of self.

> "Now he expressly does things differently than is expected or asked of him. For instance, if you ask him: 'Give Mom a kiss?' he gives everyone a kiss, walks to me and says: 'Hahahahaha' and doesn't give me a kiss. It seems to me that he wants to show that he's his own person. That he's no longer one with me, but a separate person. That's all."
>
> **Thomas' mom, 80th week, or just over 18 months**

Your toddler begins to understand that mom and dad are separate people. They start using terms as "you" and "me" and are also very interested in both mom and dad's physiques. A boy discovers that he has a penis just like his father, and that mom doesn't. They size up all the similarities and differences to a tee. For the first time in their life, your toddler can put themselves in someone else's place, now they realize that not all people are alike. For the first time they see that not everyone likes the same things as they do. That would have never occurred to them when they were younger. We can sum this up with one elegant word, they have become less "egocentric". That has all sorts of consequences. They are now able to comfort someone. They are at their high point in mimicry; they copy anything and everything around them. Their imagination comes to life.

Your explorer is also fascinated by other living creatures: ants, dogs and so forth. They are all systems, too.

LEAP 10

Your "teenaging" toddler starts realizing that they are part of a family, and that their family is different from their little friend's family, whom they visit twice a week. After all, their family is the first human organization they get to know from the inside, and they make no mistake in noticing that their little friend's family doesn't necessarily have a salad with dinner like their own family does. In their family, they have a different set of rules.

Just as your toddler recognizes their family as a system, they begin to distinguish their family from other families. They already do the same with their friends, house and neighborhood. They are getting better at finding their way around in the familiar surroundings outside their house.

They start paying great attention to their clothes. They can be quite vain and are very possessive of their toys. Your little artist starts to create art with a capital A. They no longer scribble, now they draw "horses," "boats" and "themselves." They also begin to appreciate music – that, too, is a system.

Your toddler starts to develop a sense of time. They are now better able to recall past experiences and have a better understand of what the future will bring.

They will now begin forming their first sentences. Not every toddler does this, though. Just as with other skills, the age children start with a certain skill differs greatly from one child to the next. All toddlers now understand much of what you say to them, but some are not ready to start talking. Others use several words and constantly mime, but don't produce sentences yet. A few, though, do speak in sentences. Whether or not your toddler does depends on how you interact with them.

A few examples from the adult world will help to clarify what we mean by a system. Take, for instance, practicing mathematics. On the level of programs, we think, use logic and handle mathematical symbols. On the level of principles, we think about thinking and therefore we think about how use mathematics. On the systems level, we look at mathematics as a whole, as an intellectual system.

In a similar way, the science of physics is a large system consisting of carefully discovered principles. This also applies to the science of biology and the theory of evolution and the accompanying principles of natural selection. This applies to other sciences as well.

World views or outlooks on life are also systems. Our everyday lives also offer examples of systems. Our approach to diet leads us to formulate principles regarding food, which in turn determines our eating programs. Another example of a system is democracy. Just as with other human organizations, some aspects are tangible and demonstrable, while others are rather superficial. By the time someone else is able to see something the same way you do, the situation could have changed completely. We can point to government, the annual budget, or employee hiring practices. What we are unable to do is point to authority, cooperation, back-room politics, compromises or organization in general. You can point to what you think is evidence of the existence of these, but you can't demonstrate them as easily as you can something simple and tangible, like a rock.

Other examples of human organizations as systems are families, schools, churches, banks, factories, armies, governments, soccer clubs, and bridge clubs. Such social institutions have the important task of encouraging their members to familiarize themselves with their goals, norms and values. Some institutions insist on it. In the family, it's called socialization. In the family unit, learning values, norms and other principles is practically automatic because toddlers imitate anything and everything they see. There are also countless learning opportunities, where such things are often not emphasized, but acted out as a matter of course.

This may seem different from a system like physics or mathematics. "That's way too advanced for such a little toddler," most people will say. "They won't learn that until high school." But when you observe your toddler playing, when you see how they hold a ball under water again and again to see it fly up out of the water, when you watch them endlessly rolling things down an incline or running up and down an incline again and again, you

can't ignore that they are experimenting with the fundamental principles of physics to establish systems of their own in their mind, which puts them in good company. It was Newton himself who once experimented with something as simple as a falling apple. Perhaps it wouldn't be a bad idea for physics teachers to seek advice from toddlers at play to come up with a few good demonstrations for their classes.

This applies to other systems as well as those of math and physics. A toddler is also interested in basic architecture. They can watch builders for hours or imitate their father making cement. They mix water and sand the whole day long and then they start "plastering walls." Their Lego buildings have also become more complex. For instance, they can lay down train tracks and run their trains along them.

Brain Changes

Between 16 and 24 months, the number of synapses in the cerebrum vastly increases, both within the various subareas of the cerebrum and in between those subareas. In the second half of the second year, a part of the cerebrum behind the forehead matures (the orbitofrontal lobe), and a cascade of new skills emerge. The right half of the brain develops in leaps and bounds in the first year and a half. Then development in the left half of the brain, where the language centers reside, takes over. As far as the comprehension of single words is concerned, at 20 months, a confinement takes place from the whole cerebrum to a few small areas in the left half.

Your Toddler's Choices: A Key to Their Personality

All toddlers have been given the ability to perceive and control systems. They need years in order to completely familiarize themselves with the wide range of new skills they have to play with, but as toddlers they take their first tender steps in the world of systems. For instance, at this age, a toddler may choose to focus on getting the hang of using their body and leave talking for later, using just a few words and no sentences. Or, they may be very busy with their family, friends, house and neighborhood. Or they might prefer the arts, drawing endlessly and listening to music. Just like every toddler, they choose what best suits their talents, mobility, preferences and circumstances. The very first choices become apparent when they are 75 weeks, or 17 months and a week. Don't compare your child with other children. Each child is unique and will choose accordingly.

Take a good look at your toddler. Figure out what their interests are. By now, you can readily see which talents and preferences they have, as well as their strong points. If your toddler has a high musical intelligence, that will now become clear. Use the list in "My Diary" on pages 384-389 to mark or highlight what your child selects. You can also see if there are some systems that you think your child could use or learn. Stop marking when your child begins with the next leap. That is usually when they are approximately 20-21 months old.

Toddlers Are Like This

Your toddler likes anything that's new to them most of all. Therefore, always react to the new skills and interests your toddler displays. In that way they learn more pleasantly, easier, quicker and more.

My Diary

How My Baby Explores the New World of Systems

THE CONSCIENCE

- ☐ Jumps and blurts out a loud "No" when caught
- ☐ Tests you by doing what's not allowed
- ☐ Imitates behavior from TV
- ☐ Is hurt and confused by unjust sanctions
- ☐ Is able to "lie"
- ☐ Other things I have noticed:

THE NOTION OF SELF

- ☐ Me and my body
- ☐ I control my body
- ☐ I can do things on my own
- ☐ I have my own will
- ☐ I can decide for myself
- ☐ I want power
- ☐ Other things I have noticed:

OUT OF SIGHT BUT NOT OUT OF MIND

- ☐ Hides and wants to be found
- ☐ Looks for people without just going back to where they were
- ☐ Other things I have noticed:

ME AND YOU

- ☐ Grasps that mom and dad are not the same person
- ☐ Sizes up similarities and differences to a tee
- ☐ Wants to be recognized as their own person
- ☐ Can put themselves in the place of others
- ☐ Can realize that another child wants something different
- ☐ Can console another person
- ☐ Is at their high point in mimicry
- ☐ Imagination takes off
- ☐ Starts treating toys as autonomous agents
- ☐ Other things I have noticed:

OTHER LIVING CREATURES

- ☐ Waves at birds and planes
- ☐ Smells the plants
- ☐ Likes feeding the chickens
- ☐ Is interested in bees, ants, ladybugs and the like
- ☐ Laughs at nature films with animals doing unusual things
- ☐ Wants to water the plants
- ☐ Other things I have noticed:

THE NUCLEAR FAMILY

☐ Grasps that members of their nuclear family are separate people but still belong together

☐ Plays the whole day long with stuffed animals, feeds them and puts them to bed

☐ Grasps that there are other nuclear families with other moms and dads, brothers and sisters

☐ Other things I have noticed:

FAMILY AND FRIENDS

☐ Grasps the difference between their family and that of their friends

☐ Knows exactly who belongs to who

☐ Wants to phone Grandma and Grandpa

☐ Wants to visit Grandma and Grandpa

☐ Other things I have noticed:

HOUSE, NEIGHBORHOOD AND FINDING THE WAY

☐ They have a good idea of the lay of the land in their surroundings

☐ Knows exactly where to find things in and around the house

☐ Recognizes their own house and that of Grandma & Grandpa

☐ Can point the way to the supermarket or the park

☐ Recognizes things even if they are in less familiar surroundings

☐ Other things I have noticed:

OWNERSHIP

- ☐ Knows perfectly well whose clothes are whose when sorting the laundry
- ☐ Knows exactly which bag and jacket belongs to which kid
- ☐ Knows exactly which toy belongs to whom and what's off limits
- ☐ No longer wishes to share their toys with other children
- ☐ Collects things and insists they're not to be thrown away
- ☐ Doesn't like mess. Wants everything systematically put away
- ☐ Other things I have noticed:

PUZZLES AND LITTLE THINGS

- ☐ Is now good at doing puzzles. Puzzles consisting of 7, 12 or at the most 20 pieces
- ☐ Motor skills are increasingly more refined than before
- ☐ Finds the sewing kit interesting, or a vast assortment of buttons
- ☐ Is a stickler for detail
- ☐ Other things I have noticed:

MAKING UP THEIR OWN GAMES

- ☐ Makes up a game with its own rules
- ☐ Makes up their own magic tricks
- ☐ Other things I have noticed:

ART

☐ Grasps that toys symbolize real world things or people

☐ Starts drawing in a completely different way. Random scribbling makes way for circles, squares and the like

☐ Draws horses, boats, planes, their dog, Grandma, Grandpa and themselves

☐ Likes it when you draw, too

☐ Music lovers can listen to music for quite a long time

☐ Likes playing the keyboard

☐ Erects more buildings than they used to

☐ Other things I have noticed:

SENSE OF TIME

☐ Remembers past experiences

☐ Predicts familiar, daily events and programs

☐ Reminds you the whole day long of your promise to go to Grandma and Grandpa's house

☐ Makes plans; if you promise to do something and forget, they are upset and insulted

☐ Remembers in the morning what we did the night before

☐ Other things I have noticed:

BASIC PHYSICS

☐ Holds a ball under water to watch it pop up

☐ Is endlessly occupied pouring their special mixture from one container to the next

☐ Pays attention to colors

☐ Found their first snow intimidating

☐ Is frightened of the electric toothbrush

☐ Is busy with basic phenomena of physics

☐ Other things I have noticed:

BASIC ARCHITECTURE

☐ Watches builders for hours

☐ Imitates making cement by mixing sand and water

☐ Imitates plastering walls

☐ Lays down Lego train tracks

☐ Tries building with Lego blocks

☐ Other things I have noticed:

LANGUAGE

☐ Understands most of what is said

☐ If they're exposed to different languages, they can distinguish between them and can ignore one

☐ Produces more and more words

☐ Sooner or later is able to combine words to form sentences

☐ Imitates animal noises

☐ Mimes a lot. Is able to communicate with gestures

☐ Loves books. Listens attentively to short stories till the end

☐ Other things I have noticed:

LEAP 10

What You Can Do to Help

In the world of systems, your toddler will discover that they can choose their principles. They will discover themselves, their family, their friends, their house, their neighborhood, their art and more. Give your toddler the opportunity to experience all sorts of systems. They learn how the world of systems is made up through their ingenuity, from seeing your reactions, and through much practice.

Me and My Conscience

The conscience is a system of moral principles, of values, norms and rules. The development of a conscience is not to be taken for granted. Your toddler has to construct their conscience using examples they take from you. You must demonstrate right and wrong. It takes time, a lot of time, before your toddler has seen enough examples from which to draw conclusions. Hopefully, your actions have been consistent. If you say one thing one time and something else the other, it will take your toddler much longer. The same applies if you give them confusing signals. They will have a hard time figuring it all out. From this age on, your little one tries to discover a system in everything, also in values, norms and rules. They crave rules and test the boundaries. Just as they are entitled to their daily meals, likewise they are entitled to their daily portion of rules.

"She knows that the things on the top shelf of the closet are her brother's. Now she climbs in the closet to grab and sneak something out. If she's seen, she drops it and looks at you with a look of 'How did that get there?'"
Victoria's mom, 76th week, or 17 ½ months

"He tests us by doing what he's not allowed."
Harry's mom, 77th week, or about 17 ¾ months

"He laughs when he surprises his father or me by suddenly doing something unexpected and expressly forbidden. He also laughs when we catch him."

John's mom, 79th week, or just over 18 months

"He imitates everything he sees on TV. For instance, he falls to the floor on purpose, and in one film, he saw children fighting. He observed this and hit himself."

Thomas' mom, 80th week, or 18 ½ months

"I also noticed that he wouldn't listen and he's behaving badly. I've never seen him like this. He hit someone on the head for no reason and threw another to the ground by his shirt. It's very irritating and a couple of times I have gotten really angry. I keep explaining that it hurts if he does that. Maybe I talk to him too much, so that he only listens when he wants. It has no effect on him if I tell him he can't do something or I ask him to help with something. I figured out that I need to tell him that we can do the chore together. Like putting a bottle back where it belongs instead of just throwing it."

Jim's mom, 81st week, or about 18 ¾ months

"I noticed if he falls down, he doesn't cry too quickly and takes his bumps well. But if he thinks that he's corrected unfairly, he's very hurt and confused. For instance, he bawled because he wasn't allowed on the bed with his boots. I said it was fine because they were clean, but the nanny didn't know and didn't understand. I could tell from the way he cried that it really upset and hurt him, even though it wasn't that big of a deal. I rarely hear him like that. I do hear the same cry after he has been staying with his father who tells him yes where I say no."

Taylor's mom, 81st week, or about 18 ¾ months

LEAP 10

"We changed the bedtime routine. She didn't used to go to bed until 10 and then she wanted to fall asleep on our lap first, and only then could we put her to bed. Last Saturday, we put her to bed at 8 o'clock, after she had been very tiresome. She yelled her lungs out for 45 minutes before she finally fell asleep. Since that night, she goes to bed between 8 and 8:30. We sing songs with her, her father talks with her a little bit more and then she falls asleep and sleeps through until 7 the next morning. Dad does have to put her to bed though."

Jenny's mom, 84th week, or just over 19 months

"The latest fad is making things up. He finished playing a flight simulator game on the computer with his dad and told me that his dad didn't do well and that he had crashed on landing. That wasn't at all the case, as it turned out, but he said it on purpose. He likes that he can make things up. He laughs heartily when Dad sets the record straight."

Jim's mom, 85th week, or 19 ½ months

"He is now able to 'lie.' For instance, he is eating a cookie and his mouth is full of chocolate and then the next round of cookies is handed out. When it's his turn, he hides the cookie in his hand behind his back and says that he hasn't gotten one yet. If he is allowed to take another one, he laughs and then shows the one he already had in his hand."

Thomas' mom, 87th week, or 20 months

Me and My Notion of Self

The system your toddler comes into contact with the most is themselves. That is what they get to know first, and it has all sorts of consequences. Your toddler discovers that they own their own body and that they have control over their own body. They also discover that they can make things happen, that they have their own will and can make their own decisions, and that they have power to influence. They think in terms of me, me, me.

Me and My Body

"He is very interested in his 'weenie.' He plucks at it and rubs it wherever he can. I often let him walk around naked."

Mark's mom, 72nd week, or 16 ½ months

"It seems as if she has rediscovered her toes. She studies them bit by bit, for minutes at a time."

Victoria's mom, 73th week, or 16 ¾ months

"She calls herself Mita. She gave herself that name."

Victoria's mom, 75th week, or 17 months and a week

"Often he hits his head hard against the wall. It makes me feel ill. I'd like him to stop. I think he does it to experience his notion of self."

Kevin's mom, 76th week, about 17 ½ months

"She cracked up at a silly doll in the supermarket."

Maria's mom, 81st week, or just over 18 ½ months

"She's obsessed with angels. I asked: 'Is that you?' 'Yes,' she said."

Nina's mom, 82nd week, or 18 ¾ months

"No one is allowed to touch him. Not the doctor while weighing and measuring him, nor the hairdresser, even though she was a friend. Not even his Grandma while getting dressed."

Matt's mom, 82nd week, or 18 ¾ months

"She also says: 'Is me.'"

Hannah's mom, 83rd week, or 19 months

"If anyone says to him: 'Nice curls,' he runs his hands through his hair like the star in the movie Grease."

Thomas' mom, 86th week, or approaching 20 months

LEAP 10

"She is really busy with putting on and taking off her clothes. She even puts her slippers, her socks and pants on. She is also very vain. When she has new clothes on, she gets on our bed in front of the mirror to examine herself better. Once she insisted on putting on a dress when I tried to get her in pants. She loves getting her hair done at the hairdresser."

Vera's mom, 74th-87th week, or 17-20 months

I Have Control Over My Body

"He walks the stairs, standing erect, taking big steps. Right foot on one step and the left foot on the next and so on."

Bob's mom, 72nd week, or 16 ½ months

"I already got angry once this week. She climbed up a dangerous flight of stairs after I'd already forbidden it."

Eve's mom, 74th week, or 17 months

"He pulls himself up on a bar, swings back and forth a bit then drops to the ground laughing."

Paul's mom, 74th week, or 17 months

"He climbs on everything. Nothing is too much. He is careful however. He is aware of the dangers."

James' mom, 76th week, or about 17 ½ months

"She finds all kinds of ways to get to where she's not allowed. I have put certain things away and protected others. That's no use anymore. She finds a way to get to them. Even if she needs to drag over a chair or get a ladder."

Victoria's mom, 76th week, or about 17 ½ months

"She climbs like an acrobat. She climbs on me while holding my hands. She pushes off my stomach diving backwards."

Laura's mom, 80th week, or 18 ½ months

"He went down the plastic slide at MacDonald's for the first time on his stomach."

Steven's mom, 81st week, or about 18 ¾ months

"She learned to somersault, slide down the slide by herself and climb back up by herself. She now gets in and out of bed by herself."

Nora's mom, 81st-83rd week, or about 18 ¾-19 months

"He likes to jump from high places if he thinks he can do it. When he can't, he says 'Scary' and sticks his arms out, which says: 'It's too high for me, can we do it together?' He also likes to walk along little walls, practicing his balance. He enjoys it if the wall is about four feet tall. I act calm, but inside it scares me."

Luke's mom, 83rd-86th week, or 19 to almost 20 months

"Since a month ago, the new thing is to try to make herself fall while going across the waterbed."

Eve's mom, 82nd week, or approaching 19 months

"She enjoyed shooting little blocks away with her mouth, it made her laugh. Running down the sand dunes and chasing after the dog on the beach was the best thing."

Hannah's mom, 86th-88th week, or approximately 20 months

I Can Do It Myself

"She peels and eats an orange by herself, opens doors and can say her own name. She winds up her toy radio herself and goes around listening to it."

Juliette's mom, 72nd week, or 16 ½ months

"She grasps that she can use her potty to do her business. Twice she went and sat down with a diaper and relieved herself."

Josie's mom, 73rd week, or approaching 17 months

"She doesn't want to sit in her highchair much anymore. She wants to sit in a normal chair at the dinner table. Also, she doesn't want to wear a bib and she wants to feed herself."

Julia's mom, 73rd-75th week, or around 17 months

"This week he walked around with napkins. He used them as a bib or towel, but particularly as an oven glove. I mean, when he goes to pick up something, he puts the napkin on top and then picks the thing up. He mainly did this in the kitchen with the grips on the drawers."

Paul's mom, 74th week, or 17 months

"Now he is busy with spatial aspects. Putting things in or under something is very interesting to him. It's not so much that something fits somewhere, it's more that he's the one putting things in and taking things out. He's more interested in researching his own potential, instead of the qualities of the things themselves. He now has a renewed urgency to look into the pans. Now it's not about me showing him what we are eating and telling him what it's called, but that he looks and identifies it himself. Playing with the bucket with the shape-sorting lid has taken on a new twist. It's now about him putting the pieces in as he wants. He purposefully tries to ram the shapes through the wrong holes. If he accidently puts one in the proper hole, he quickly pulls it out. He wants to put the pieces in as he sees fit, not according to the rules of the game."

Frankie's mom, 76th week, or about 17 ½ months

"This week he likes drawing. I think it's because it's something he does himself. He makes something by himself."

John's mom, 77th week, or 17 ¾ months

"She makes drawings and then laughs about it herself."

Maria's mom, 77th week, or 17 ¾ months

"These days he wants to feed himself dinner. That's not without its problems, but in general, he does well. He imitates more and more. He cleans the floor with a sponge, he blows his nose with a handkerchief and vacuums with the vacuum cleaner attachment. He now knows exactly what things are for."

James' mom, 77th week, or 17 ¾ months

"If I ask, 'Do you want Mom to do it?' she says: 'No, Anna.' Even if she has broken something and we ask who has done it, she says: 'Anna.' She is very conscious of herself. She laughs if she drops something or throws something on the ground."

Anna's mom, 77th week, or 17 ¾ months

"This week he came walking up proudly with a full potty. I was just as proud as he was. If he goes around without a diaper, he's indicating that he wants to use his potty or that he has used it before I even know about it. He waits to pee until he has the potty. He uses all his might to do a number two and every little bit must be done in the toilet. Endearing. Then he says 'More.' That means he wants to use it again. When he's all done, he says 'Finished.'"

Mark's mom, 78th-79th week, or around 18 months

"Now she releases her belt and climbs out of her chair herself."

Ashley's mom, 80th week, or 18 ½ months

"He can now function as an 'errand boy'. He gets whatever is asked of him. He gets the remote control, the TV guide, socks. He turns on the washing machine, 'Medium heat please.' He gets the shoes. Gets the cleaning products. And if he and Dad are playing the flight simulator on the computer, he follows his commands: 'Gas!'–'Landing gear!'–'Eject!'.
I am proud of my big little boy. He really gives it his all and does everything asked of him right away. But I feel for the poor child. He really gets put to work."

Thomas' mom, 80th week, or 18 ½ months

LEAP 10

"She is an expert with the toy doctor's instruments."

Elisabeth's mom, 81st week, or 18 ¾ months

"She did her business on the potty. She says 'Poo-poo' if she goes in her diaper, which means that she wants a clean diaper. Now and then she does her business on the toilet."

Nina's mom, 80th-83rd week, or 18 to 19 months

"He likes to walk around naked after his bath. Then he crouches down and strains to go pee. Once, he peed in his closet."

Robin's mom, 82nd week, or approaching 19 months

"It never ceases to amaze me how well she understands what's going on. Now and then, she has it all figured out. For instance, if she can't reach something, she goes to the bathroom, gets a stool and puts it where she needs it. That's just one of the many moments I see her solving her own problems."

Vera's mom, 82nd week, or approaching 19 months

"She colors with crayons now."

Laura's mom, 83rd week, or 19 months

"She is able to arrange the colors. She saw that one of the markers had the wrong color top on it."

Victoria's mom, 84th week, or just over 19 months

"He tells me ahead of time that he needs to use the bathroom."

Taylor's mom, 84th week, or just over 19 months

"Now and again she wants to use her potty. She sits down for a second and goes to wiping furiously, but has yet to do anything on the potty."

Eve's mom, 85th week, or 19 ½ months

"He's increasingly more helpful and he imitates more. He brings his cup to the kitchen and puts it on the counter or grabs a plate. He also likes to play like he's hammering something. He wants to drink out of a big person's cup and not a bottle or baby's cup."

Bob' mom, 86th week, or approaching 20 months

"She did a little business once on the toilet."

Anna's mom, 87th week, or 20 months

"She gets onto the potty herself if she's already naked. If she's wearing pants, she does it in her pants, but alerts us directly."

Hannah's mom, 87th week, or 20 months

"Completely potty trained. After only three nights, she completely stopped wetting the bed."

Emily's mom, 87th week, or 20 months

"He can blow his nose. Now he tries to blow his nose into everything, even the coasters."

Gregory's mom, 88th week, or just over 20 months

I Have My Own Will

"The last few months he's been naughty and has been testing the waters to see what's allowed and what's not, as well as the consequences. At the moment, he knows full well what's allowed. Now he's just naughty to show: 'I do what I want. So, what are you going to do about it?'"

Harr y's mom, 76th week, or about 17 ½ months

LEAP 10

"He doesn't listen to warnings anymore. It looks as if he's proclaiming that he knows what he's doing. Experimenting has taken priority: falling down, heat, strong spices, etc. He decides what he eats, when and how."

Matt's mom, 76th week, or about 17 ½ months

"He really goes his own way. Preferably looking for trouble."

James' mom, 77th week, or about 17 ¾ months

"She wanted a lot of attention if she wasn't allowed something or if getting something took too long. She kept tugging on me, was very stubborn, whiny, pig-headed, naughty, hot-tempered and uncontrollable."

Josie's mom, 77th week, or about 17 ¾ months

"He gets into everything, but I have to keep a close watch on him. It's too dangerous to leave him unattended because he's always defying the rules. I really got angry when he tried to light the stove with a hot pan on it. It really made me jump. Fortunately, he only received slight burns, and there was only minimal damage, but he certainly got a physical warning. I hope it's sunk in that he's not allowed to touch the gas. It's really fun to cook together, but if he hasn't learned his lesson we'll no longer be able to."

Steven's mom, 78th week, or around 18 months

"Recently, she has abandoned her toys for the things that she's not allowed to touch, like the DVD player."

Laura's mom, 78th week, or around 18 months

"I have to accompany him everywhere. He's very enterprising and quite the prospector. Everything must be turned upside down and inside out with me looking on. We had a run-in because he makes a mess faster than I can clean it up."

Luke's mom, 79th week, or just over 18 months

"He is a real clown. He pays no mind to anything, just does his own thing. He loves to kid around. We call him the 'little elf.'"

James' mom, 80th week, or about 18 ½ months

"She's increasingly independent. She goes off by herself or along with others. A quick wave and off she goes."

Elisabeth's mom, 80th-81st week, or 18 ½ to 18 ¾ months

"The last few days he's been playing with cars. On Wednesday, I ended up with a half-hour all to myself. He played happily with his blocks and cars and I didn't hear him for a whole half-hour."

James' mom, 81st week, or 18 ¾ months

"She put her finger in the hot tea. Ouch!"

Julia's mom, 84th week, or just over 19 months

"Now and then she really amuses herself well. She plays by herself if I'm around, but I'm not allowed to read. I sometimes get a bit of reading in, which is more than I used to."

Nina's mom, 83rd-86th week, or 19 to almost 20 months

"Her personal awareness grows daily. She indicates what she wants and what she doesn't want. She blows kisses when bidding farewell and if she gives something to you, it's a conscious decision."

Ashley's mom, 83rd-86th week, or 19 to almost 20 months

"She doesn't want me to brush her teeth, but if she does it, she doesn't brush but eats the paste and then she's finished. One time when I went ahead and brushed her teeth for her, she was angry with me for the next half-hour."

Anna's mom, 86th week, or approaching 20 months

I Can Decide For Myself

"She starts to laugh already when she's planning something naughty."
Eve's mom, 76th week, or about 17 ½ months

"He announces everything he does. He always points to himself."
Kevin's mom, 76th week, or about 17 ½ months

"She really knows that it's 'bah' when she has messed her pants. She comes up and says 'Bah.' If she can choose the spot where she gets changed, then she doesn't make a scene and will consent to it. She finds the strangest spots to be changed. Changing clothes is the same: 'Find your spot,' and there she goes."
Nora's mom, 86th week, or approaching 20 months

"He wants to pick out his own clothes these days. He really has certain preferences. His comfortable jogging pants with mice print is 'out.' Sometimes he puts Daddy's jacket on with a tie and goes and wakes Mom up."
Thomas' mom, 86th week, or approaching 20 months

I Want Power

"The temper tantrums have really picked up. She can really scream loud. It's short but powerful. She also watches her brother very carefully when he misbehaves. It looks like she's taking mental notes."
Victoria's mom, 72nd week, or 16 ½ months

"If she doesn't agree, she starts to scream. The rolling around on the ground has lessened. She tries to get her way by screaming."
Jenny's mom, 72nd week, or 16 ½ months

"He scares me with snakes and mice and does the same to the girl next door."

Frankie's mom, 74th week, or 17 months

"He tries putting oversized cars into his tiny toy garage. He didn't ever try this before."

Robin's mom, 76th week, or about 17 ½ months

"He constantly hits and sometimes pinches if he doesn't get his way. If he's angry, he punches hard, softer when he's joking. The general idea is that I try to break his bad habit by calmly correcting him, and offering him a pillow to pound or by urging him to calm down. I do sometimes get angry if he really hurts. This makes him sad and then he starts handing out kisses."

Luke's mom, 76th week, or about 17 ½ months

"He insists on eating and drinking what I have, even if he already has the same. He wants what I have. He takes my food and drink from me. We fight it out like two children."

Gregory's mom, 76th week, or about 17 ½ months

"She screams so loudly and in a high pitch if she doesn't get her way or she fails at something. That really annoys me and I want to break her of that soon. We have had several squabbles this week because of it."

Juliette's mom, 77th week, or 17 ¾ months

"A couple of times a day she gets in a rage, especially if she doesn't get her way. It generally blows over all by itself. Sometimes, I have to intervene in order to calm her down. She's quite fierce."

Maria's mom, 77th week, or 17 ¾ months

"He has gotten notably rougher. He also forcefully throws things and really can't stand not getting his way. He sometimes throws things at the cat, like the alarm clock."

Matt's mom, 77th week, or 17 ¾ months

"He is very well tempered and exceedingly energetic. He's so very busy with what he seems to need to do, that he doesn't even flinch when I express my displeasure at certain things. He throws and hits with anything he can get a hold of, with all his might. I think he flings things like that because he feels a certain power over his possessions. The same goes for hitting. I try to make it clear to him when I take action against him by threatening punishment. If he persists in throwing and hitting, I put him in his playpen. He sits there quietly waiting it out, only to pick up where he left off, throwing and hitting. The only thing that helps is to distract him. It seems like we are dealing with a new learning pattern."

Kevin's mom, 78th week, or around 18 months

"If he doesn't get his way he gets angry. For instance, if he wants to go outside, he points to his jacket. If I say no, he gets angry. He also gets angry if he doesn't get more candy or if his friend isn't home."

Robin's mom, 77th week, or 17 ¾ months

"If she has to come inside from the garden, she cries and stamps her feet. In these cases, I give her a time-out."

Vera's mom, 79th week, or just over 18 months

"Sometimes I doubt whether or not I can manage his headstrong, dynamic activities."

Harry's mom, 79th week, or just over 18 months

"He throws everything to the ground and away from himself. He bites and hits. I really got angry this week when he smeared his food and drink all over the floor."

John's mom, 79th week, or just over 18 months

"I try anger and demanding obedience, insisting that he has to stop, but nothing helps. He's not at all impressed. It's difficult when he acts this way. If he is tired, it's even worse. Then it really is overwhelming."

Paul's mom, 79th week, or just over 18 months

"If I leave the room briefly or neglect her in the slightest, she starts digging in my plant."

Laura's mom, 80th week, or about 18 ½ months

"She was very annoying this week. She kept insisting on getting her way. If she didn't get her way, then she started screaming and threw herself on the ground. If we just left her, she would come around on her own."

Emily's mom, 81st week, or 18 ¾ months

"If she can't get something, has to go to bed or doesn't get her way, she cries and stamps her feet."

Ashley's mom, 84th week, or just over 19 months

"The throwing and hitting seem to be lessening. But the biting is sometimes very serious. Harsh scolding, explaining, a spanking: nothing seems to help."

John's mom, 83rd-86th week, or 19 to almost 20 months

"He terrorizes the cats. He constantly keeps tabs on where they both are. Then he has to be able to pet them."

Jim's mom, 83rd-86th week, or 19 to almost 20 months

"She doesn't want to be seen as 'small.' We went to get ice cream in a nice place, where the scoops are pricy and Dad said: 'Elisabeth can have some of ours.' When the ice cream came, she could lick it but she wasn't allowed to hold it. That brought on a temper tantrum. She wanted to leave. She was insulted that she was thought to be small. Dad then went to a lesser ice cream parlor for some more ice cream. She held it but didn't eat it. Her tantrum continued all the while. She was deeply insulted. For the next half-hour to 45 minutes, she was no fun. She hit Dad, too."

Elisabeth's mom, 86th week, or approaching 20 months

"She is very willful, which is sometimes difficult. She cries if she isn't allowed something or she doesn't get her way. Real tears are reserved for when she falls or hurts herself."

Julia's mom, 87th week, or 20 months

I Am Out of Sight But Not Out of Mind

Because your toddler now understands that they are a separate system, they also understand that the same principles that apply to the people and objects around them also apply to them. They understand that people and objects continue to exist, even though they may not be in their field of vision. They also understand that they still exist for mom and dad even when they can't see them. Furthermore, they now understand that other people don't necessarily remain in the same place where they last saw them. It starts to dawn on them that they can move about and change their positions. When they look for dad, they now understand that they may have to look elsewhere than where they last saw him.

"He likes to crawl into closets and shut all the doors."

Steven's mom, 81st week, or 18 ¾ months

"She hides in the closet, slides the doors shut and then calls 'Mom.' It really makes her laugh when we finally find her."

Josie's mom, 85th week, or 19 ½ months

Me and You

Now that your toddler sees themselves as an individual, they will start using terms like "me" and "you." They grasp that mom and dad are individuals too who lead their own lives. They start to compare themselves with them and map out the similarities and differences to a tee.

"She has discovered that her father has a penis. She calls it 'Pino.'"

Victoria's mom, 72nd week, or 16 ½ months

"His own weenie is really an item. So is his father's and the absence of mine."

Bob's mom, 73rd week, or approaching 17 months

"These days he points first to himself and then to me, as if he wants to point out the difference."

Mark's mom, 75th week, or just over 17 months

"If I propose: 'Shall we go out together?' she points to herself as if saying: 'You mean me?' as if there are other people in the room."

Nina's mom, 75th week, or just over 17 months

"He loves it when I make special reference to him. He points to himself to distinguish himself from me and as a confirmation that it's for him."

Luke's mom, 77th week, or 17 ¾ months

"If I imitate certain stereotypical statements or behavior of hers, it makes her laugh."

Hannah's mom, 78th week, or approaching 18 months

LEAP 10

> *"He is very interested in his father – in the shower, in bed, on the 'john.' He follows him everywhere and always talks about him."*
>
> **Frankie's mom, 79th-86th week, or 18 to almost 20 months**

> *"She learned the terms 'me' and 'you.'"*
>
> **Juliette's mom, 86th week, or approaching 20 months**

Now that your toddler can distinguish between themselves and others, they can also put themselves in another person's position. In a simple experiment, it was shown that toddlers of 13 to 15 months were unable to fathom that another person could make a choice that was different from theirs. They will be able to do this for the first time at 18 months. That has all kinds of consequences.

The Dangling Carrot

> *"We came out of the store and there was a helicopter ride for the kids there. If you put money in, it moves around for a while with lights flashing. Nora loves it and was allowed to go on once. But there was already a kid in it, who didn't want to get out after his turn. Nora looked around and ran to a mini-shopping cart and started pushing it around. The other kid came out of the helicopter right away and wanted to push that cart around too. Nora shot over to the helicopter and got in."*
>
> **Nora's mom, 87th week, or 20 months**

I Can Console

> *"She says to us that we have to cry and then she will give us a kiss and a gentle caress."*
>
> **Jenny's mom, 79th-80th week, or 18 months**

Me and My Mimicry

"He re-enacts moods. He says for instance 'Stop!' in a way that a girl does, a bit sassy. He imitates certain gestures, like turning his head and body and putting his hand up, and talking to the hand."

Taylor's mom, 80th week, or around 18 ½ months

"Imitating certain postures and movements is a favorite pastime. She even tries to imitate the cat."

Maria's mom, 83rd-86th week, or 19 to almost 20 months

"He observed the monkeys and how they open nuts. We collect hazelnuts in the neighborhood and at home he really gets in to shelling them."

Bob's mom, 83rd-86th week, or 19 to almost 20 months

"She imitates the other children quite a bit. If they climb a fence, she tries too. If they knock on a window, she does the same. If they do it, she copies it."

Vera's mom, 87th week, or 20 months

Me and My Fantasy Play

In their make-believe play they start to treat their toys like they play along too, like people capable of doing things.

"She grabbed an imaginary something from her hand and put it in her mouth. She did it a couple of times. It was very peculiar. It looked like her first game of make-believe."

Josie's mom, 71st week, or just over 16 months

"Suddenly she has become more independent. She plays by herself very well. Now and then it looks like she's in a dream world. She fantasizes. I had yet to see her do that. She plays the game with her doll. Sometimes she tells me her fantasies."

Victoria's mom, 75th week, or just over 17 months

"He made a drawing of a turd and then stamped on it. I don't allow him to stamp on turds in the street."

Paul's mom, 77th week, or 17 ¾ months

"After having seen his baby pictures one afternoon, he decided that all his animals were his babies and played with them the whole afternoon in his bed."

Gregory's mom, 84th week, or just over 19 months

"She indicates much more clearly what she wants and gets frustrated if I don't get what she means. Playing make-believe has much to do with it. She gives me a dog and I have to understand that the dog needs to be breast fed."

Emily's mom, 86th week, or approaching 20 months

"He does play make-believe a lot, like having a tea party, sitting together in his Lego car on the steps. He pats the ground beside him in the most inviting way and loves if we sit there together."

Thomas' mom, 86th week, or approaching 20 months

Other Living Creatures

Other living creatures are all separate systems with their own behavioral rules and programs. Your toddler is fascinated by this fact.

"This week she was very interested in birds. She laughed when a bird she was watching returned from out of sight. She laughed more when she saw where the sounds came from, the sounds she had heard before even seeing the bird. It's the same with airplanes. She also likes to investigate how plants smell."

Eve's mom, 73rd week, or approaching 17 months

"She waves at planes and birds and sometimes to people."

Eve's mom, 74th week, or 17 months

"This week he liked feeding the chickens. He stayed with his grandfather on the farm."

Jim's mom, 77th week, or 17 ¾ months

"He saw a snail in the street and then before I noticed it, he said that the snail was dead. It turned out that he and his father had covered this topic a few times."

Harry's mom, 79th week, or 18 months

"He enjoyed the bees with his grandfather, the beekeeper."

Steven's mom, 83rd week, or 19 months

"She cracked up when she saw a snake eat a mouse in a nature film."

Laura's mom, 84th week, or just over 19 months

"This week he was really interested in an ant outside in the garden."

Matt's mom, 84th week, or just over 19 months

"She is really into bugs this week – ladybugs and ants."

Anna's mom, 85th week, or 19 ½ months

"She likes watering the plants these days. She starts by making smacking noises as if the plants are hungry: 'The plants want to eat.' Preferably, she feeds them twice a day. For Ashley, it's the filling up and pouring out of the watering can that makes her feel she has done her deed for the day."

Ashley's mom, 85th week, or 19 ½ months

> "At the beach he was able to play endlessly in the sand, digging and pushing shells into the sand and then pronouncing them dead."

Kevin's mom, 87th week, or 20 months

I Am Part of a Nuclear Family

The nuclear family is a system like other human organizations. And it's the first human organization that your toddler experiences from the inside, right from the start. However, it is only now that they begin to see that a nuclear family is a unit, a system.

> "She now has a strict division of tasks. Mom gets her glass and Dad fills it."

Victoria's mom, 73rd week, or approaching 17 months

> "She now grasps that we are a family, a group. If I just use the names Xaviera, Marco and Thomas in a sentence, she corrects the omissions of Mita (Victoria) and Kitan (Christian)."

Victoria's mom, 74th week, or 17 months

> "She is busy with her dolls and stuffed animals all day long. One goes in the highchair. If she gets something to eat, she first gives some to her 'friends.' She also puts them all to bed in her doll wagon and then goes and lays in the big bed."

Elisabeth's mom, 74th-75th week, or around 17 months

> "She knows exactly who belongs with who or who gave her what."

Vera's mom, 75th week, or just over 17 months

> "She laughs when we play with the cats or if the cats get riled up."

Jenny's mom, 71st-76th week, or just over 16 till about 17 ½ months

"He points to his father, to me and to himself. Then I am supposed to say that we all are separate people and yet we belong together. Then he nods approvingly 'yes' and sighs in contentment."

Frankie's mom, 76th week, or about 17 ½ months

"Nowadays, he is a real 'pal.' He asks me to accompany him in the Lego car. He wants to read together. He wants to color together."

Thomas' mom, 78th week, or about 18 months

"When we would take her brother to school or pick him up, she had a hard time with me calling other women 'mom of so-and-so.' There was only one mom and that was me. Now she understands that there are other families and that those women are mothers of other children. She still protests though if she hears them called 'mom.' The only unequivocal mom is her mom."

Victoria's mom, 79th week, or just over 18 months

"If his older brother or sister is on my lap, he gets angry, and remains that way until my lap is vacated."

James' mom, 82nd week, or approaching 19 months

"This week he enjoyed getting in bed and snuggling with Mom and Dad."

Gregory's mom, 83rd week, or 19 months

"He is very bold and already teases his brother and sister, sometimes getting on their nerves."

James' mom, 83rd week, or 19 months

"Now she grasps that ours is not the only family. Recently, we went to pick up her brother who was playing at a friend's house. We stayed to have coffee. She was clearly upset and kept calling the name of the boy's sister and asking where she was. But the sister was playing at friend's. The family was incomplete without the sister and that troubled her. She saw that as being wrong."

Victoria's mom, 84th week, or just over 19 months

LEAP 10

"James sometimes gets left out by his brother and sister when they want to play a game. They put him in the hall and shut the door in his face. He comes to me shattered and needs to be consoled."

James' mom, 87th week, or 20 months

"She knows her father is called Hank and her mother Miko."

Julia's mom, 87th week, or 20 months

Me and My Family or Friends

Just as a nuclear family is a system, so too is the extended family and the circle of friends. Your toddler starts to recognize that now as well. They also learn the differences between their family and their friends' families.

"She came to me with the telephone and a picture of her grandparents and signaled that she wanted to call them."

Juliette's mom, 78th week, or about 18 months

"If I speak about his friend, he knows who that is and he says his name enthusiastically. He certainly knows his friend."

Steven's mom, 78th week, or about 18 months

"We are really close. He follows my conversations and interactions with others. He reacts to statements, even if they're not directed at him. When my friend called her son, who was pretty far away, she said that he doesn't listen to her, so my son rushed out to go get him. He tried to drag him along, but his friend got him in a hold which resulted in a screaming match, because my son does not like to be pinned down."

Luke's mom, 79th week, or just over 18 months

"When the neighbor went home to cook, he wanted to go with her. That was fine and I waved him off. I had expected that my boy would want to come back soon. That wasn't the case. After an hour and a half, I got worried and went to see what was going on. But Thomas didn't want to come home. He wanted me to stay, too. Then he showed me everything he'd seen there, the refrigerator, the grapes, etc. He has a great time there because he's allowed to do what he wants. While she was cooking, he sat on the kitchen counter with his feet in the sink playing in the water."

Thomas' mom, 80th week, or 18 ½ months

"Grandma and Grandpa live around the corner. We stop by often and naturally we don't always go inside. If we pass by, she always calls out 'Ama' or 'Apa'."

Victoria's mom, 82nd week, or almost 19 months

Finding My Way Around My House and My Neighborhood

Your own home is a system as is the surrounding neighborhood. Your toddler learns to recognize that now and starts learning how to find their way. They construct a map in their head of their surroundings. Such a mental map is actually a system, too.

"He's finding his bearings. Even when he's not in familiar surroundings, he looks for other points of recognition and he's very pleased when he finds them. He wants to share this immediately, as well as what's coming up."

Harry's mom, 74th week, or 17 months

"A month ago, he didn't notice the sea while at the beach. This time he shouted for joy when he spied the sea from the top of the dune. He was practically overcome with joy when he saw the sea. Day after day, a constant reminder."

Bob's mom, 74th week, or 17 months

"He knows where we are going. If I ask him, he answers correctly."

John's mom, 79th week, or 18 months

"He knows the way from the campground to the sea."

Jim's mom, 80th-81st week, or around 18½ months

"Taylor and I have moved to another floor in the same building. Taylor felt at home in his new abode and after settling in, started going around with his buggy. He was familiar with the house because the previous inhabitants had two kids of their own. He seemed used to it already."

Taylor's mom, 82nd week, or approaching 19 months

"A few times she didn't want to come with me inside to visit, regardless if they were strangers or Grandma and Grandpa. Really strange, she's never done this before. When she finally made it in, she was fine."

Maria's mom, 82nd week, or approaching 19 months

"He has a good map of the vicinity in his head. He knows exactly where to find things, at home, outside, or at Dad's work. He can point me the way to the grocery store or the way to Dad's work as well as the way inside the building to his office. He also knows the next-door neighbor's house very well. He knows where everything is, the grapes and so on. She usually has them. He gets disappointed, though, if they are not in the right place."

Thomas' mom, 83rd week, or 19 months

> "If we let the dog out in the neighborhood, she says 'Ama' or 'Apa' [Grandma or Grandpa] and points in the right direction to their house, even though the house is still out of sight around the corner. Clearly, she wants to visit."

Victoria's mom, 86th week, or approaching 20 months

> "This summer, my friend and I went to the beach regularly. Our two boys got along well. They are still good friends. Jim had expected to meet up with his friend before we went. He kept asking where he was. This time they were waiting for us at the beach."

Jim's mom, 87th week, or 20 months

Me and My Belongings

In a nuclear family system there are all sorts of principles, among which there are values, norms and rules. Consider for instance "We will share fair and square" or "Thou shalt not steal." There are rules for what belongs to whom and what we are entitled to. Your toddler learns these rules by doing. Sometimes they pick it up unnoticed and it's a pleasant surprise to find out what they've learned on their own. Other times it takes some persuasion.

Me and My Clothes

> "She knows exactly which bags, coats and what-not belong to which kids and when we leave she fetches our things."

Nina's mom, 82nd week, or approaching 19 months

"When I empty the washing machine, I lay out every piece on the machine and pull them into shape before I put them into the dryer. She is right on top of everything, sorting things in her own way. She knows precisely who everything belongs to: 'Is Thomas,' 'Is mommy,' 'Is Mita.'"

Victoria's mom, 83rd week, or 19 months

"He seems aware of his new clothes, underwear and undershirt instead of onesies. He finds it very interesting. He loves his new shoes."

Paul's mom, 83rd-86th week, or 19 to almost 20 months

Me and My Stuff

"While visiting a friend, Robin played with one of his toy cars, which he wasn't allowed to take home with him. He cried the whole way back to the house and at home, he threw away his own cars."

Robin's mom, 76th week, or about 17 ½ months

"She remembers where she left things. If I ask where something is, she remembers."

Emily's mom, 78th week, or around 18 months

"She finds one 'diamond' after the other. Her brother collects nice stones and lays them out in his room. So she scavenges for rocks too. Pieces of gravel go into her pocket one after the other and absolutely none of them can be thrown away."

Victoria's mom, 78th week, or around 18 months

"One day she came up to me, took my hand and led me to the room where all the toys are. She pointed: 'Is Thomas, is Thomas, is Thomas... and Mita?' This was a hefty protest. Recently, Thomas hadn't allow her to touch his toys, because she had broken some things. And indeed, this left her with very little to play with!"

Mita/Victoria's mom, 83rd week, or 19 months

No Mess

You've never seen anything like it before. They can't stand a mess. Enjoy it while it lasts. It lasts until the next leap and won't be back for a number of years – if it ever comes back at all. They want everything arranged systematically.

Doing Puzzles

A puzzle is a system too – an organized unit that is a whole due to the interdependence of the components from which it is comprised.

LEAP 10

"Her motor skills continue to improve. This week she enjoyed putting beads on sticks and then the sticks in holes. She also likes to take my money out and spread it out."

Anna's mom, 73rd week, or approaching 17 months

"She does the puzzles herself."

Laura's mom, 75th week, or just over 17 months

"He is good at puzzles, with a bit of help. Even puzzles he hasn't seen yet."

Matt's mom, 76th week, or around 17½ months

"I pretended that I couldn't do the puzzle. Every time I went astray he said: 'No, no' and then told me where I should put the piece. After repeating this act several times, I'd had enough. I pulled the puzzle apart and put it back together in a flash. I acted like I was very proud and said: 'See, I can do it too.' He responded with: 'No.' It turned out that a tiny corner of a piece of the puzzle was sticking up. He pushed it in and then it was right!"

Thomas' mom, 80th week, or about 18 ½ months

"All of a sudden he did the puzzle right. He turns the pieces so that they fit well. Not always, but mostly."

Frankie's mom, 82nd week, or approaching 19 months

"She enjoys the box of buttons and all the various tops."

Jenny's mom, 82nd week, or approaching 19 months

"She does many puzzles now. Her first puzzles, the easier ones, are no longer fun. Now she has a difficult one, 13 pieces."

Julia's mom, 86th week, or approaching 20 months

"He pays attention to the minutest of details. Like the smallest piece of the puzzle that's not quite right. He seems rather nit-picky. For instance, in the fairy tale 'Snow White' the expectant mother says that she would like to have a baby girl. One with skin as white as snow and lips as red as blood. The mother had just pricked her finger and there was a tiny drop of blood visible on the picture. He noticed this even though he'd never seen anything like 'pricking a finger.' He pointed to the picture where the nice red was."

Thomas' mom, 86th week, or approaching 20 months

"All of a sudden she did a 20-piece puzzle without batting an eye. She'd not done the puzzle before. After that she was no longer interested in puzzles."

Xaviera's mom, 87th week, or 20 months

Creating a Game

A puzzle is a system devised by someone else. Your toddler is now able to think up systems by themselves, for instance a game where they make up the rules, or magic tricks.

"He made up a game himself, taking turns throwing dice. One person throws, the other has to pick it up. He's strict in keeping the sequence. He keeps looking for tight corners to throw the die."

Mark's mom, 83rd-86th week, or 19 to almost 20 months

"Today she did a magic trick she had come up with herself. She watches her brother doing tricks a lot. She put a marble into a bottle and said: 'Uh, oh.' She shook the bottle up and down and said: 'No.' She meant that the marble was stuck. Then she turned in a circle (like a magician does) and held the bottle upside down. Tada!"

Victoria's mom, 83rd week, or 19 months

Me and My Art

After a year and a half, your toddler starts to use toys in a way that signifies they know what the toys stand for, what or who they represent. In their play, it shows that they are familiar with the people, the objects and the situations from everyday life that are represented by the toys. The toys symbolize someone or something from the real world. Your toddler can play with these symbols in their imagination.

Their ability to symbolize enables them to create drawings that are completely different from their earlier drawings and that represent something from the real world – for example a car, a dog, or even themselves. This new ability to symbolize did not emerge gradually, it came into being all of a sudden with a leap and is a new quality. Art is born. If your little artist loves making drawings, you will have a hard time keeping them supplied with paper. The beginning of a huge collection is at hand. If they experience something exciting, like fireworks at New Year's Eve, it's likely they will make a drawing to capture the moment.

Not only do they start making drawings, but they start building constructions as well. And if you have a little music lover, they will be playing their keyboard and can listen to music for quite a long time and enjoy it.

"Her drawings are very different now. The scribbles have made way for small circles, tiny, tiny. She is really into details."
Victoria's mom, 78th week, or about 18 months

"She now colors in her drawings. She is very precise and hardly colors outside the lines."
Victoria's mom, 79th week, or just over 18 months

"He draws horses and boats now and this morning he meticulously drew a circle and a square and then pointed to himself. He had drawn himself."
Luke's mom, 79th week, or just over 18 months

"He has started building more, whereas he used to be more into destruction."

Taylor's mom, 83rd week, or 19 months

"He drew a car. It was a good drawing of a car. He can only do this if he is lying down on his side with his head resting on his other outstretched arm. What does his car look like? It's two circles, the wheels, with a line in between. Circles are 'vroom vroom'. He also draws airplanes and just recently, legs. A spiral is a steering wheel — a steering wheel turns."

Thomas' mom, 83rd week, or 19 months

"She has a Bambi book. In it is a picture of possums hanging by their tails from a tree branch. 'Hey,' Elisabeth thought, 'that's not right.' So she turned the book upside down, so she could see it better."

Elisabeth's mom, 85th week, or 19 ½ months

"He loves music. He likes playing his electric keyboard. He puts on a certain rhythm to accompany his lead. At the store, he listened to practically a whole CD of classical music. It lasted almost an hour. He was upset when I disturbed him halfway through to go on with our shopping. He had to listen to the end."

Thomas' mom, 86th week, or approaching 20 months

There is good reason that toddlers in Japan can play the violin fairly well at the age of two. Of course, they use special, small violins. In Western culture, not many people are eager to drill their toddlers this early in life in pursuit of such mastery. "Freedom and happiness" is the motto. However, we are not addressing cultural differences here. The point is that toddlers at this age normally have the ability to learn such things.

LEAP 10

" wrong... wrong... wrong... , wrong... Grandpa "

The Evolution of Art

Art appeared late in the evolution of our species. While we consider our evolution to have covered of millions of years, most evidence of the emergence of art is dated as recently as 35,000 years ago. About that time so many artifacts were found that there was talk of an art explosion. All of a sudden there was a surplus. We are talking about cave drawings, small stone carvings and musical instruments. A very rare find of the remains of a flute dates back 90,000 years. Art is characteristically human. The emergence of art was preceded by a massive increase in our brain size. We are, however, still in the dark about how this came to be. But the notion of self, fantasy and language certainly play a large role, just as the increase in the size of the frontal lobe placed just behind our forehead does.

Me and My Sense of Time: Past, Present and Future

Your toddler starts to develop a sense of time now. Their memory of past experiences improves and they get better at anticipating the future.

"I can't tell her anymore in the morning that we are going to do something fun in the afternoon. Otherwise, she reminds me the whole day until it happens: 'Now Apa Ama [Grandma Grandpa] to?'"

Victoria's mom, 78th week, or around 18 months

"She makes plans. When we sit down for dinner, she asks if she may draw. I tell her that first we're going to eat. Then she tells me where her pen and paper will need to be. I am supposed to say that I understand and that it will happen. If I forget after dinner, she gets very angry, and she is offended."

Victoria's mom, 80th week, or just over 18 months

"He remembers promises. If I promise that we'll do something after his bath, he reminds me. When he wakes up in the morning, he refers to what we did before he went to sleep."

Gregory's mom, 82nd week, or approaching 19 months

Basic Physics

If you observe their play well, you cannot ignore that they are busy with the basic phenomena of physics.

"He dunks things like a ball under water to experience the resistance. He also disassembled a small electric telephone. He now looks at it differently than he did before when it just made noise. It doesn't work anymore after his experiment. He finds throwing things and taking them apart really interesting. He tries things out."

Harry's mom, 77th week, 17 ¾ months

"She can spend hours pouring some liquid from one vessel into another. She uses bottles, glasses, plates or cups. While she's busy she likes to add the necessary commentary."

Ashley's mom, 78th week, or around 18 months

"She pays close attention to colors: green, red, yellow. Red and yellow go together. I was kidding with her when I told her that it's supposed to be that way."

Josie's mom, 78th week, or around 18 months

"It snowed at Easter. It was his first snow. He was a bit weary and out of sorts. He just couldn't place it and wanted to be alone after taking in all the new impressions."

Thomas' mom, 80th week, or just over 18 months

With principles, we have seen how your toddler started to "think about thinking." Once they have entered the world of systems, for the first time they can hone their principles into a system, principles they have learned through experience. It's quite possible they are doing this while taking their "thinking break."

"Sometimes he likes to be alone. He says: 'Bye' and goes in his room to be alone. He's pondering life. Sometimes he does that a half-hour at a time, with a toy. Other times he stares and thinks for ten minutes like a 50-year-old. He just wants a bit of peace after having such fun playing. After he's taken his break to collect his thoughts, he returns cheerful, says 'Hi,' wants to nurse a bit and then goes to sleep or to play a bit. He really needs his privacy."

Thomas' mom, 80th week, or just over 18 months

"Initially, he was afraid of the electric toothbrush, but now that he's gotten used to it, it's fine and he says 'On.'"

John's mom, 83rd week, or 19 months

"She grasps that the train takes batteries, and understood that they were drained. She went and found new ones."

Hannah's mom, 86th week, or approaching 20 months

"When playing the flight simulator on the computer, he doesn't treat the joystick carelessly like he used to; he's very aware. He puts the landing gear down right. He checks to see if it happened like he wanted it to by having the plane climb a bit and then back down."

Jim's mom, 86th week, or approaching 20 months

Basic Architecture

Their interest in the phenomena of physics extends to more systems than just physics. They are also interested in basic architecture. They can spend hours watching builders, and you will notice their play will produce more structures since their latest leap, like towers of cups pushed together, and more elaborate structures.

"My husband cemented the fish pond this week. He explained to my eldest son how to mix cement. He then explained the same to Victoria. Now they are together the whole day long mixing sand and water for cementing. She does everything he does. She looks up to Thomas."

Victoria's mom, 79th week, or 18 months

LEAP 10

"Cars have fallen out of favor. Now it's more the alternative transportation, like motor bikes, semis, dump trucks, trolley cars. He loves to watch the builders."

Mark's mom, 80th week, or just over 18 months

"She was chosen as a test person for new Lego toys for toddlers. She was rewarded for her efforts with an electric train for 3-year-olds. Much to everyone's surprise, she quickly laid down the rails for the train. She approached it like a puzzle. The straight pieces were easy. The curved pieces were a little more of a chore. It was one track with a beginning and an end. When she had finished fiddling around with the track, she put the crossing guard arm on the train and went riding around. It struck me as strange and I said that to her. She didn't change anything though, which surprised me, until I discovered that she had copied this from the picture on the box, which showed the guard arm on the train just as she had done it. She isn't really interested in running the train, though. She prefers to lay the tracks. She constantly takes the track apart and starts over."

Emily's mom, 82nd week, or approaching 19 months

"He tries putting the small Lego blocks together these days. He can't quite manage because it takes a bit of strength. But he tries. He doesn't use the bigger blocks."

Matt's mom, 86th week, or approaching 20 months

Me and My Talking

Between 17 and 22 months, toddlers start using the adult language system with an explosive increase in the spoken vocabulary and the average duration of a speaking turn. They also start combining words to form sentences. They are now able to distinguish two different languages from each other and ignore one of the two. Furthermore, there is an impressive increase in verbal language comprehension around 18 months.

There is large individual variation in the budding development of speech. Some toddlers don't use many words (approximately six) around the time this leap takes place. The parents know that they actually know and understand many more words, which causes some irritation. Other children use many words, repeating after you (sometimes just the first syllable) or taking the initiative, but no sentences yet. They can make themselves understood, though, literally with hands and feet. They mime their part. A third group already produces sentences, while they are still miming.

Understands All, or A Few Words

"The words he now uses are limited: 'cookie,' 'bottle,' 'ouch,' 'thank,' 'Mom,' 'Dad,' 'bread' and 'pel' (= apple; he only pronounces the last syllable). He understands everything and follows instructions well."
James' mom, 76th week, or about 17 ½ months

"He puts his arms up in the air at 'hip, hip, hooray' and shouts something like 'Oora!' He knows all the gestures too like 'clap your hands.' And if he doesn't succeed he says 'Oot' (shoot)."
Robin's mom, 76th week, or about 17 ½ months

"She uses more and more words. Not yet very clearly pronounced, mostly the heavy syllables."
Anna's mom, 79th week, or 18 months

"He says three words: 'Di dah' is tick-tack, 'Moo' is moon, and 'Hi hi' is horse."
Robin's mom, 80th week, or a good 18 months

LEAP 10

"She repeats more and more. If she picks up the phone, she says 'Hello.' The words she says now are 'Daddy,' 'Mommy,' 'up,' 'hi,' 'bottle,' 'bread,' 'cookie,' 'apple,' and 'out.' She shakes her head 'no' if she doesn't want something. She nods her head 'yes' if she wants something."

Laura's mom, 80th week, or just over 18 months

"He doesn't say much yet, but he understands everything! And he communicates exactly what he wants."

James' mom, 81st week, or 18 ¾ months

"Now she says 'cheese,' 'boom,' 'Daddy,' and 'Mommy.'"

Anna's mom, 82nd week, or approaching 19 months

"He understands everything you say and ask. He is very enterprising, always doing something, walking through the house all day long singing or mumbling something."

James' mom, 83rd week, or 19 months

"She is using some more new words."

Laura's mom, 83rd week, or 19 months

"He uses more and more words, although his vocabulary is limited. He speaks his own language a lot. This week he clearly said 'Grandma' to get her attention. The words that he now occasionally uses are 'Grandma,' 'Grandpa,' 'ow,' 'hi,' 'bottle,' 'bite,' 'sit,' 'me,' and 'look.'"

James' mom, 84th week, just over 19 months

"He picks up more and more words. Now he knows 'Dad,' 'Mom,' 'cheese,' 'ouw,' 'boom,' 'ant,' 'more,' 'di dah,' 'moon,' and 'sars' (= stars)."

Robin's mom, 84th week, or just over 19 months

"She imitates animal sounds."

Laura's mom, 85th week, or 19 ½ months

"He definitely uses more words now. He answers sometimes now with 'Yes.' 'Eese' (cheese) and 'food' are now part of his repertoire. In general, he's not yet very talkative. By pointing and a few oohs and ahs we understand him. He gets what he needs."

James' mom, 86th week, or 19 ¾ months

"She talks a lot and repeats a lot."

Anna's mom, 86th week, or 19 ¾ months

Understands All, or Many Words, a Lot of Mime, No Sentences

"The most understandable word at the moment is 'cheese.' 'Ird' (= bird) is also clear. He says 'Papa' like he spent the summer in Italy. It's charming."

Taylor's mom, 72nd week, or 16 ½ months

"He talks more and more. Now he likes to make noises with his tongue: 'lllll.' We play a lot of language games. He loves that."

Luke's mom, 72nd week, or 16 ½ months

"A great moment this week was the comprehensive contact we had when we were playing a game making noises. It was really funny. We tried to stick our tongues in and out of our mouths while making noise. Later we tried to push our tongues against the back of our front teeth to produce the 'lll' sound as in: 'Lala.' She found it exciting and challenging and wanted to do what I did. At the same time, it looked like she was thinking 'I'll get you.' I saw so many different expressions in her face. We both loved it and the laughter grew, especially when she said 'Lala' spontaneously with a kiss."

Ashley's mom, 73rd week, or approaching 17 months

"His way he talks has changed again. Even though his speech is, for the most part, incomprehensible, it does seem that he's forming more sentences, and I think: 'Heck, I'm getting this!' He explains clearly through gestures and words what has happened to him in my absence. For instance, when he was at Grandma's in the kitchen and I asked him what he'd done. He said something I couldn't understand with the word 'cheese' in it, which led me to understand that he had gotten a piece of cheese from Grandma. When asked, he nodded yes."

Taylor's mom, 74th-77th week, or 17 to almost 18 months

"It looks like she's talking. She has been curious for a long time about what everything is called, but it seems that she's developed in some way. She asks the name intending to repeat the name to herself. Some are perfectly pronounced. Most are only with the first syllable: ball is 'ba,' water is 'wa,' and breast is 'bre.' It is great to hear the sound of her voice. She's proud, too, and repeats when requested."

Elisabeth's mom, 74th week, or 17 months

"The way he communicated this week was interesting. He seems to be forming sentences in his own language. He keeps it up until I understand him. An example: we walk across the street to the sea for the second time, Luke on Daddy's back. I had the bag with gear and the sand shovel was sticking out. All of a sudden he shrieks: 'Da, da, da.' It takes a bit before I get that he means the shovel. When I say 'The shovel?' he says 'Ya' and points from the shovel to the sea. I repeat in words: 'Yeah, we're taking the shovel to the beach.' He sighed contentedly and leaned back. We have this type of conversation often."

Luke's mom, 74th week, or 17 months

"We can now actually have a dialogue. We communicate extensively. What she wants to communicate to me most is her world plan. For instance, track down dirt and then say 'Bah, bah,' to show that she can find dirt and that she knows what it is and what to do with it."

Elisabeth's mom, 75th week, or just over 17 months

"She makes sentences that seem like a long word missing some letters. But I can understand her if I pay close attention. She saw that the stop light was red and pointed to it. I hadn't seen it yet, but heard her say it, and she was right, although I don't know exactly what she said. Rather strange! It was like she herself didn't know what she was saying, but did utter some sounds that seemed to fit the picture."

Ashley's mom, 76th week, or around 17 ½ months

"I can keep him occupied with stories while changing his diaper."

Luke's mom, 76th week, or around 17 ½ months

"He uses a lot of words. He repeats them or starts them himself. He says the first syllable and that's usually good. He doesn't really try sentences. He jabbers on sometimes."

Bob's mom, 76th week, or around 17 ½ months

"This week it was interesting to witness his desire to give everything a name. What an endless desire to learn a language is buried inside such a little person. Another gem is how he can communicate so well. He literally uses his hands and feet to get his message across. He's a mimic. Even when I'm talking with other people, he chimes in. He mimes his part."

Luke's mom, 76th week, or around 17 ½ months

"She is interested in repeating words and practicing with me more than before."

Ashley's mom, 77th week, or 17 ¾ months

"He uses a lot of words, especially the first syllable. More and more words I don't have to cue. The joy he gets from speaking is touching."

Bob's mom, 77th week, or 17 ¾ months

"Communicating about what he does and wants to do and about what he's done is central. He's very creative in saying what he wants with body language that he can't say yet in words. He enunciates much better. Words aren't trimmed at the root. He's starting to use words that have not been cued, so from memory."

Kevin's mom, 78th week, or around 18 months

"She knows new words: 'horse,' 'cow,' and 'melon.' She also knows the name of the children she has played with. She can pronounce 'Nina' best of all."

Ashley's mom, 80th week, or just over 18 months

"I think that he basically can repeat everything I say first. It depends on his mood if he will or not."

Taylor's mom, 81st week, or 18 ¾ months

"She uses many words now. She starts them with the proper letters but puts them in the wrong order, like 'flower' becomes 'fowler.' Every day brings new words. She practices for a while until she has the letters right. With some letters that is very difficult, like the 'h' and the 'r'."

Ashley's mom, 82nd week, or approaching 19 months

"The way he expresses himself is very creative. He points to his eyes if he wants to peek in the diaper that I whisk away."

Kevin's mom, 82nd week, or approaching 19 months

"If I don't understand him and he doesn't know the word, he refers back to words that have been used in that context before. Usually, we are able to figure it out."

Luke's mom, 82nd week, or approaching 19 months

"He now uses the word 'nice.' He comes with a book in his hand, points to the cover and says: 'Nice.'"

Taylor's mom, 83rd week, or 19 months

"He comes up to me with his index finger pressed to his thumb and that means 'money.'"

Taylor's mom, 84th week, or just over 19 months

"All of a sudden he gets an idea and says words completely. When I praise him, he's proud as can be. He still doesn't take the trouble to make sentences. He prefers body language. It happens a hundred times a day that he wants to see something I'm doing or something I prohibit. He points to his eyes. That means 'I just want to have a look.' He broadcasts his other sensory needs in the same way, by pointing to the relative sense."

Kevin's mom, 83rd-86th week, or 19 to almost 20 months

"He says something if he's scared. I'm not sure whether or not he understands the word 'scary', but things he doesn't like or that are overwhelming, such as loud noises or being physically held down, he calls scary. He finds some animals scary, and some dangerous situations, like if he almost falls down. 'Scary' doesn't always mean 'run away.' He tries to overcome his fears by confronting what's scary."

Luke's mom, 83rd-86th week, or 19 to almost 20 months

"He doesn't enjoy repeating words anymore. But he's still improving. There are more and more words he repeats, as well as more and more words with more than one syllable."

Luke's mom, 83rd-86th week, or 19 to almost 20 months

Understands All, or Many Words, and Sentences, Too

"She is starting to sing. For instance, when I sing 'Kitty Meow,' I sing 'kitty' and she sings 'meow.'"

Jenny's mom, 73rd week, or approaching 17 months

"She really 'reads' books now. She tells a story while she looks at the pictures. Can't understand a word, but very touching. Moreover, she can speak in intelligible sentences, too."

Victoria's mom, 75th week, or 17 months and a week

"If she wants the cat to come to her she calls: 'Wittie, come here.'"

Jenny's mom, 75th week, or 17 months and a week

"She repeats every word we say and knows exactly what is what. She doesn't repeat it unless she knows what she's saying."

Emily's mom, 76th week, or 17 ½ months

"Recently he's been having some nightmares. Towards the end of his REM sleep, he uttered many new words. I think he is very frustrated because he really wants to talk. He now dreams out loud. After his visit to the petting zoo, he imitated all the animals."

Thomas' mom, 80th week, or a just over 18 months

"She says several things together, like 'that's good,' 'not now' or 'Mommy and Daddy.'"

Emily's mom, 81st week, or around 18 ¾ months

"He wanted the soap. But I didn't feel like reacting to 'eh, eh' and said: 'Tell me what you want?' Then he said: 'Yes, that that, me.'"

Thomas' mom, 82nd week, or approaching 19 months

"In the garden center, he had another nice sentence: 'That....nice.'"

Thomas' mom, 82nd week, or approaching 19 months

"She now puts two and three words together."

Emily's mom, 83rd week, or 19 months

"She keeps making headway with speaking. She sometimes puts three words together. For instance: 'Daddy sit me.'"

Jenny's mom, 84th week, or just over 19 months

"He loves his books. Now he listens to and reads fairy tales. Those are little books with very short stories that he got when he visited the amusement park. When I read to him, I always let Prince Thomas play the lead role. He listens all the way to the end of the tale."

Thomas' mom, 86th week, or approaching 20 months

"She already speaks in complete sentences, one after the other."

Emily's mom, 87th week, or 20 months

LEAP 10

Show Understanding for Irrational Fears

When your toddler is busy exploring their new world, and elaborating their newfound ability, they will encounter things and situations that are new and foreign to them. They are actually discovering new dangers, dangers that did not exist for them until now. Only after they come to understand things more fully will their fears disappear. Show sympathy.

"She is afraid of thunder and lightning. She says: 'scary, boom.'"
Maria's mom, 71st week, or just over 16 months

"He really disliked the vacuum cleaner and a running tap. They had to stop."
Paul's mom, 72nd week, or 16 ½ months

"He is scared of balloons. He also won't go between the sheep and goats at the petting zoo. He wants to be picked up then. Nor does he like sitting on an animal at the carousel. He does like to watch though."
Matt's mom, 73rd week, or approaching 17 months

"She is afraid of loud noises (trains, airplanes, drills) and of the dark."
Nina's mom, week 75th-76th week, or just over 17 months

"He found vomiting nasty. He'd vomited in his bed and kept saying 'Bah,' even after it had been cleaned up."
Jim's mom, 80th week, or a just over 18 months

"The crow of the rooster, as well as spiders, horses, dogs. This was new. I think this is part of his newfound autonomy."
Gregory's mom, 80th-81st week, or around 18 ½ months

"After his bath he always goes and sits down to pee. He tried so hard that this time a turd came out. He found that odd."
Robin's mom, 82nd week, or approaching 19 months

"She has a wind-up Bert for her bath, but Bert's nose is loose and if the nose is lying in the water or Bert is lying there without a nose, then she is really scared and pulls herself back in a corner."

Josie's mom, 83rd week, or 19 months

"He's been frightened of the vacuum cleaner for a while. He used to get on top of it when I turned it on. Now, he gets well out of the way in a corner until the cleaning is done."

Steven's mom, 85th week, or 19 ½ months

"He keeps showing his father the 'troll king' he saw at the amusement park. Dad has to tell him a story about him. At the amusement park he was a bit frightened of the 'troll king.'"

Thomas' mom, 86th week, or approaching 20 months

"He was afraid of a goat that came toward him at the petting zoo."

Frankie's mom, 87th week, or 20 months

"Flies, mosquitoes and wasps scare her."

Eve's mom, 87th week, or 20 months

"He was afraid of a spider in the garden and of flies."

Harr y's mom, 88th week, or just over 20 months

After the Leap

After 79 weeks or just over 18 months most toddlers become a little less troublesome than they were, although their budding notion of self and a tendency to want get their own way and the struggle for power are not making it any easier. However, those behaviors make them troublesome in a different way. They are not difficult in the sense of **the three C's**: CRYING, CLINGINESS and CRANKINESS. They are occasionally just plain irritating. The trick is to place yourself above it all. Stop and count to ten, remember that your little darling is progressing and do your best to manage the situation. After all, this is a very good opportunity to phase in some rules of conduct for your toddler so they learn that the world doesn't revolve around them, and that they must take others into account as well.

It's good to know that for adults, thinking and reasoning or logic are not the highest attainable goals, as some people like to think. Logic belongs in the world of programs and is subordinate to the worlds of principles and systems. If you really want to make a change, you will have to change your principles, and in order to change your principles, you will first have to change the accompanying system. The problem is that concepts at system level are not easily changed in adults. That is in part due to the fact that every change at the system level has far reaching effects for all levels under the world of systems. And that doesn't happen without a struggle. History has taught us that such upheaval often brings with it revolutions or wars using words and even arms.

Concepts at the system and principle level are more easily formed than they are changed. Children learn them by observing their surroundings and then start to use them themselves. Sometimes adults place emphasis on certain system concepts. This is a textbook example of socialization and upbringing.

Your toddler is, of course, new to the show. Their world is still very small and close to home. It will be many years, until after their childhood, until they have developed what we adults call an outlook on life, but a tender start has been made. However tender this start may be, it's important and has far-reaching consequences. Among other things, a beginning is made with forming a conscience and learning norms and values. If a poor start is made here, the negative consequences will be most noticeable a few years down the road. If you give this all your attention, it will be a very good in-depth investment. It will save you, your child and everyone around them a lot of misery.

The importance of this early start applies, of course, to all the other areas in the world of systems. Whether your toddler likes music, likes to build, talk, play with physical phenomena or practice body control, give this rising star a chance. You will be amazed at the pleasure you will have together.

Top Games for This Wonder Week

Here are games and activities that most 17-20-month-old toddlers like best now and that help develop the new ability into many new skills:

- Playing silly together by pronouncing words differently and making silly movements
- Play wrestling
- Recognizing people
- Standing on their head, scrambling about, practicing balance
- Drawing
- Blowing bubbles
- Jumping and balancing on walls (up to 5 feet)
- Playing the fool
- Tickling and physical play
- Playing physical with Dad and joking around
- Playing outside
- Playing with other children
- Playing ball games
- Feeding the dog
- Ghost games
- Twirling around getting dizzy
- Playing circus
- Riding horse game
- Tag
- Hide-and-seek
- Reading stories
- Tongue games: You push your tongue against the inside of your cheek. Your toddler pushes your cheek in, whereby you stick your tongue out.

Top Toys for This Wonder Week

Here are toys and things that most 17-20-month-old toddlers like best now and that help elaborate the new ability into many new skills:

- Cars
- Clay
- Children's TV
- Children's books
- Small trinkets, things that belong together
- Garages with cars
- Toy airports
- Drawing on paper
- Buckets with sand and water
- Push cars
- Plastic chairs
- Balls
- Bicycles
- Stuffed animals, bears and dolls
- Stickers
- Sandboxes
- Digging in the yard
- Sesame Street music
- Slides
- Coloring pencils
- Tractor trailer trucks
- Blowing bubbles
- Pinocchio
- Trains
- Swings
- Rocking horses
- Puzzles (up to 20 pieces)
- Clickers for the bike

Be Careful with the Following:

- The toilet
- The garbage cans

Sleep and Leaps

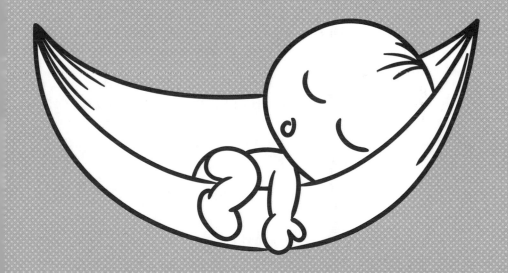

Introduction

Sleep: only five letters, but you only notice the massive impact of sleep on your life once you've had a baby... That's why we have decided to add a full chapter about sleep to the bestseller *The Wonder Weeks*. Every day we get hundreds of emails from parents from all over the world, and most are about sleep. Or rather: about their baby not sleeping, not sleeping enough or restless sleep. Fathers, mothers, brothers and sisters will all notice: when a baby arrives, their sleep patterns are disturbed. As a new parent, no doubt you would love a wonderful sleep solution: a kind of magic formula that makes your baby fall asleep. You would like a calendar to tick off the days. Another three months and the nights will get better... you want to know when your baby will sleep through the night. You want to know at what age your baby will (finally) sleep for a few hours. When the problems overwhelm you, having such a tick-off calendar could give you hope. But I must disappoint you right now: there is no such fixed list with times and months. The magic formula to get a baby to sleep does not exist either. The reasons?

1. Babies have other sleep needs than we do. And just to give you a little hint: a baby's sleep needs and sleep cycle and ours are like fire and water, they don't mix that well together.
2. A quick fix is rarely a good long-term solution.
3. An average number of hours doesn't say anything about your baby in your circumstances.

After you read this 'spoiler' and you feel like you've had cold water thrown on you: don't worry, there is hope and we have a lot of good news to share with you. We hope to give you insight into the challenging, but beautiful and healthy sleeping pattern of your baby. We give you tips to help your baby, as long as your baby is open to them, and you let your baby set the pace. But what we really want to get across is how important it is to value the natural development of the sleep process, without intervening. We also want to show you the link between sleep and leaps, which will resolve many questions about sleep. We give you insight into the sleep development of your baby, just as we do in the rest of the book about your baby's mental development. Armed with these insights you can make the right choice for your baby, yourself and your family. We hope to empower you with this sleep information so you can make your own unique choices.

From Sleep Problems to 'Different' Sleeping

We often speak about 'different' sleep. Yes, we get that in day-to-day life it's simply all about your baby's sleeping problems, but as you will read it's usually not the babies who have problems, but us, the adults. We really understand the frustration that your baby's 'sleep problems' cause, but we don't want to call it a problem. It is not fair to the baby to call their completely normal sleeping behavior problematic. That's why we talk about 'different' sleeping.

Sleep and Us: An Ideal Combination

Few adults without children really get enough sleep, even though they know how important it is for them. Compared to someone who doesn't get enough sleep, a person who does looks better, is often slimmer (!), is better able to concentrate, is happier, healthier and we could go on. Yet there is something inside us that rarely allows us that daily rest. Simply because we can function even when we steal a little from our body's sleep requirements. In fact, we need seven to eight hours' sleep at least, and sometimes even more. We are, of course, talking about consecutive sleeping hours. You can guess what's coming...

Sleep and Your Baby: Also an Ideal Combination

Just like us your baby needs sleep. Without enough sleep, they don't develop as well as they should physically, emotionally and mentally. The quantity of sleep your baby needs depends on their age and personality. Some children need far more sleep than others, just like adults. But one thing's for sure: the sleep rhythm is faster; the sleep cycle is shorter–and that makes their sleep needs very different from those of an adult. If a baby wakes up after a few hours and then falls asleep again, they had a perfect sleep, if you are only looking at their needs from their viewpoint! As an adult you quickly tend to think that your little one didn't have enough sleep and that not sleeping has immediate, negative consequences for their development. It doesn't have to be like that at all: the idea that your baby has a problem comes up because we, as adults, project our sleep needs and rhythm onto the baby and that is unfair.

Your Sleep and Your Baby's Sleep: Not a Great Match

Your baby and you have different sleeping needs and they clash. Usually you are the one who suffers, and not your baby. Your baby's sleep requirements often indirectly define your sleep rhythm, and that can be really difficult. Your little one is perfectly fine waking up three times a night (and it's normal too). But you have to get out of bed disturbing your sleeping cycle and then fall asleep again leaving you completely exhausted in the morning. Not to mention that your morning starts earlier than before you were a parent. If you also have an older child that wakes during the night, you are dealing with three different sleep rhythms, sleep cycles and sleep requirements and it becomes even more difficult for you and your partner, often not so much for your children. That in itself is a reassuring message, but then again, it's not that simple either. If we don't sleep enough we become moody, irritated–in short, extremely tired, so tired that it will affect our daily life in a negative way. Of course you need to prevent this, or at least minimize it. If you understand your baby's sleep behavior, know what to expect and what to do to make it easier for yourself, you prevent real sleep problems.

Nice to know and Need to know:

After having a baby, 90% of parents have sleep problems. It's not down to you. It's not down to your baby. Your baby's sleeping requirements and yours clash by nature.

(Not) sleeping is only a problem if you, your family, or your baby suffer severely from sleep deprivation. That's when you need to get help.

As your baby gets older, you need to align your sleeping requirements even more. And think about it: as soon as they hit puberty you won't be able to get them out of bed in the morning!

Now and then you need to remember that even though this is an extremely difficult phase, you will (as countless parents before you have) get through this. Luckily, women also have the luxury of make-up to mask some of the physical effects of the lack of sleep! Sorry gentlemen!

Day-Night Rhythms and Sleep-Wake Rhythm

To understand what your baby's sleep entails, you also need to understand what 'sleeping' is. Sleeping is much more than closing your eyes and letting go: sleep is a very complicated process that directly influences our health and development. To sleep like we adults do, you need the part of your brain that is not fully developed yet in babies, and that is the actual 'problem'.

When we think of the day-night rhythm we automatically think of sleeping and waking up. But that sleep-wake rhythm is only one of the many day-night rhythms! There is a part at the center of the human brain that regulates all the various day-night rhythms. That part is connected to the eyes and registers if there is light, and if it is day or night.

Examples of day-night rhythms in adults are:

- A change in the heartrate during the day and at night (faster during the day, slower at night);
- Change in temperature during the day and at night (drops slightly at dusk);
- Change in the volume of urine production (less at night);
- Production of the sleep hormone at night and decrease in the stress hormone at night;
- Difference between day and night in the quantity of growth hormones or testosterone produced;
- ... And last, but not least: the sleep-wake rhythm.

Our Biological Clock: Reset Every 24 Hours!

In the center of an adult brain there is an element that underlies all those different day-night rhythms. That part of the brain is called the 'biological clock' and has a rhythm of just under 24 hours that goes up and down (or 'oscillates' if you're looking for a more scientific word), without outside influence. This part is connected to the eyes and registers when there is light and when it is night or day. And that's fine, because if the biological clock is left alone, it will progressively deviate more and more from the earth's light-dark cycle that lasts exactly 24 hours. The biological clock is 'reset' every day and runs in synchronicity with the earth's light-dark cycle.

Melatonin: The Sleep Hormone

One of the day-night rhythms in adults concerns the production of melatonin a.k.a. 'the sleep hormone'. Your brain (the pineal gland) produces this as soon as it gets dark. And here too... when babies are born they cannot yet produce that substance! Your body produces less of other substances too when you go to sleep, e.g. cortisol. Cortisol is a stress hormone that makes you alert. Once you produce less of it, you automatically relax more and the decrease in this hormone makes sure you fall and stay asleep more easily.

In short, to have a lovely night's rest you need – among other things – a sleep-wake rhythm and the production of specific substances in the brain. When it's dark at night you are sleepy, and when it's light during the day, you are awake. You let go, or on the contrary, you are alert. Since your newborn baby does not fully have that sleep-wake rhythm system yet, your baby is biologically not able to have a day-night rhythm. It's just not possible! That knowledge can be reassuring. You aren't doing anything wrong, nor is your baby doing anything wrong, it's just biologically impossible during the first weeks and months.

A Biological Process: The Development of a Sleep-Wake Rhythm

The question now is: When does a child have a full sleep-wake rhythm along with all the other day-night rhythms? That's why we have listed the various elements of a mature sleep-wake rhythm for you.

Pregnancy:

In the womb, your baby does not yet contribute to a sleep-wake rhythm or other day-night rhythms. The day-night rhythms they display are caused by substances like melatonin that enter their body through the mother's blood via the umbilical cord.

Halfway through Pregnancy:

The first form of the biological clock appears in your baby's brain, but it is still far from complete. It seems that the eyes already have a connection to the part of the brain that you can call the biological clock.

Biological Clock and Premature Babies

The fact that the biological clock emerges halfway through the pregnancy is important to know for very premature babies. Because the foundation of day-night rhythms is already present in a certain form and the eyes are probably already connected to the biological clock, premature babies could get a certain day-night rhythm earlier than full-term babies. That's why there is a lot of debate as to whether or not it is better for premature babies to quickly get used to the light and darkness of day and night.

Newborn Babies:

After cutting the umbilical cord there is no longer a melatonin supply through the mother's blood, there is no reserve, and a baby is not able to produce it yet. A newborn baby does not display day and night rhythms yet and that's why the sleep-wake rhythm is chaotic. Short sleeps, long sleeps, in daytime, at night; your baby sleeps when they feel like it. The difference between dark and light has no effect (yet) on them when it comes to producing sleep hormones.

Birth Up to Six Weeks:

Your baby takes naps spread over the 24 hours of the day. You do not notice a difference in the hours and times they sleep during the day or at night. They are not yet guided by the presence of light or darkness. They sleep when they want to sleep.

Week One:

The day-night rhythm of your baby's body temperature starts. You don't notice that as a sleep-wake rhythm, but it is the first step in that direction. To obtain a good sleep-wake rhythm your baby first needs the day-night rhythm of the body temperature. You could say that the day-night rhythm of the body temperature is the mold in which the sleep-wake rhythm is shaped.

Six Weeks:

Your baby now has the foundations of a waking rhythm. Not a sleep rhythm yet! The waking rhythm develops earlier than the sleep rhythm! But the sleep-wake rhythm has developed a bit further. Also, researchers have already found a small concentration of melatonin (the substance produced at night to sleep through the night) in 7-week-old babies. You will notice that the times of being really awake and the times of being tired cannot be so

clearly distinguished anymore. Where at first being awake or sleepy were spread out in complete disarray over the day and night, those short chaotic moments now seem to get closer together. This is far from a true pattern, but the process has started!

Two Months:

Your baby begins to develop the very first precursors of a sleep-wake rhythm. You won't notice that immediately, but it is great to know that biologically the night rhythm has started in the developmental process! Don't expect miracles, but observe the subtle progress in the development of a healthy day-night rhythm.

Three Months:

The time your baby sleeps during the day decreases and the time they sleep at night increases. Always remember: right now it's only about the number of minutes, the sum of time. This doesn't say anything about how often your baby wakes up. Even if a baby sleeps six hours (and that almost never happens), it doesn't mean that these are consecutive hours. In short: your baby wakes up a few times and that is completely normal at this age. At a biochemical level you can only measure a day-night rhythm if it concerns melatonin production.

Three-Six Months:

A pattern increasingly develops in the production of melatonin at night. From now on, a difference in cortisol levels between night and day can also be measured. From 15 weeks onwards you will notice that your baby has a clear sleep pattern over 24 hours. Your baby has set sleeping hours during the day and night. You will also notice that the new pattern acquired around three months will be greatly disturbed when they reach the fourth leap at about four months. Apart from that (temporary) disruption, it is great to see that your baby has started to develop a rhythm. But be warned, all this applies to the majority of babies, but... every baby is unique and there's nothing wrong if your baby doesn't yet have set sleeping and waking hours.

Actually, you can learn two important things here. Firstly, a newborn baby can't sleep through the night yet as they simply don't have a day-night rhythm – it is biologically impossible. Secondly, of all the different day-night rhythms (difference in body temperature, difference in heart rate, difference in urine production, difference in alertness etc.), the sleep-wake rhythm that is so often important to parents always develops last. So, your baby already has a number of day-night rhythms long before we notice them in the form of sleep.

When there are Day-Night Rhythms: Does Your Baby then Sleep through the Night?

No, it's just not that simple. Even if the sleep-wake rhythm is already present at a given moment, every baby is different and every baby sleeps differently. Some fall asleep by themselves without waking you up. Those babies do not need you to comfort them if they wake up from time to time during the night. Other babies only sleep well if they are with you all the time. Why is that good to know? Because you then realize that any lists with times and averages are simply irrelevant and you can't expect a young baby to sleep through the night. Lists with averages and times can be more frustrating than reassuring and you could even say that they are not honest or respectful to your baby. These types of lists could suggest that your baby falls outside the margin and is 'lacking'. And, of course, that's not true.

Babies Sleep Differently Than We Do

It's not just the day-night rhythm of babies that is different to ours, there also are numerous differences in the way we sleep and the way your baby sleeps. One of the major differences is your baby's sleep cycle. Those differences with ours exist for a reason: they are biological advantages for your little one and they help them to survive. In short, you don't want to change the sleep cycle, even if that means that your baby wakes up in the night more often than you do. But it is still good to understand the background of the sleep cycle. You start to understand your baby's sleep behavior and by understanding it, you get to know when you can put your little one down, or leave the room without them waking up and then having to start again from scratch. The biggest differences in the way babies and adults sleep are in the sleep cycle and the sleep phases.

Non-REM

Everyone has roughly two types of sleep: Non-REM sleep (Non-Rapid Eye Movement) and REM sleep (Rapid Eye Movement). The Non-REM sleep is the tranquil sleep. We are not stimulating the brain in a special way, we are not busy processing things–we just are resting deeply. But then again, not all phases of the Non-REM sleep are equally deep. Your child has three different Non-REM sleep phases:

Non-REM-Sleep Phase 1:

Sleep is very light. You could almost call it a phase of very intense relaxation or lethargy. The eyes are shut, but it is very easy to wake from this phase. You can recognize that phase in yourself when your eyes are closing, when you nod off while watching a movie for example. It is the phase just between being awake and asleep, but leaning more towards sleep.

Non-REM-Sleep Phase 2:

The body starts to reach 'sleep status' in this phase. The heartbeat slows, the body temperature starts lowering slightly and the muscles relax even more.

Non-REM-Sleep Phase 3:

This is the phase of very deep sleep. It is difficult to wake up in this phase. The body relaxes completely and the body temperature and heartbeat are considerably lower. That phase is followed by REM sleep.

Did you know...

People who sleepwalk or talk in their sleep are at the start of phase 3 of the Non-REM sleep. Nightmares and night terrors occur at the end of Non-REM phase 3. In short: many things can happen in the phase when a body rests most deeply!

Babies : Active Sleep is Twice as Long!

The REM sleep is also called 'active sleep' and that actually explains everything. During this phase people sleep lightly and wake easily. Your mind is actively processing and learning. When you look at the eyes, you see just how active the mind is: the eyes move very fast, faster than you could move them when awake. Hence the name: Rapid Eye Movement. The strange thing is that the rest of your body is completely at rest. The activity is really focused in your head at this time. It's the same for babies. Sometimes you can even see the eyes move. That shows how actively your baby is processing everything in this sleep!

REM: Extremely Important for a Good Development!

In the past it was thought that the REM sleep was only important for processing your day in your dreams. But more recent research has increasingly shown many other crucial benefits of REM sleep in babies. During the REM sleep the neurons in the brain are further stimulated. The blood flow to the brain almost doubles in REM sleep! That stimulation may well be essential to the creation of new brain connections. Therefore, the REM sleep is thought to hugely influence brain development!

REM Sleep and Leaps

During a leap most babies don't sleep as well as they normally do. The slightest thing wakes them. Parents say they daren't put their baby down, because they wake up again and they have to start from the beginning again. In a leap, babies often seem not to reach the restful deep sleep. It may be good for babies to enjoy a relatively longer period in REM sleep during leaps to create new brain connections. So, it's no wonder that your little one is woken by the slightest thing: they are in REM sleep and humans wake more easily in that sleep. Give your child the chance to grab those extra periods of REM sleep especially during the leaps. If they only want to do so on the familiar lap of a parent, let them. It is tempting to put them down for a while and quickly finish something you'd been planning to do, but just pick up a book instead. If your baby wakes up more relaxed, because they can more easily process the leaps after those superficial REM sleep-naps, it is not only they who benefit, but ultimately you and your family too.

Nice to know and Need to know:

There are 'activity- or experience-independent' brain connections and 'activity- or experience-dependent' brain connections. To put it more simply: for the first you don't have to do anything (the independent variant), and for the other, you have to do or experience something (the dependent variant). A leap in mental development is an example of an independent variant. Your baby makes a leap, whether they want to or not, and they will not occur earlier or later, no matter what you do. So, actually, you don't have to do anything. Those brain connections are generated spontaneously and that leads to new sensory abilities.

Those spontaneously generated brain connections are plentiful. If they are not used, they disappear again. But… the connections that are used remain. In other words: with appropriate stimulation, your baby maintains the many brain connections that have been created. Or as the saying goes: 'Use it or lose it.' As a parent, if you respond to the leaps and play the games that help your baby to process the leaps and the skills they bring, they will keep as many brain connections as possible. These are of the dependent variant. It depends on your little one's activities and experiences. The good news is that if you take the leaps into account and react by stimulating your baby, then you will maintain as many brain connections as possible. Very good news when you consider that the creation of brain connections is especially crucial in those first two years.

Did you know?

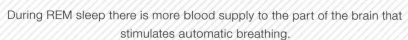

During REM sleep there is more blood supply to the part of the brain that stimulates automatic breathing.

Non-REM + REM = Sleep Cycle

And now comes the first part in which you as a parent can really 'do something'. If you get the theory and take the time to get to know your baby's sleep cycle, you will know when you can put your little one down without waking them. You then know when it is 'safe' to leave the room. The sleep cycle is simply the Non-REM-sleep + REM-sleep one after the other. After these two, humans start the Non-REM again, then the REM (second cycle), then the Non-REM again, then the REM again (third cycle), until they wake.

Difference Between a Baby and Adult's Sleep Cycle

Even though both babies and adults go through the same sleep cycle, the time duration differs enormously. Whereas a newborn baby has a cycle of some forty minutes, and a baby a few months old (up to approx. nine months) has a sleep cycle of 50/60 minutes, an adult has one of 120 minutes. Also remember that the ratio of Non-REM to REM is completely different in babies than in adults; babies spend more than twice as much time in REM sleep and much less time in Non-REM sleep.

Even Children's Sleep Cycles Differ to Adult's

The change in sleep cycle is a progressive process. It takes years before your little one's sleep cycle looks like yours. It is only when children reach school age that their sleep cycle approaches ours lasting some 90 to 100 minutes. The difference in the number of minutes someone spends in Non-REM and REM sleep does not disappear after infancy either. Even by the time your little one is three years old they still spend 50% of the time in REM sleep whereas we are only in REM sleep for 20% of the time. So, sleep is not something that you 'fix' in infancy. It takes a lot of time before children sleep like we do. And that's as it should be, because the way babies sleep is good for them. It has survival benefits and makes them healthy and strong.

Conclusions:

- Your baby wakes up more easily when they are in REM sleep and just at the start of Non-REM sleep.
- Your baby spends about twice as much time in REM sleep.
- The total day-night rhythm is more than just being awake or asleep. The rest of the body also participates. For example, during sleep, the body temperature decreases, the heartrate slows, less urine is produced, the stress hormone levels drop, and there is more blood supply to the brain in REM sleep.
- The Non-REM sleep (non-active sleep) has three phases.
- During phase three of the Non-REM sleep the body increasingly relaxes, the blood pressure and body temperature drop; your baby wakes up less quickly in this phase. In phase three a child sleeps very deeply; everything relaxes and they do not wake up easily.
- Non-REM + REM = sleep cycle.
- The sleep cycle is a lot shorter in babies than in adults.
- You experience several sleep cycles during the night.
- At the end of a sleep cycle you wake up or a new sleep cycle begins.

Sleep Cycle

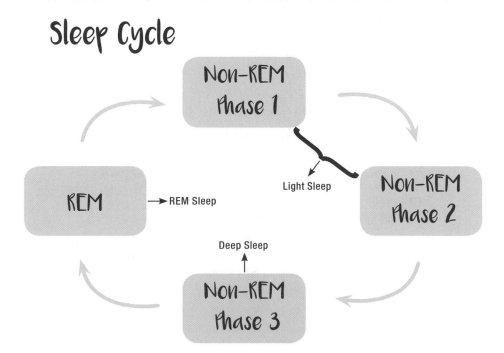

Content

- Sleeps very lightly
- Eyes are closed
- Very easy (extremely easy) to wake up

Differences between Baby and Adult

- This phase is a lot shorter in adults than in babies (only 2-4% of sleep time)
- In adults this is often seen as lethargy or napping on the couch
- Babies often have a moment of Non-REM sleep phase 1

Practically

- Baby wakes up easily, not enough time to put them down or sneak away

Non-REM Sleep Phase 1

REM Sleep

Content

- Active sleep
- Dreams
- Body stationary, eyes moving a lot
- Active brain stimulation
- Creation of many brain connections
- Blood supply to the brain doubles!

Differences between Baby and Adult

- Babies in REM sleep twice as long
- In babies, you see the eyes moving quickly under the eyelids

Practically

- REM sleep helps to process leaps
- Does your baby seem to sleep longer and have more REM sleeps during a leap? That's quite normal and therefore good for them. Don't try to make them sleep longer or more deeply.
- Your baby wakes up more easily, so this is not the right time to put them down or to sneak away.

Content

- Body relaxes more, feels limper
- Heart rate slows
- Body temperature decreases further

Differences between Baby and Adult

- An adult spends 45-55% of the time in this phase, a baby much less than this
- The older a child gets, the more time is spent in this phase and less in the REM phase

Practically

- Test whether your baby is already sleeping deeply enough to put them down/ leave the room etc. by lifting an arm and 'dropping' it. If it falls limply, your baby is in the end of phase 2 or even already in phase three and is deeply asleep. If the arm falls but is still 'under control', not really limp yet, they are still in phase 2 and you have to be very careful when you put them down or leave the room. Or you have to wait a few minutes until phase 3 starts

Non-REM Sleep Phase 2

Non-REM Sleep Phase 3

Content

- Deep sleep
- The whole body relaxes
- Sleep talking and sleepwalking are possible at the start of this phase
- Possible nightmares and night terrors at the end of this phase
- Even when you relax very deeply, this phase doesn't last the longest

Differences between Baby and Adult

- Adults have a deeper and longer sleep in this phase

Practically

- It is now very easy to put your baby down, to leave the room, etc. Your little one is in a deep sleep
- This phase starts approximately halfway into the whole sleep cycle of a baby
- Keep in mind that a new cycle starts after this phase and the sleep (if your baby does not wake up) becomes a light sleep again!)

Tip:

Keep track of your baby's sleep cycle. If you frequently 'test' how long it takes until your baby sleeps deeply, how many minutes they sleep more lightly and when they wake or continue to sleep, you can act on it. You will then know when to put your little one down or to leave the room to do something. Then you know for how many minutes you must carry on quietly and when you can be rest assured that you can start vacuuming without waking your baby. Don't forget: another rhythm starts with every leap, so you will have to learn about new cycles and rhythms regularly.

1. Check how many minutes after closing their eyes your baby's body seems to relax completely.

2. Do the 'arm test': carefully lift an arm, let it 'fall' (sounds more dramatic than it is!). If it drops limply, the baby is in a deep sleep. Write down the number of minutes it took after closing the eyes. If the arm drops, but is still controlled by the muscles and not completely limp, they are not in a deep sleep yet.

3. Check your baby's movements regularly. If you notice body movements, they have come out of a deep sleep and are sleeping more lightly. This phase is 'do or die' as it were: start another sleep cycle, or wake up.

4. By writing down all times for three days, you will be able to predict your baby's sleep cycle.

Note: this does not work for babies younger than fifteen weeks and it is not an absolute prediction like calculating leaps. This can only give you an idea of your baby's rhythm so you can respond to it more easily.

Waking Up: For the Safety of Your Baby

You would think that we are made in such a way that the sleep cycles of parents and babies are seamlessly adapted to each other to create a beautiful, harmonious start in life. But no... So why does this difference in sleep cycle and sleep rhythm exist? It looks like frequently waking during the night is a kind of safety advantage for your baby. Babies are vulnerable, and the younger they are, the more vulnerable they are. There are a few survival factors that can explain why a baby wakes up a few times at night:

- Their stomachs are still very small and milk digests rather quickly. A baby needs milk to survive and because milk digests more quickly, they need a 'ration' more often than we need food. If a baby didn't wake, they wouldn't get food during those hours, which is not good for growth. We are talking about young babies who are not eating solid food yet. Solid food, including puree, is a lot heavier to digest. You will notice that a baby, as soon as they are old enough to eat solids, will wake from hunger less frequently.

- Being in a deep sleep for a shorter time also has safety advantages. It is important that a baby wakes up if there is something that discomforts them or something that could harm their body. Think here of 'simple' things like a dirty diaper. If worn for too long it causes irritation, and your little one can be in discomfort due to the acidic substances in urine. So, it's good that their deep sleep is not so long that their skin could suffer from wearing the wet diaper.

- Think also of a little nose full of mucus that obstructs breathing. Since their breathing is not as developed as ours, it is important that your little one can wake easily if something bothers them in their sleep. If your baby was in a deep sleep for too long, it could be dangerous.

- Babies seem to sleep best when they are with you and not when they're completely alone. That too seems to have a logical explanation if you think about the fact that a baby can't survive without you. A baby depends completely on you. And they 'know' it. Not consciously of course, but it is a primeval instinct. They are safe with you, alone is just alone. Hearing your voice or feeling your hand etc. can be enough. The amount of contact a baby wants to sleep peacefully depends on the baby and their age. The older they are, the less need for direct contact. But there are no guidelines here. Many (self-appointed) sleep professionals are wary of body contact or speaking, because they believe that babies then never learn to fall or stay asleep on their own. But experience shows that if you let nature run its course, babies can increasingly be on their own, and fall and stay asleep by themselves. You can look at it in a different way: if a baby feels from the start that they are safe, that you are there for them, they become more self-confident and in the long term that leads to very strong self-confidence, that allows them to fall asleep and stay asleep by themselves with a safe feeling.

- Another reason why it is a safety advantage that your baby is not in a long and deep sleep is the fact that they can't yet control their body temperature like adults can. Besides, if we get cold, it's not that bad. But it is for your baby. It is important that they can easily wake if they are too hot or cold. But remember, your baby takes longer to react to feeling too hot or cold, and so by the time your baby starts crying they may already be feeling discomfort. That's why checking the temperature frequently is very important.

- Also, think of things that could go wrong: a small toe getting stuck in a loose stitch of the blanket. We would feel it, immediately remove the toe, etc. Your baby 'puts up with' a lot more and doesn't protest straightaway.

When they start crying it often already hurts. You have to be quick and that would be impossible if your little one didn't wake up and cry to indicate there really is something wrong. It should be added that crying is a real sign of discomfort: something doesn't feel right. A baby never cries without reason. As adults we might think the reason is exaggerated, but for your baby the reason is real, and that's what it's all about, right? Of course, a stuck toe is obvious, but not feeling good is also a reason. A reason that is very real to your baby, and that we must handle with love.

The above is intended to reassure you and to make you understand that waking up during the night has benefits for your baby. You mustn't read it the other way around and become scared when your baby seems to sleep longer and more soundly once in a while. With all our experience, and that of thousands of pediatricians all over the world, we can say: a baby seems to be pre-programmed in such a way that they feel what is best for them. There always seems to be a good explanation for all the natural rhythms, a natural explanation.

Increasingly more physicians and professionals are opposing (certain types of) sleep training with the purpose of keeping your baby in a deep sleep for longer than your baby needs by nature. Many professionals state that this sleep training "comes at a price, and perhaps at a risk." Helping your baby get the sleep they need at that time is good all round. That's how you respond to your baby. You create the conditions your baby needs to give them the chance to do what they need. If you rely on sleep training to solve your "problem" and teach your child almost unnaturally to sleep when forced, this is not beneficial to your baby. You then disturb the natural processes, which doesn't help to build a tight bond with your baby. There are many sleep coaches and sleep trainers online that write about The Wonder Weeks and link that to conclusions about sleep. We very rarely endorse these conclusions, simply because the conclusions made have never been proved.

Do Remember

Not everything you hear is equally true: not all parents are equally open about the sleep behavior of their baby. Some parents make the story sound better than in reality. Parents don't do this out of malice, but we live in a society in which a baby sleeping well or not is often considered proof of good or bad parenting. And here too, we can honestly tell you: the fact that your baby sleeps 'well' or 'badly' says more about their personality and age than your parenting!

Important to Remember!

Let this become your mantra, because it is what it is really all about: no one sleeps the whole night through. Not even you. After the sleep cycle is completed, you enter the twilight zone between being asleep and being awake, but you continue into the next sleep cycle. Your baby cannot, we repeat: not (!) sleep through the night. Not a single baby. However, some babies will start another sleep cycle by themselves. But that doesn't mean these babies sleep through the night. That is simply impossible!

Sleep and Leaps

Once your baby has developed a day-night rhythm, you will notice that the rhythm and the way your baby sleeps will change during a leap. We also have to point out that there are exceptions: babies who sleep marvelously during a leap. But these are really exceptions. It is also not that strange that a leap affects your baby's sleep: there is a lot going on in their mind. They go through a difficult phase and experience stress. These are enough ingredients to considerably affect sleep.

Sleep Disturbance: Unfortunately Not Only During Leaps

During each leap your little one suffers from the 3 C's: Crying, Clinginess and Crankiness. They eat differently, feed differently from the breast (your baby will often want to breastfeed a lot more) and sleep differently (often more lightly and superficially). When the leap is over, you notice that your little one doesn't cry as much anymore, is in a better mood, eats and sleeps better, but… as far as sleep is concerned, the sleep disturbance is still there after the end of the leap. Sleep disturbance is more prevalent during a leap, but it is also there when the difficult phase of a leap is over, albeit to a lesser extent. This is also a reason why parents experience so many problems with sleep disturbance. It comes, but it rarely 'goes away completely'.

Sleep and The First Three Leaps

Because your baby doesn't yet have a day-night rhythm in the first three leaps, you will find it difficult to determine that the rhythm was disturbed by the leap. How can you detect a change in rhythm if there is no rhythm yet? Still, you will notice changes in your baby's sleep during those leaps, especially with daytime naps. Your baby sleeps more lightly, for shorter periods, or even longer than normal! Some babies are continuously busy with getting to know the world in their heads. Those babies sleep more lightly and for shorter periods at this time. Babies who sleep longer know they have enough to deal with already and they know how to create a good balance including a good portion of sleep. The way your baby deals with these leaps is influenced by their personality and their circumstances. On the one hand, you have no influence on this (with regards to personality), but on the other hand, you do! It is good for the baby to have the chance to sleep. It seems unnecessary to mention this, but it isn't. During a leap, you need to bear in mind that things can quickly become too much for them as they are very open to all the stimuli around them. So, take the time, quietly sit or lie on the sofa with your baby. Do you notice that your baby is tired? Do not over-stimulate them; give them the chance to get some sleep when they want it.

Sleep Regression Periods? Or: Welcome to Leap 4, 6 and 10, Physical Milestones and Biological Changes.

Many people mention sleep regression periods. These are longer periods in which a child suddenly sleeps much 'worse' than before. It is clear we don't want to link it to the term 'worse', but of course we get what they mean by the term. The periods people refer to when speaking about sleep regression do not appear out of thin air. Those periods are much easier understood when you look at the leaps. All leaps are a step forward for your baby. After making a leap they can observe more complex aspects of the world and understand the world at a higher level. With each leap they are mentally able to do things they did not have the mental capacity for before that leap. Some leaps seem to bring about even more than others. These are sort of 'overarching' leaps through which the previous leaps are even better integrated. Compare it with building a brick wall. Every brick is a part added, but the brick that is finally placed on the bottom bricks, is not just a part of the wall, but keeps the rest connected and sturdy. This is a simplistic representation, but it clarifies it well. Take three guesses which leaps they are... four, six and ten, at respectively four, eight and seventeen months. These leaps are experienced by parents throughout the world, irrespective of culture and religion, as the most difficult in every way: in terms of Clinginess, Crankiness, Crying, but also with regards to 'eating or breastfeeding' and... sleeping. Because the effect of the sleep rhythm is twofold (not only on your baby, but on your mood too) it is experienced as particularly difficult during these leaps. Remember: sleep regression periods (although the word choice is unfortunate) contrary to what you often read, do not appear out of thin air and they are there for a reason. Your baby does not have a problem that needs resolving, but needs your love and help to get through the leap. Once the leap is over, sleeping is a lot easier. However, it is possible that your little one experiences more sleep regression after the difficult phase of this leap too. The sleep regression

phase can, therefore, last somewhat longer than the difficult phase of the leap. This is due to two other reasons that affect these periods of 'worse' sleep. Firstly, the consequences of those leaps are huge. Your little one can do more things mentally following the leaps, but with the consequence they will also actually train their body to do what they can already do in their mind. This varies from learning how to use their hands (in particular leap four), to learning to crawl, or in a few cases to already make the first steps in leap six, and learning to run, wriggle and perform other physical antics by leap 10. Your baby's sleep is affected by the mental leaps, and then again by the physical consequences, and as if that weren't enough, biology plays a role too. Think for example of teething. In short: enough reasons to explain that your little one enters a period in which they will sleep a bit 'worse' for a while.

For All Babies and Parents In Leap Four and The Weeks Thereafter...

We won't sugarcoat it: out of all the leaps and sleep regression periods, this is the one experienced as the most intense. Sleep problems, sleep questions and sleep dramas and despair hit a high here. Remember: after this, you have made it through the worst. But if it really gets you down, you feel desperate or you just want to let off some steam: that's what our Facebook group The Wonder Weeks Talk is for!

"Usually he fell asleep as long as I touched him. Now he is in the fourth leap it's no longer enough. I have to talk to him too. When he feels and hears me, he falls asleep, although it's more difficult than normal and he sleeps worse than normal."

Angelica's mom, 17 weeks

Bad Sleep... Has the Leap Started?

Out of all the characteristics of a leap (Clinginess, Crankiness, Crying, wanting to be breastfeed more often, being more single-minded, etc.) there is one that you notice virtually immediately when your little one enters a leap. A kind of first signal. You get it: 'worse' sleep. You can notice it from the fourth leap, when there truly is a day-night rhythm. With each further leap it becomes increasingly clearer because your child invariably develops a more stable rhythm. Remember: your baby can't help that they wake up more often and cry more often or just want to be close to you more. Nights are difficult: there is so much to discover! And the world is so new, different, and scary in your baby's perception. So, they want to be with you. As a parent, you are their rock. Their safe base to rely on in times of trouble.

Daytime Naps and Leaps

You will also notice from the fourth leap that daytime naps are influenced by the leaps. Your little one faces so much that they sleep more lightly and for shorter periods or finds it harder to fall asleep. On the one hand, that's because your little one does not stop processing everything; there is so much to be discovered. On the other hand, it's is because, during those light REM sleeps, extra blood is pumped to the brain and there is extra brain activity to create good brain connections. Fine for the brain, but this biological process keeps the baby active, which influences the daytime naps during the leap. After a leap, you may notice a new pattern in the daytime naps. That does not happen from one day to the next, but progressively. Until another leap occurs that influences the daytime naps (temporarily).

Nightmares and Night Terrors

A good day or night rest can be terribly disturbed by a nightmare or a night terror. A night terror is something that you generally see around three years of age, but can also happen earlier, sometimes from the second year of life. A night terror is a real panic attack during sleep. Your little one cries, screams, or may even lash out and is inconsolable. You can't get through

to them and whatever you do only seems to make it worse. This is contrary to a nightmare. Your little one could have those a lot earlier, sometimes even at four months. With a nightmare, you can get through to them and your baby is not in a completely deep sleep. Another difference between these two things is that a child can remember a nightmare the next day but not a night terror. You then come up against the following problem with regards to your baby: it is not possible to 'talk it over' the next day. Neither can you ask them what the matter is. And that can make you feel quite desperate. Especially if your little one goes through a period in which they often have nightmares.

"He will just begin crying out in his sleep. It doesn't wake him up, so he will cry for a bit as I shush him and put a hand on him to calm him and then stops crying, all while remaining asleep."
Desmonds' mom, 23 weeks

"Sometimes my baby girl wakes up screaming with all her might. I literally jump out of the bed to pick her up and comfort her. It usually takes a couple minutes till she opens her eyes and realizes that I am holding her. Then she settles down and goes back to sleep. However, sometimes it doesn't help at all because it looks like she can't wake up–she keeps her eyes closed and keeps screaming. Then I put her down and gently stroke her cheeks calling her by name till she opens her eyes and sees me."
Ivy's mom, 22 weeks

Nightmares and Separation Anxiety

During the period when separation anxiety plays a part, babies will have more nightmares. You can't prevent separation anxiety, and you don't want to prevent it: it's a part of normal development. Of course, you can make sure

that the intensity of the fear is as low as possible. And that your baby gets through this period as easily as possible, one in which they learn that you can in fact leave, but that this doesn't mean that you will never come back. You can do this from the leap of relationships (when your baby is around six months old) by playing the games we described on page 184. By assisting them from that moment, the peak of separation anxiety between eight and ten months will be less severe, which also influences the nightmares that a child can have during that period. You can't completely prevent nightmares, and you don't have to, they are completely normal things to have And so long as your little one knows you are there for them, everything will be fine.

"She has yelped out in her sleep during this most recent leap (7), but when observed on the monitor it was clear she wasn't awake."
Sarah's mom, 46 weeks

To Wake Them, or not to Wake Them?

Opinions differ, among physicians too, but the majority still thinks that the smartest thing to do is to let your baby sleep when they are having a nightmare. You could place a reassuring hand on their tummy or head or soothingly say that everything is okay, but that is different from waking them. You then reassure them and try to bring them back to the peaceful phase of sleep. But don't underestimate your intuition! If you think it is so bad that it's better to wake them, you need to follow your intuition. Ultimately, the combination of you and your baby is unique, and you have to find out what works best for you both.

"She screamed in her sleep and I saw the pain and fear in her face. It happens to her quite often and every time I picked her up and calmed her down, it seemed to just get worse, until she woke up abruptly, and that did not feel good either. I now let her be and only talk to her soothingly. That seems to work better. She continues to have nightmares, even though she is always happy and cheerful during the day. I'm glad I found a way that seems to work for her."
Mindy's father, 37 weeks

Do Remember

Nightmare Stats:

Some parents noticed that their baby had already had a nightmare at four months. By the time babies are in leap six (the second difficult sleep period, known as the second sleep regression period) around 40% of babies have a nightmare. At leap 10 (17 months) it's more than half. The percentage rises steadily because ultimately, we all have nightmares now and then.

By Parents for Parents

Okay, now that you know your baby sleeps differently from you as an adult, and that yes, it can be really exhausting. You can't and due to the natural benefits, you don't want to change anything about their sleep. Your child sleeps in a different way and at other times than you do, and they do so for various good reasons. The solution, therefore, is to adjust your (sleep) behavior. Here are some tips by parents for parents. They have helped them and could help you too. See what suits you and try it. It's worth it!

- Fresh air helps! Go for a walk on your own regularly, after you've fed your little one and if someone stays with them of course. Fresh air does wonders, especially if you are very tired.

- Have a power nap when your partner is home. A half-hour nap is often enough to recharge your batteries.

- Take turns sleeping in the guest room for a night, or even on the couch. Express milk, and get a night's rest.

- Try a bath during the day. Usually a child sleeps more soundly after a hot bath, and you can do that during the day too instead of only in the evening!

- Ask for help. This is an important one! Even if there is nothing wrong with your baby, even if it is normal that you are tired, it's not easy. Everyone with children knows this and will be glad to help. Sometimes an hour is enough. Just having a nice shower, having a walk, exercising, doing something for yourself. Don't be embarrassed, everyone will understand!

- Some babies love being swaddled. You need to get lots of information if you want to try this. Choose a good cloth and find films that show you how to do it.

- Co-sleeping. Most babies sleep more soundly when they are with their parents. In addition, you don't have to get out of bed if your baby wakes. If you opt for co-sleeping, do it safely. The University of Notre Dame (Indiana, USA) has a Behavioral Sleep Laboratory and a website where they describe all the ins and outs of co-sleeping. It's a good source of information on the subject.

- A sling can work wonders too. Your baby feels safe close to you and you can still do things because your hands are free. Your little one will wake up less quickly and fall asleep faster because they can feel you.

- Eat healthy. Yes, coffee, sugar and energy drinks seem like a good solution, but only in the short term. The good effect is followed by the dip and then you are twice as tired. You can't cope with those kinds of dips now because you're already living on your reserves. Healthy eating does wonders and you will soon feel the difference in energy. Eat lots of wholegrain products, fruit and vegetables.

- One of the most effective tips is to rest during the day too. Is baby going to sleep? Have a nap too. Yes, that means you can't do those things you wanted to do while they are sleeping. Just do them later. Sometimes it's smart just to leave the mess be. And you know, with that new energy from those extra daytime naps you'll do the things you have to do a lot faster afterwards!

> "I really lost it one time with my first baby. I became hysterical with my husband, screaming, crying, I was a wreck. With baby number two we started co-sleeping. Yes, I'm still tired, but luckily never that tired that I lose it and return to that place."
>
> **Lisa, mom of two (3 years, 6 months)**

So: Does Your Baby Sleep Yet? Mine Sleeps Like a Dream!

We hope we have given you more insight into the normal, natural pattern of your baby and their sleep. We hope you understand that we can't give you ready-made, quick-fix answers, and that wouldn't be good for your baby anyway. We hope you find strength in this information. And that this information helps you not to let the comments of others drive you mad. Trust yourself, trust your baby and your interaction. Give yourself space to accept that you simply have to go through this phase together and that ultimately everything will be fine. Try the tips that helped other parents. And don't be afraid to ask for help from family and friends, but also from doctors if you feel the need.

Who actually came up with the saying:

"Sleep like a baby"???

Postscript

Countless Wonders

By now you know that every parent will, at some time, have to deal with a baby who is tearful, cranky, or fussy; a baby who is difficult to please; a baby who, in fact, just needs to touch base.

It's our hope that when you find yourself trying to cope with these types of behaviors exhibited by your baby, you will now understand that you are not alone. Every parent is faces problems like these. All mothers and fathers experience worries and irritations when their infants reach certain ages. All parents forget–or would like to forget–these trying times as soon as possible; as soon as the difficult period is over, in fact. It's human nature to play down the misery we have to go through, once the dark clouds have parted.

Now that you understand that your child's difficult behaviors and your own anxieties and irritability are all part of a healthy and normal development as your infant struggles towards independence, you can feel more secure and confident. You know what you're doing.

Even without an instruction manual, you know that your baby will explore each "new world" in their own individual way. You know that the best thing you can do is to "listen" to your baby, in order to help them on their way. You know how to have fun with them. You also know that you are the person who understands them best, and the person who can really help them unlike any other. We hope that the information and findings we've shared with you about the Wonder Weeks that mark developmental stages will make it easier for you to understand and support your baby during these traumatic times.

Our Dutch parental support and education program "Hordenlopen" ["Leaping Hurdles"] was evaluated in a research project. That program was based on "The Wonder Weeks." It was shown that understanding and supporting your baby using this program makes a huge, positive difference to the parents themselves and for the further development of their babies. So your baby's development is in your hands, and not in those of your family, neighbors, or friends. Everyone's baby is completely different. We have made this abundantly clear in this book and we hope that we have empowered parents to be immune to unwelcome and conflicting advice from others.

We have shown that every baby is "reborn" ten times in the first twenty months, or the so-called sensorimotor period. Ten times over their world was turned upside down by a "big change" in their brain. Ten times over they were bewildered and did everything in their power to cling to mom or dad. Ten times over they touched base. And ten times over they took a "mom or dad refill" before making the next leap in their development. Obviously, your toddler still has a long way to go.

More Wonders Await

Research into the development of brain waves (EEG) of children aged one and a half to sixteen has shown that major changes occur at the transition between well-known stages in their mental development. The beginning of puberty is one such leap at a later age. For a long time it has been common knowledge that surging hormones trigger the onset of puberty. But recent discoveries have shown that big changes in the brain also co-occur with the onset of puberty. These are not only changes in brain waves (EEG), but also sudden and extremely rapid increases in the volume of certain parts of the brain. For the umpteenth time these youths enter a new perceptual world, enabling them to gain a new insight that they could not possibly have developed at an earlier age. Teenagers are not keen to admit this, because they think they are on top of the world already. As parents, we cannot help but smile at the thought that babies are of the same opinion.

Yet, even teenagers still have a long way to go. Further leaps occur several more times before they become fully independent. There are even indications that adults experience these phases, too.

As the Colombian author and journalist Gabriel Garcia Marquez wrote in *Love in the Time of Cholera,*

"People are not born once and for all on the day that their mother puts them on to the Earth, but ...time and again, life forces them to enter a new world on their own."

Gabriel Garcia Marquez

Further Reading

Readers who want to know more about the scientific literature behind the book *The Wonder Weeks* may consult the literary sources listed below.

Bell, M., & Wolfe, C.D. (2004). Emotion and cognition: An intricately bound developmental process. Child Development, 75, 366-370.

Bever, T.G. (1982). Regressions in mental development: Basic phenomena and theories. Hillsdale, NJ: Erlbaum.

Cools, A. R. (1985). Brain and behavior: Hierarchy of feedback systems and control of input. In P. P. G. Bateson & P. H. Klopfer (Eds.), Perspectives in Ethology (pp. 109-168). New York: Plenum.

Feldman, D.H. & Benjamin, A.C. (2004). Going backward to go forward: The critical role of regressive moment in cognitive development. Journal of Cognition and Development, 5(1), 97-102.

Gardner, T., Chiarelli, B., & Plooij, F. X. (Eds.), The ethological roots of culture (pp. 357-373). Dordrecht: Kluwer Academic Publishers.

Heimann, M. (Ed.). (2003). Regression periods in human infancy. Mahwah, New Jersey: Erlbaum.

Horwich, R.H. (1974). Regressive periods in primate behavioral development with reference to other mammals. Primates, 15, 141-149.

MacLaughlin, S., New Infant Sleep Recommendations and Strategies, zerotothree.org, 2016, Web. 16-2-2017

McKay, P., The myth of baby sleep regressions – what's really happening to your baby's sleep?, Pinkymckay.com, 2014, Web. 5-3-2017

Ockwell-Smith, S., The Gentle Sleep Book: For calm babies, toddlers and pre-schoolers, Piatkus, 5 Mar. 2015

Plooij, F. (1978). Some basic traits of language in wild chimpanzees? In A. Lock (Ed.), Action, gesture and symbol: The emergence of language (pp. 111-131). London: Academic Press.

Plooij, F. (1979). How wild chimpanzee babies trigger the onset of mother-infant play and what the mother makes of it. In M. Bullowa (Ed.), Before speech: the beginning of interpersonal communication (pp. 223-243). Cambridge, England: Cambridge University Press.

Plooij, F. (1984). The behavioral development of free-living chimpanzee babies and infants. Norwood, N.J.: Ablex.

Plooij, F. (1987). Infant-ape behavioral development, the control of perception, types of learning and symbolism. In J. Montangero (Ed.), Symbolism and Knowledge (pp. 35-64). Geneva: Archives Jean Piaget Foundation.

Plooij, F. (1990). Developmental psychology: Developmental stages as successive reorganizations of the hierarchy. In R. J. Robertson (Ed.), Introduction to modern psychology: The control-theory view (pp. 123-133). Gravel Switch, Kentucky: The Control Systems Group, Inc. distributed by Benchmark Publ., Bloomfield NJ

Plooij, F. X. (2003). The trilogy of mind. In M. Heimann (Ed.), Regression periods in human infancy (pp. 185-205). Mahwah, NJ: Erlbaum.

Plooij, F.X. (2010). The 4 WHY's of age-linked regression periods in infancy. In Barry M. Lester & Joshua D. Sparrow (Eds.), Nurturing Children and Families: Building on the Legacy of T. Berry Brazelton. Malden, MA: Wiley-Blackwell.

Plooij, F., & Van de Rijt-Plooij, H. (1989). Vulnerable periods during infancy: Hierarchically reorganized systems control, stress and disease. Ethology and Sociobiology, 10, 279-296.

Plooij, F., & Van de Rijt-Plooij, H. (1990). Developmental transitions as successive reorganizations of a control hierarchy. American Behavioral Scientist, 34, 67-80.

Plooij, F., & Van de Rijt-Plooij, H. (1994). Vulnerable periods during infancy: Regression, transition, and conflict. In J. Richer (Ed.), The clinical application of ethology and attachment theory (pp. 25-35). London: Association for Child Psychology and Psychiatry.

Plooij, F., & Van de Rijt-Plooij, H. (1994). Learning by instincts, developmental transitions, and the roots of culture in infancy. In R. A. Gardner, B.

Plooij, F., & Van de Rijt-Plooij, H. (2003). The effects of sources of "noise" on direct observation measures of regression periods: Case studies of four infants' adaptations to special parental conditions. In M. Heimann (Ed.), Regression periods in human infancy (pp. 57-80). Mahwah, NJ: Erlbaum.

Plooij, F., Van de Rijt-Plooij, H. H. C., Van der Stelt, J. M., van Es, B., & Helmers, R. (2003). Illness-peaks during infancy and regression periods. In M. Heimann (Ed.), Regression periods in human infancy (pp. 81- 95). Mahwah, NJ: Erlbaum.

Plooij, F. X., Van de Rijt-Plooij, H., & Helmers, R. (2003). Multimodal distribution of SIDS and regression periods. In M. Heimann (Ed.), Regression periods in human infancy (pp. 97-106). Mahwah, NJ: Erlbaum.

Powers, William T. (1973). Behavior: The control of perception. Chicago: Aldine. Second edition (2005), revised and expanded, Bloomfield NJ: Benchmark Publications.

Sadurni, M., & Rostan, C. (2003). Reflections on regression periods in the development of Catalan infants. In M. Heimann (Ed.), Regression periods in human infancy (pp. 7-22). Mahwah, NJ: Erlbaum.

Schwab et al. Nonlinear analysis and modeling of cortical activation and deactivation patterns in the immature fetal electrocorticogram. Chaos An Interdisciplinary Journal of Nonlinear Science, 2009; 19 (1): 015111 DOI: 10.1063/1.3100546

Sears, 8 Infant Sleep Facts Every Parent Should Know, askdrsears.com, Web. 19-12-2016

Seehagen, S., Konrad, C., Herbert, J. S., Schneider, S. Timely sleep facilitates declarative memory consolidation in infants. Proceedings of the National Academy of Sciences, 2015; 201414000 DOI: 10.1073/pnas.1414000112

St. James-Roberts, I., Roberts, M., Hovish, K., Owen, C. Video Evidence That London Infants Can Resettle Themselves Back to Sleep After Waking in the Night, as well as Sleep for Long Periods, by 3 Months of Age. Journal of Developmental & Behavioral Pediatrics, 2015; 36 (5): 324 DOI: 10.1097/DBP.0000000000000166

Trevarthen, C. & Aitken, K. (2003). Regulation of brain development and age-related changes in infants' motives: The developmental function of regressive periods. In M. Heimann (Ed.), Regression periods in human infancy (pp. 107-184). Mahwah, NJ: Erlbaum.

Van de Rijt-Plooij, H., & Plooij, F. (1987). Growing independence, conflict and learning in mother-infant relations in free-ranging chimpanzees. Behaviour, 101, 1-86.

Van de Rijt-Plooij, H., & Plooij, F. (1988). Mother-infant relations, conflict, stress and illness among free-ranging chimpanzees. Developmental Medicine and Child Neurology, 30, 306-315.

Van de Rijt-Plooij, H., & Plooij, F. (1992). Infantile regressions: Disorganization and the onset of transition periods. Journal of Reproductive and Infant Psychology, 10, 129-149.

Van de Rijt-Plooij, H., & Plooij, F. (1993). Distinct periods of mother-infant conflict in normal development: Sources of progress and germs of pathology. Journal of Child Psychology and Psychiatry, 34, 229-245.

Woolmore, A., & Richer, J. (2003). Detecting infant regression periods: weak signals in a noisy environment. In M. Heimann (Ed.), Regression periods in human infancy (pp. 23-39). Mahwah, NJ: Erlbaum.

www.livingcontrolsystems.com (Living Control Systems Publishing)

For those who are interested in further information on the Perceptual Control Theory (PCT) concerning the functioning of the human brain that inspired much of the thinking behind The Wonder Weeks, this resource site features books, introductions and commentary, simula tion programs for your computer, and more.

Index

week 5, 45-46, 48

week 8, 66-67, 67, 71

week 12, 93, 93, 96-97

week 19, 119-21, 126-27

week 26, 159, 164-66

week 37, 221-13, 213

week 46, 247, 253-54

week 55, 284-85, 289

week 64, 324-30, 330

week 75, 377-82, 382

Body movement

games, 177, 186-89, 264-65, 334-36, 364,
394-95

investigative behavior and, 105–6, 128-30,
172-73, 221-22, 396

nakedness and, 130, 393, 398-99

walking, 179, 205, 240, 272, 334-36, 379,
393, 396-98, 430

week 12 developmental leap, 105-6

week 19 developmental leap, 128-30

week 26 developmental leap, 166, 176-80

week 64 developmental leap, 334-35

week 75 developmental leap, 394-95

Body postures, 76

Boredom, alleviating, 33, 297

Brain changes

week 5 developmental leap, 46

week 8 developmental leap, 67

week 12 developmental leap, 93

week 19 developmental leap, 121

week 37 developmental leap, 213

week 55 developmental leap, 285

week 64 developmental leap, 330

week 75 developmental leap, 382

Breathing reflex, 32-34

C

Caretaking time for babies, 97

Clinginess

week 5 developmental leap, 40

week 8 developmental leap, 59

week 12 developmental leap, 86

week 19 developmental leap, 111

week 26 developmental leap, 152

week 37 developmental leap, 184–86

week 46 developmental leap, 234-35

week 55 developmental leap, 273-74

week 64 developmental leap, 307, 309-10,
320-21

week 75 developmental leap, 373, 374,
375, 376-77, 439

Comforting baby

in good and bad moods, 23

importance of, 49-50, 66

slings for, 43

tips, 43

Concern, parental

week 5 developmental leap, 40-43

week 8 developmental leap, 61-65

week 12 developmental leap, 87-92

week 26 developmental leap, 157

week 75 developmental leap, 376

Conscience, 378, 384, 390-92, 442

Confidence in handling newborn, 20-23

Consistency, importance of, 228, 362-63, 390

Control, maintaining, 118, 142, 158, 210-14

Copycat games, 224–25

Crankiness, 10

week 5 developmental leap, 39

week 8 developmental leap, 57

week 12 developmental leap, 85

week 19 developmental leap, 114

week 26 developmental leap, 149, 152, 154

week 37 developmental leap, 199, 205, 208

week 46 developmental leap, 237

week 55 developmental leap, 275

week 64 developmental leap, 313, 320,

week 75 developmental leap, 374, 375,
376, 439

Crawling, 130, 172-74

Creativity, 297, 352, 359, 422-24, 434-35

Crying

in fussy phases, 2, 10, 13, 16

D

E

week 64 developmental leap, 322
Gripping reflex, 32–33
Grooming games, 262-63
Growth spurts, 2, 10-11

H

Habits, breaking old, 18, 297, 362-63, 440
Hand control, 93, 131-34, 179
Head circumference changes
  week 5 developmental leap, 46
  week 8 developmental leap, 67
  week 12 developmental leap, 93
  week 19 developmental leap, 121
  week 37 developmental leap, 213
  week 55 developmental leap, 285
Head support, 113
Hearing
  investigative behavior and, 52, 75
  newborn's, 25
  reflex to turn toward sound and, 32, 93
  sound relationships and, 165
  week 5 developmental leap, 52
  week 8 developmental leap, 75
  week 12 developmental leap, 93
  week 19 developmental leap, 140-41
  week 26 developmental leap, 182
Helping baby. See Parental roles
Helping behavior, 295, 327, 333, 341, 357-59,
  399
Helping out games, 262-63, 298-99, 366
Human contact. See Physical contact needs

I

Imitation, 75, 121, 163, 214, 224-25, 248,
  251-52, 292, 303, 327, 332, 339-42,
  366-67, 372, 381-82, 384, 389, 391,
  397, 399, 409, 430, 437
Impatience, curbing, 142
Independence
  games promoting, 298-99

Investigative behavior and, 257, 289-91
  week 8 developmental leap, 77
  week 46 developmental leap, 258
  week 55 developmental leap, 289-91
  week 64 developmental leap, 309, 313, 318
  week 75 developmental leap, 395-402, 409
Individuals, differences between, 385, 407-8
Insecurity, parental
  week 5 developmental leap, 40
  week 37 developmental leap, 207
  week 46 developmental leap, 244
  week 55 developmental leap, 281
Intelligence, first appearance of, 212
Investigative behavior
  body movement and, 105–7, 120-30
  body postures and, 76
  creativity and, 297
  examination and, 131-134
  experimentation and, 255-57, 296-97
  exploring games and, 222-23
  hearing and, 52, 75
  independence and, 257, 289–91
  language and, 138, 140, 180-82, 293-95
  manipulation and, 131-34
  music and, 138, 140, 180-82, 293-95
  play-acting and, 226, 229
  space for, 220-21
  touch and, 52, 73-75, 100, 101, 120
  toys and, 292-93
  vision and, 51, 73, 135
  week 37 developmental leap, 216-21
  week 55 developmental leap, 296-97
  week 64 developmental leap, 334-43
  week 75 developmental leap, 394-400, 411,
    415, 424-27
Irritability, parental
  week 8 developmental leap, 64
  week 12 developmental leap, 87
  week 19 developmental leap, 117
  week 26 developmental leap, 159
  week 37 developmental leap, 192-93
  week 46 developmental leap, 230

week 55 developmental leap, 266-67
week 64 developmental leap, 321-22
week 75 developmental leap, 376-77, 391,
    429, 440

Jealousy
   week 46 developmental leap, 237
   week 55 developmental leap, 275
   week 64 developmental leap, 312-313
   week 75 developmental leap, 375

L

Language skills
   - baby talk, 121
   - first sentences, 121, 380, 389, 428, 432,
      436-37
   - first words, 181
   - Investigative behavior and, 138, 140, 180-
      82, 293-95, 339-40, 431-33, 435
   - sound recognition and, 121
   - talking games and, 185
   - thinking skills and, 211
   - week 19 developmental leap, 138, 140
   - week 26 developmental leap, 180-82
   - week 37 developmental leap, 198, 212,
      214, 223-24
   - week 46 developmental leap, 260-61
   - week 55 developmental leap, 293-94
   - week 64 developmental leap, 321, 339-40
   - week 75 developmental leap, 382, 389,
      424, 428-437
   - word games and, 223-24
Laughter, generating baby's, 52, 99, 100, 103,
      104, 132, 136-37, 168, 174, 177, 215,
      259, 266, 352, 366-67, 384, 391-92,
      407, 412, 431
Learning. See New skills
Listlessness
   - week 12 developmental leap, 87

- week 19 developmental leap, 115-16
- week 26 developmental leap, 153
- week 37 developmental leap, 204
- week 46 developmental leap, 238
- week 64 developmental leap, 324
- week 75 developmental leap, 375
Living creatures, other, 410-12

Manipulating objects, 131-34, 164, 174-75,
      216-20, 253, 255-56, 259, 292-93,
      296-97, 332-33, 336-38, 382, 388-89,
      419-21, 425-28
Map of surroundings, mental, 415-17
Massage, 36
Mental development
   "big change" and, 12-13
   milestones in, 12
   studies on, 10
Mimicry, 379, 385, 409
Mischievous behavior
   week 46 developmental leap, 243
   week 55 developmental leap, 278-79
   week 64 developmental leap, 318-19
   week 75 developmental leap, 375
Moodiness
   week 19 developmental leap, 114
   week 37 developmental leap, 208
   week 46 developmental leap, 237
   week 55 developmental leap, 275
   week 64 developmental leap, 313-14, 324
   week 75 developmental leap, 375
Moro reflex, 32
Motion. See Body movement
Movement. See Body movement
Music
   investigative behavior and, 138, 140,
      180-82, 293-95, 422-24
   recognizing, 121
   song and movement games, 136, 186-87,
      264-65, 294-96, 299

Q

R

S

Internet

Readers You may be interested to know that *The Wonder Weeks* is available in several languages and that there is plenty of supporting information on childhood development available on the Internet. A convenient way to access information on the Internet is to go to the website that is designed to support the English edition.

www.thewonderweeks.com

This website provides a great deal of additional information, including scientific research, the many languages into which *The Wonder Weeks* has been translated, how to order the book in any of these languages, and how to find blogs, forums, and other web pages with comments about *The Wonder Weeks* around the world in any language by searching the Internet using either the title or the ISBN number.

You can also subscribe to a free email service called *Leap Alarm*. See page 8.

The Wonder Weeks series

your Baby's Development, Sleep and Crying Explained

The Wonder Weeks Milestone Guide

The Milestone Guide provides information on other topics than those related t[o] mental health as they are explained in The Wonder Weeks. Used together wit[h] The Wonder Weeks, they are the most complete resources for you to turn to.

My Wonder Weeks Diary

This luxury diary is your ultimate keepsake. It is based on a unique method that enables you to track the things that really matter. A real must have!

- Deluxe Edition -

But there's more!